BOSTON WAYS

BOSTON WAYS

HIGH, BY, AND FOLK

Third Edition

GEORGE F. WESTON, JR.

Updated by Charlotte Cecil Raymond

Beacon Press   Boston

We are deeply grateful to the following persons and organizations for allowing us to reprint photographs from their collections:

The pictures on pages 4, 49, 156, 188, and 279 appear by courtesy of the *Boston Redevelopment Authority*; the pictures on pages 15, 17, 20, 21, 33, 35, 42, 53, 99, 115, and 202 by courtesy of *The Bostonian Society, Old State House*; the picture on page 294 by courtesy of *The First Church of Christ, Scientist*; the picture on page 252 by courtesy of the *Harvard University Portrait Collection*; the pictures on pages 160 and 162 by courtesy of the *Isabella Stewart Gardner Museum, Boston*; the pictures on pages 217, 260, and 269 by courtesy of the *Massachusetts Historical Society*; the picture on page 233 by courtesy of the *Secretary of the Commonwealth of Massachusetts*; the pictures on pages 132 and 235 by courtesy of the photographer, Judythe Wilbur. All of the remaining pictures appear by courtesy of the photographer, Alan G. Raymond.

Grain and Flour Exchange Building (half title photograph)

Brewer Fountain (frontispiece)

© 1957 by George F. Weston, Jr.

Revised and enlarged edition copyright © 1967 by George F. Weston, Jr.

Third edition, revised and updated, copyright © 1974 by Beacon Press

Beacon Press books are published under the auspices
of the Unitarian Universalist Association

Simultaneous publication in Canada by Saunders of Toronto, Ltd.

Printed in the United States of America

9   8   7   6   5   4   3   2   1

Library of Congress Cataloging in Publication Data

Weston, George F
    Boston ways: high, by, and folk.
    1. Boston — History.   2. Boston — Description —
1951–   I. Raymond, Charlotte Cecil.   II. Title.
F73.3W5   1974   917.44'61'03   74–213
ISBN 0–8070–5180–2

I HAVE CONSIDERED THE DAYS OF OLD:
AND THE YEARS THAT ARE PAST.
Book of Common Prayer

The Old Meets the New: Boston City Hall and Faneuil Hall

Contents

Old City Hall and Josiah Quincy (left)

Editor's Preface

George Weston had a love affair with the city of Boston. For over twenty-five years, he followed the leisurely habit of walking the streets of the city, notebook in hand, and observing. *Boston Ways* is a result of those observations. Neither a history nor a guidebook, it is instead a portrayal of Boston's color and flavor— a book that is meant to be enjoyed as Mr. Weston enjoyed Boston.

In the late months of 1973, we at Beacon Press set out to see how George Weston's Boston had withstood seven years of change, a job both gratifying and frustrating. Many of his "high, by, and folkways" remain. The venerable Brattle Book Shop is still going strong although it has undertaken yet another book giveaway and change of location; Lyndeboro Place stands like a lone ship on an angry sea of urban renewal; Beacon Hill is protected by its designation as a National Historic District; and Lindall Place continues to withstand the insulting roar of the elevated passing within feet of its tidy windowboxes.

However, despite the timeless quality of George Weston's Boston, change has taken its toll. Streets have disappeared, buildings have burned down, statues have been decapitated, plaques have been stolen, and mementos have vanished. How many times did we search in vain for some sign of Corn Court or Change Avenue? Could a skyscraper have completely obliterated Leather Square?

But George Weston would not have mourned the loss of these and other landmarks. *Boston Ways* acknowledges change, change that will continue long after this revision is set in print. When Mr. Weston last revised *Boston Ways* in 1967, two years before his death, he realized the city he loved was engaged in a running battle with progress. In his final chapters he wrote:

Charles Street Meeting House (left)

The face of the city is changing with such rapidity that it will not sit still long enough for a portrait, and the only true picture of the Boston of today would have to be a moving picture. A book about it should really be of the loose-leaf type with the possibility of removing and adding pages at least once a week.

Primarily *Boston Ways* is the story of what is enduring in this city—those things which will never change, either because they are a part of Boston's unique history and character or because they are, thanks in part to people like George Weston, valued and loved by its residents and friends.

Boston Ways has been revised by deleting reference to those streets and landmarks which have been obliterated since 1967, except in cases of particular historic interest. In some instances, "new" nooks and shortcuts have been found to replace the old. Facts and photos have been updated, and material has been added to describe today's Boston. But our primary goal has been to retain the style, character, and viewpoint of what was first written twenty years ago.

We would like this revised edition of *Boston Ways* to be a tribute to George Weston and the city he loved. If we have succeeded, it is due in large part to the many people who knowingly (or unknowingly) contributed invaluable advice and information. We are especially grateful to Vicki Kayser and Skip Smallridge of the Boston Redevelopment Authority, Caroline Chang, and John Codman for their generous assistance in providing information for the textual updating. Special thanks are also due to Alan G. Raymond, who provided most of the photographs expressly for this volume.

C.C.R.

Preface to the Second Edition

In this book, *Boston Ways*, I have attempted to present unusual stories of Boston's ancient, winding streets and of the people who made and used them. Here is the lore, the romance, and the history of the market district, of Beacon Hill, of the Waterfront, of Chinatown, and the North End—from early Colonial days, through the era of Provincial government down to the present.

The hobby of nosing into nooks and crannies and of tracking down little-known legends has persisted for a long time. It began some twenty-five years ago in the delightful little town of Hancock, New Hampshire, which is my summer home. It began with a ruptured appendix. The little village had no ambulance but my wife, being clever and resourceful, made all necessary arrangements, and presently the local undertaker arrived. With her by my side, I rode comfortably to the hospital in the hearse.

The mortician helped to carry "the body" into the hospital, laid it out on a cot, and with a cheery "I'll be seeing you," departed. Seven pain-filled weeks later I also departed. Before leaving I received a fatherly talk from the attending physician, the text of which was: "If you care to go on living you will take a walk of at least two miles in the open air each day."

There is little pleasure in aimless walking, but a chance-read paragraph in a Boston newspaper furnished an objective. The item said: "There are more points of historic interest in Boston within easy walking distance than in any other city in the United States." Walking to these "points of historic interest" one could not fail to observe many other odd and interesting places and buildings. Looking these up in the voluminous literature about Boston opened further vistas, and thus my interest in the ancient city grew and the file of data about it thickened as a rolling snowball grows.

The exploration of Boston's notoriously tangled and twisted streets became, for me, a fascinating pastime and one which I am delighted to share with the reader of this volume. When, in 1960, the Boston Redevelopment Authority was created, a fifteen-year renewal plan was announced and the work of destroying the old and creating the new was begun.

Six of the fifteen years have already passed and many changes have been made in the old city. More are contemplated. In this, the revised edition of *Boston Ways: High, By, and Folk,* these changes have been noted and an attempt has been made to present the city as it will be when the redevelopment is completed.

It is both a pleasure and a duty for me to express my deepest appreciation to the Boston *Herald-Traveler* for permission to quote freely from my articles which have appeared weekly in the *Traveler.*

I am also grateful to the Boston Department of Commerce and the Massachusetts Chamber of Commerce. The following members of the staff of The Boston Redevelopment Authority have been of tremendous help in furnishing information regarding the "New Boston"; Edward J. Logue, Administrator; Janet Bowler, Administrative Assistant; Robert Hazen, Central Business Director; Richard R. Green, South End Project Director; Robert Litke, Waterfront Project Director; Mace Wenninger, Back Bay Project Director; Evarts Erickson, Publicity Director.

Our thanks are also due to Arthur Monks Associates, Inc., for material regarding the State Street Bank Building.

I especially wish to thank my wife, Mildred Weston, for her many helpful suggestions and for many patient hours spent in reading and correcting both manuscript and galley proof.

1967   *G. F. W., Jr.*

Paul Revere (right)

54 and 55 Beacon Street

1. Presenting Boston

THIS IS BOSTON

"A city that is set on a hill cannot be hid." Boston, which was set on three hills, cannot escape notice; nor has she ever attempted to do so.

Opinions as to Boston's worth are varied. John Adams, in a singularly uninhibited moment, wrote of his fellow Bostonians, "The morals of our people are much better; their manners are more polite and agreeable; they are purer English; our language is better; our taste is better; our persons are handsomer; our spirit is greater; our laws are wiser; our religion is superior." A minority report, equally unrestrained, from no less an authority than the Rev. Cotton Mather reads, "This town of Boston is become almost a Hell upon earth, a City full of Lies and Murders and Blasphemies; a dismal Picture and an Emblem of Hell. Satan seems to take a strange possession of it."

Who shall decide when authorities disagree to such an alarming extent? Perhaps the wisest course is for one to examine the city for himself and to form his own conclusions, which will assuredly lie somewhere between the estimates quoted above.

The geographical center of Boston is in Roxbury—at the corner of Westminster and Walnut Avenues, if one cares to be precise. Due north of the center we find the South End. This is not to be confused with South Boston, which lies directly east from the South End. North of South Boston is East Boston and southwest of that is the North End.

In widely separated parts of the city we find four different Adams Streets, four Chestnut Streets, five Franklin Streets, and five Park Streets. The reason for this is that Boston has, from time to time, annexed various communities and has seldom bothered to change the names of any of their highways. There is occasional confusion in mail deliveries, but otherwise no one seems to care.

Nature and man have combined to divide Boston proper into eight distinct and sharply defined districts, each with its own personality, its own flavor, and its own romantic history. Each district has its colorful past, its vivid present, and its promising future.

Beacon Hill, though mixed in its population, is most commonly noted as the residence of Boston's oldest and wealthiest families. After the hill was cut down to size in the "great digging" which started about 1803, it became the home of the affluent and socially prominent—the "Proper Bostonians." Though many have removed to Duxbury, Beverly Farms, or to other exclusive suburbs, the Boston Brahmin remains a Beacon Hill fixture. In recent years increasing numbers of the old houses have been turned into apartments and condominiums, but the quality of "The Hill" does not change appreciably. Periodic attempts by entrepreneurs to "update" the area have met with strong community resistance, and, as an additional safeguard, much of the region has been designated a National Historic Landmark. This and the magnetic appeal of "The Hill's" ancient streets and hidden courtyards continue to attract residents who respect its particular charm.

The *North End* was, in Colonial days, the home of the leaders in social affairs, in military matters, and in religion. In the latter part of the nineteenth century it was a purely Irish community while today it is inhabited by people of Italian descent. These, following their ethnic tradition, have turned much of the district into a huge market place. Thus this part of the city has become a mecca alike for the tourist in search of interesting historical monuments, the epicure seeking choice delicacies, and the artist hoping to find local color.

The *West End*, or various parts of it, used to be known by such pleasant names as Valley Acres, New Fields, Bowling Green, and Elm Pasture. None of these names would be appropriate now, for the West End, once a polyglot region which, in places, approached a semislum status, is now char-

"Boston's Window on the World": The Waterfront

acterized by luxury high-rise apartments and monuments to the bureaucracy of government.

Colorful *Chinatown* is located, as are most Chinatowns, right in the heart of the business district. Gay restaurants, interesting curio shops, street signs in Chinese, and the decorative phone booths and streetlights are features which attract the visitor, while noodle plants, bean-sprout factories, and firms making soybean cake provide the staples for the residents. A Chinese drugstore stocks sea horses, snake jelly, ground tiger bone, dried bat skins, and other wonders of the Oriental pharmacopoeia.

The nostalgic *Waterfront* seems to sit and dream of a past magnificence, when—in a single year, 1748—540 vessels cleared from, and 430 entered, the port of Boston, not counting coasting or fishing vessels. In one day of that year, seventy ships sailed from Boston for ports throughout the world. It is not that the Waterfront is now dead or dying. The transformation of nineteenth-century warehouses into apartments, shops, and offices promises to rebuild the Waterfront into the thriving and exciting area it once was.

Commonwealth Mall: Back Bay

The *South End* is considered by many to be a much maligned district. Here are the homes of many of Boston's solid citizens. Here, also, are numerous business concerns and major health centers; but, to many Bostonians, crime, poverty, and the location of Boston's Skid Row in the area have overshadowed the South End's unique character. Walking down Tremont Street through the center of the district, one can find Syrian restaurants, Puerto Rican bookstores and record shops, Greek and Chinese groceries, and other signs of a culturally mixed neighborhood. Certainly the South End has a great deal to offer—and, in recent years, its renovated townhouses have attracted many of those middle class families returning from the suburbs.

Diverse *Back Bay* is the cultural center of the city, as well as Boston's major student stronghold. If your interests lie in the field of art, music, or education, a visit to the Back Bay—or, still better, a series of visits—will be most rewarding.

4

The *Central Business District* is a region of twofold interest. It was here that history was made during the Colonial days and also in the pre-Revolutionary period. Today it is the locale of the great department stores and office buildings. Set foot anywhere in the Central Business District and you will find yourself in a fascinating department or specialty store or at some site famous in the history of our nation—probably both.

Boston is a city of contrasts and contradictions, with some of the best streets and some of the worst streets in America. It is near the top of the list of cities in per capita wealth and still nearer the top in its per capita municipal debt. It is a Yankee city with an Irish majority. It owns palatial residences and disgraceful slums. Having more agencies and associations for the amelioration and uplift of mankind than most cities, it still has as large a percentage of hopelessly degraded unfortunates as any. Boston raises no sheep, yet awards sheepskins in fabulous quantities.

FOOT NOTES

You may "see" Boston in various ways. From the air, you get the impression of a crowded city with meaningless little streets running aimlessly in all directions and meeting at the oddest angles. From an automobile, you see overly narrow streets, restricted to one-way traffic in the direction you do not wish to go. They are also filled with eccentric pedestrians who obey no traffic laws.

You may take a sightseeing bus and acquire an informative, although necessarily superficial, view of Boston's historic sites, her buildings, and her parks. But if you would penetrate to the essence—the very soul of the city—you will *walk*. In this way, and in this way only, you can acquire a very special, very personal ownership of the city. Others may hold the title deeds, but to you belong the things that are real and vital. These are the flaming sunsets across the Charles River, the recurrent miracle of spring in the Public Garden, the reverent jollity of Christmas

5

Eve on Beacon Hill, the multilingual cacophony of the market district, and the pleasant serenity of unexpected courts.

Then there is the sumptuous beauty of Trinity Church in Copley Square and the pathetic ornamentation of the store-front churches of Columbus Avenue; and there is the emotional impact of visiting the very places and buildings where history was made. All of these belong only to the one who visits them in the contemplative mood induced by easy rambling.

Seeing Boston on foot does not call for the rapid, purposeful walk of a man going to a business appointment, nor the brisk heel-and-toe, chin-in, chest-out stride of one walking for exercise. On the contrary, it requires the slow, thoughtful saunter—slouching a little, perhaps, with frequent pauses to note a choice bit of architecture, an unexpected vista, or an animated street scene. It means accepting the invitation of an alluring little alley or changing one's direction as the mood of the moment dictates; it means capturing and holding the elusive scene and the fleeting picture. Above all it demands the observant eye, the harkening ear, and the mind in tune with the warm, friendly tempo of the city.

In a leisurely walking of the streets, one has time to note the subtle differences and charming idiosyncracies which give Boston its incomparable flavor—the striking yet delicate balance between the old and the new along the major thoroughfares; the enjoyment of a family outing along the Charles; the pontil glass, violet windowpanes, delightful doorways, and secret gardens of Beacon Hill. He can explore the meandering pathways through the groves of beeves and muttons hanging in Quincy Market; can savor the displays of strong cheeses, yard-long sausages, ragged tripes, and live snails in the North End. He can muse over the old burying grounds with their ancient stones and enjoy both swan boats in the Garden and baseball on the Common. Or he can stroll past the intersection of Batterymarch & Batterymarch on the way from Water to Well.

One may also note the patrician ladies of Boylston Street and the "winos" of Skid Row; streets that turn into flights of steps; streets that pass through tunnels and others that go nowhere with an air of busy importance. These are all part of the Boston scene and are all to be had for the taking.

Give yourself time to observe the contours of the streets. They have a meaning. This curving highway once followed the shore line—now a full half-mile away; this widened place is where the town pump stood; the angle beyond was made to avoid Elder Oliver's house—which was torn down in 1680; the sharp turn here went around an almost forgotten pond; and the convergence of several streets marks this as the spot where there was a favorite tavern in the olden days.

While strolling the highways do not neglect the rewarding upward look. Many of the old-time architects lavished their finest artistry on the upper stories. The "remodelers" and "modernizers" have touched them with a lighter hand than they used on the ground floors.

Looking Upward: The Old State House

There is also a world underfoot that is worthy of attention. The very pavements upon which you walk have a story to tell. The round, waterworn stones from the beaches still form the floor of some of the Beacon Hill streets and the North End courtyards. These gave wonderful traction for the horses of an earlier era but are not appreciated by the automobiles of today.

The ancient brick sidewalks of Beacon Hill are so beloved by the residents that they fought—and won—a considerable legal war to retain them. There are other sidewalks of packed earth, of tar, of pebbles, of granite blocks, and of cement. Sometimes all five will be found in one short highway. In the pleasant reaches of Commonwealth Avenue one finds occasional variants of the brick sidewalk. These, locally known as "rich men's sidewalks," are of a highly vitrified, polished, and shining tile. They are slippery when wet and should be approached with extreme caution. Cement is a highly functional material. But while "green" it lends itself to the literary and artistic efforts of our youth and to the wandering footsteps of animals. These then belong to the ages.

> The evanescent romance and the fugitive event
> Endure throughout the ages when enshrined in wet cement.
> Generations yet unborn see where the puppy chased the cat,
> And learn that "Joe loves Susie" and that "Tommy is a rat."
> In the streets beside the Common are the marks of pigeons' feet,
> And a devious minded sea gull promenaded Brattle Street.
> We forget our loves and hatreds; we forget our grief and pain;
> We forget our solemn pledges—but these foolish things remain.

II. Genesis

BEFORE BOSTON

The birth and location of many cities is an accidental thing. Some fisherman's hut, some crossroad tavern, or some wilderness trading post grows, by a process of accretion, into a metropolis. Not so with Boston. Boston was planned.

The Puritans set out with the full determination of founding a permanent colony somewhere in New England and they had something to guide them. There was a sketchy map or two for examination and they had the opportunity to study the records of the previous expeditions which had failed in their attempts to colonize the same region. Each of the earlier bands of adventurers had added to the store of general information about the country, and each had left a few hardy individuals who found wilderness life congenial.

A few families lived at Wessagusset (Weymouth), a few straggling people were at Natuscot (Hull). Morton and his dissolute companions were "frisking with ye Indians" at Passangesset (Quincy) and there were groups of five or six at Thompson's Island, Noddle's Island, and Charlestown. At Salem and Plymouth were struggling communities under Governor Endicott and Governor Bradford respectively. In Shawmut, later to become Boston, lived the hermit Blackstone. So the Puritans were not to be entirely without neighbors.

The prospective colonists were no mere adventurers. They were, for the most part, well educated and deeply religious men. There was a higher percentage of college graduates among them than there was in England as a whole. Their guide and book of laws was the Bible, which, as Wycliff wrote in 1384, was "for the Government of the People, by the People, and for the People"—a neat phrase usually credited to a later writer.

Nathaniel Morton, secretary of the colony, noted the arrival of the Puritans in his journal: "This year (1630) it pleased God of his rich grace to transport into the Bay of Massachusetts divers honorable Personages, and many worthy Christians. A chief one among them was that famous Pattern of Piety and Justice, Mr. John Winthrop, accompanied with divers other precious Sons of Sion, who might be compared to the most fine gold."

This estimate of the Puritan character was only partially shared by Edward Ward, a roving reporter of the *London Spy* in 1699. Edward evidently thought that some of the "fine gold" contained considerable dross, for he wrote that, while many of the colonists were seeking an opportunity to worship God as they saw fit, there were some who left England to escape imprisonment for debt, and still others who were fleeing from the results of domestic indiscretions. To quote him exactly, "Bishops, Bailiffs and Bastards were the three Terrible Persecutions which chiefly drove our unhappy Brethren to seek their Fortunes in Foreign Colonies."

The truth probably lies, as it usually does, midway between these estimates, and without doubt the Puritans were ordinary folk with the usual human virtues and vices.

ON THE WAY

Crude sailing ships—inaccurate charts—unreliable instruments. With these aids to navigation, it is a mystery how the captains of the ships of the Puritans contrived to find the broad side of North America, to say nothing of so small a dot on the map as Salem. But they made it, after seventy-six days of exceedingly rough going, and were welcomed by Governor Endicott with "a good venison pasty and good beer."

They found the people of Salem in a desolate and sickly condition with little food for themselves and nothing to share with the new arrivals. Governor Winthrop's assistant, Dudley, summed up the situation in four words, "Salem pleased us not."

Returning to their ship, they cruised south along the shore.

"We seek," wrote Winthrop in his diary, "a place for our sitting down." They came to Charlestown and there they sat. Salem had "pleased them not" and it took but a few days for them to decide that Charlestown pleased them even less. There were no good springs, and the only water they could find was brackish and unpalatable. Even today there is very little water drunk in Charlestown.

Across the harbor, the Puritans could see a hilly peninsula which the Indians called Shawmut. Had they taken a census of the region, it would have shown a white population of one, and he had been a resident for eight years.

In 1622, Sir Fernando Gorges sent his son to found a colony near Shawmut under a royal grant from James I. He used little judgment in selecting his associates, and prospective colonists were, for the most part, the sweepings of the London docks and slums. The type of people who made up the company is well illustrated by an incident which is said to have occurred during their stay. A young man of their group stole a quantity of corn from the Indians. His victims insisted that the guilty man be put to death. The colony could not afford to offend the natives nor could they spare a young and vigorous man, so they tied up an old infirm weaver and hanged him instead. The Indians were satisfied, the colony no longer had to feed the unproductive member, and everybody was happy except, perhaps, the weaver. Son Robert, having found that a sea voyage did nothing toward transforming a set of lazy vagabonds into industrious laborers, was glad enough to return with his dissolute ruffians to England.

Every expedition of the seventeenth century felt obliged to be accompanied by a spiritual leader. Gorges had two; he needed them. When the ship returned to England, the assistant pastor, the Rev. William Blackstone, chose to remain—and remain he did, with his library of two hundred books and a small store of tools, provisions, and seeds. Perhaps he felt safer with the wild animals and the Indians than with Robert's assorted rascals.

By the time Winthrop's company arrived, Blackstone had built a frame house near a beautiful spring on the sunny slope of Beacon Hill, about where Louisburg Square is located. His garden and orchard extended down across the site of Park Street and the Common. He had a canoe landing on the Charles—and he had caught up on his reading.

There is some doubt as to the exact location of Blackstone's spring or, rather, there is far too much certainty about it. The City of Boston has located it—probably by a majority vote of the City Council—as being at the Beacon Street Mall of the Common, where a tablet marks the exact spot. The Proprietors of Louisburg Square are sure that it was in the very center of their little park and every third resident of "The Hill" knows positively that it was exactly where his cellar is located.

When Blackstone heard of the plight of his thirsty neighbors, his sympathy overcame his judgment and he invited them to come over to his peninsula, assuring them of gushing springs of purest water. They accepted with alacrity and moved in with promptitude.

The Puritans did the right thing by Blackstone; they made him a member of their church—somewhat against his will—and "gave" him fifty acres of his own land. The Rev. William promptly sold the land back to them for thirty pounds and took off. When next heard from he had established a new home on a new river well away from overcrowded Boston. The town of Blackstone on the Blackstone River is there now.

It was twenty years before Boston saw Blackstone again, when he stormed into town on a huge brindle bull that he had trained to obey the reins. Having a somewhat belated urge for romantic adventure, he courted and married Mary, the widow of John Stephenson. The sixty-year-old bridegroom, his wife (age not recorded), and her sixteen-year-old daughter returned to his wilderness home, where he died at the age of seventy-six, leaving two children.

In 1834, as a tardy tribute to the colorful first settler, the city named a newly created thoroughfare Blackstone Street in his honor.

Blackstone would have liked the highway that bears his name. It is the chief street of the market district and demonstrates the fact that food, like life, can be beautiful. Blushful

"A Sunset in Vegetables": Blackstone Street

tomatoes greet the eye; red, russet, and yellow apples; jolly peppers and sweet corn grinning toothfully. A sunset in vegetables! The red, red cheeks of the salesmen matching their choicest sirloins! Everywhere prosperous-looking cats—sleek, fat, and smiling!

RESTLESS EARTH

It has been said that a woman falls in love with a man for what he is and spends the rest of her life trying to change him into something different. The Puritans fell in love with Boston and immediately set about making alterations.

They, and their successors, leveled hills and filled in marshland, bogs, and coves to such an extent that the present city— exclusive of annexations—is nearly three times its original size. It has increased from the original 783 acres to the present 1904 acres. The unimpeachable *Encyclopedia Britannica* says, "The topography of Boston has undergone greater changes at the hand of man than any other city, ancient or modern."

The original shape of the peninsula was that of a long-stemmed pear from which three considerable bites had been taken. The "stem," where Washington Street now extends between Beach and Northampton Streets, was so narrow that one of the earliest traffic problems of the town was caused by the ships tied to the wharves in the South Cove and in Back Bay. Their bowsprits interfered with passing wagons on Washington Street. This narrow strip was known as Boston Neck, and the first horse-drawn streetcar line—that from Boston to Roxbury—was called "The Shawl Line" because it went over the neck and back.

The three "bites" in the pear were the North Cove of 70 acres, the East Cove of 112 acres, and the Back Bay of nearly 600 acres.

Beacon Hill was crowned by three mountainous peaks so steep that they could be climbed only by the use of hand and foot holes dug in the earth. A considerable rise in the ground at the south end of the East Cove was known as Fort Hill, while a much higher one at the other end of the Cove was called Copp's Hill.

A knowledge of the ancient topography helps one to understand why Back Bay is dry land, why there is no water in Water Street, and why Dock Square, Salt Lane, Bay Street, Causeway Street, and Beach Street are all so far inland. The names were apt and fitting at one time, as was that of Fort Hill, later a flat park, and High Street, which is now practically at sea level.

North Cove

To use modern names, the North Cove lay between Beacon Hill and Copp's Hill. It penetrated inland to the corner of Washington and Brattle Streets, now replaced by Government Center. The North Station is almost at the center of this cove. A long, narrow island formed a natural causeway which nearly blocked its entrance. On the other side of the town, the waters of East Cove cut into the land as far as Dock Square.

Quick to realize the possibilities of this topographical arrangement, the colonists dumped earth and rock into the North Cove at the ends of the island. This transformed the island into

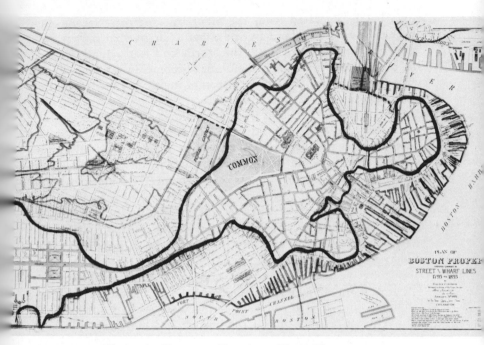

Boston's Changing Shoreline: Plan of Boston 1795–1895

a serviceable dam and impounded the water, thus forming a semi-circular lake which was called the Mill Pond. A canal was then dug connecting this pond with East Cove at Dock Square. A gristmill was erected at the north end of the dam and a sawmill at the point where the canal joined the Mill Pond. Races and water gates at each mill completed the work. At high tide, the gate at the dam would be opened and the water would rush in, turning the mill wheel. At low tide, this gate would be closed and the other opened. The water would then flow out through the canal, turning the wheel of the mill on that side. Not a bad piece of engineering, this, for a colony less than twenty years old.

Johnson in his *Wonder Working Providence*, written in 1648, speaks of this canal saying, "The north-east part of the town being separated from the other by a narrow stream, cut through the neck of land by industry, whereby that part is become an island." For a time, the North End was actually called the Island of Boston. This section has become an isolated island once more, being cut off from the rest of the city by the Fitzgerald Expressway.

The tide mills ground their grist and sawed their planks for a hundred and fifty years, during which time the population of Boston doubled and redoubled a number of times. By 1807 there were so many people that the town was in desperate need of more land, so a company of engineers conceived the idea of filling in the Mill Pond.

By using the earth from Beacon Hill, a double purpose could be served. Filling in the Mill Pond would add some seventy acres of valuable land, and leveling off Beacon Hill would make inhabitable an added territory of considerable extent. It took twenty-five years of pick and shovel work to accomplish this feat; but after it was finished, many mercantile establishments, office buildings, and a huge railroad station were erected on the new land. Thus it became one of the busiest and most valuable sections of the town.

Since the earth from Beacon Hill was used for the fill, one of the wits of the time frequently referred to the North Station as being located on the top of Beacon Hill. It was easy to be a wit in 1829.

The Mill Creek was continued as a canal through the newly created land. Enlarged and faced with stone, it formed a link in the Middlesex Canal system through which the products from a considerable distance inland were shipped by boat direct to the harbor at Dock Square. When the advent of the railroads and improved land transportation rendered the slow travel by canal boat obsolete, the waterway was filled in and became a wide street, appropriately named Canal Street. The highway which ran across the causeway became, of course, Causeway Street; and those at the sides of the Cove became North Margin and South Margin Streets.

*"Cutting Down Beacon Hill," lithograph by Bufford (1858)
after drawing by J. R. Smith (1811–1812)*

East Cove

Until about 1870, a large cove lay between Copp's Hill and
Fort Hill. It extended inland to where Washington Street met
Dock Square and covered what is now known as the Market
District as well as a part of the North End.

Fear of invasion, ever present in the Colonial mind, resulted
in some remarkable engineering feats. Possibly the most extraordinary of these was the Barricado, built in 1673. This was a
twenty-foot-wide wharf extending 2200 feet across the East Cove
from Scarlett's Wharf at the foot of Copp's Hill to India Wharf
near the bottom of Fort Hill.

Openings through this Barricado permitted vessels to pass
into the Cove, where they could be protected by the cannon
mounted on the Barricado and also by the "lowd babbling guns"
which crowned Copp's and Fort Hills. The value of this defense
was never put to the test because of the efficiency of the forts
farther down the harbor.

The ever growing need for more land finally resulted in the filling in of the East Cove. Earth for the fill was obtained by leveling Fort Hill and by cutting off about half of Copp's Hill.

Atlantic Avenue was laid out in 1868, almost exactly along the line of the old Barricado at a cost of nearly two and a half million dollars—the most expensive street in Boston with the single exception of Washington Street.

South Cove

Boston Neck, the "stem" of the pear, was so low and narrow that at extreme high tide it would be completely inundated and, for a brief time, Boston would be an island. So much land has been reclaimed from the sea that this part of the city, once the narrowest, is now the widest.

This neck of land being the only contact with the mainland, Boston was an ideal situation for a pioneer community. A slight fortification and a guard of five or six men could render the town absolutely safe from attack by land.

As the years passed and the community grew, residents found themselves again in dire need of increased room. The work already done was not enough to satisfy the need, and the shallow South Cove which lay east of Harrison Avenue along the neck offered possibilities. In 1833 a group of engineers and businessmen formed the South Cove Corporation, and the work of filling in the Cove was begun.

At about the same time came the building of the first important railroad—that from Boston to Albany, which ran across the newly created land. The officials celebrated the amazing fact that the two cities were now only fifteen hours apart by holding a banquet at the United States Hotel in Boston. The bread served at this dinner was made from the wheat which had been growing in Albany only two days before, and it was shipped in a barrel which had been a living tree the previous day. The world was beginning to shrink.

A highway paralleling the railroad was built across the new land. It was named Albany Street, of course. The streets branching from it were named after the towns and cities which the railroad had now made near neighbors. Indeed, the focus of interest in the new mode of transportation made the people conscious of the outside world to such an extent that, of the 169 streets of the South End, 84 were named for cities and towns, chiefly in New York and western Massachusetts.

Back Bay

Beacon Street now runs from Beacon Hill—which our ancestors cut down to size in the early 1800s—out through Back Bay, which other ancestors filled in around 1860. Anciently, this highway stopped at Charles Street. It had to. The waters of the Back Bay prevented progress farther.

Uriah Cotting, Boston's noted engineer, conceived and matured a tremendous, almost fantistic, idea. It was nothing less than the building of a huge dam to enclose the Back Bay—580 acres. The water thus impounded was to run a series of tide mills. As the dream grew, he envisioned a street atop the dam, bordered by magnificent mansions with delightful waterscapes on both sides. Zestful, salty sea breezes would bring warmth in winter, coolness in summer, and good health all the year.

It did not work out quite that way. A corporation was formed, money raised, and work begun. Laborers were imported from Ireland and the dam was built. Beacon Street, under the name of Western Avenue, was continued along the dam as far as Brookline, and the building of a few houses was commenced. Everything developed according to plan with one serious exception. The vigorous, delightful, and health-giving breezes were not as advertised. Much of the sewage of a considerable city emptied into the bay, and the new dam prevented its being carried out to sea. The winds across the flats at low tide, while vigorous, were neither healthful nor delightsome. In fact, the well-being and comfort of the entire city were menaced. Something drastic had to be done, and done promptly.

Mr. Cotting had died and the problem was turned over to Colonel Loammi Baldwin, who was a great engineer in spite of

Back Bay: 1855

the fact that he is now better remembered for the delicious apple which he developed. Actually, there was only one thing to be done. The Back Bay was finally filled with good clean earth from Needham.

Once a placid bay, later an offense in the nostrils of the city, Back Bay has become a beauty spot of Boston. Where the British boats left to carry the soldiers on the first stage of their tragic journey to Lexington and Concord now stands the Public Garden, whose only shipping is the swan boats on its little lake. Where enemy ships anchored during the siege of Boston has risen Copley's beautiful Square, and where our sporting ancestors fished and shot wild ducks is that perfect palace—the Gardner Museum—filled with the artistic treasures of the earth.

Of museums, schools, libraries, and residences Back Bay has many of Boston's best and some that could safely challenge comparison with any in the country.

Back Bay: 1890

THIRST

Delving into the early records of the colonists of Boston one finds frequent references to rum and beer—usually spelled Rumm and Beare and *always* capitalized. Water, although less frequently mentioned, was important too. In fact it was the report of the many bountiful springs which influenced the very first settlers to choose Boston as their permanent home. Water they had to have —at least until they could get the cider mills and breweries into production.

Governor Winthrop built his home near a great, gushing spring, and the less important—but equally thirsty—members of the colony gathered nearby. The pathway to the spring was, of course, known as Spring Lane, and Spring Lane it has remained —a short, narrow, and crooked way in the heart of the city.

Walking down the lane from Washington Street, one notices a sharp and seemingly unnecessary angle in the sidewalk on the left-hand side. This is the location of the ancient spring, as attested by a tablet in the wall of the opposite building.

As the population increased, they did not exactly drink the fountain dry, but they did sink so many wells in the neighborhood that the water table was lowered appreciably and the Great Spring ceased to flow. A well and a wooden pump repaired this deficiency, and for two centuries many of the Boston people obtained their water here.

Gradually the supply lessened until it finally disappeared altogether. It was rediscovered in 1869 when the post office was built between Milk and Water Streets. The old spring gushed with all its pristine vigor right in the cellar of the new building, much to the annoyance and expense of the contractor.

Town pumps and public springs have always been notorious centers of gossip and newsmongering. One can vividly picture Madame Winthrop, the voluble Anne Hutchinson, the wealthy Mrs. Robert Keayne, and the wife of shoemaker Marshall meeting at the Spring Gate for a refreshing drink of water of a morning and lingering for a bit of miscellaneous conversation. After Mrs. Winthrop had played the Governor's wife sufficiently, they would really get at the news of the day: how Philemon Pormont had been "intreated" to be schoolmaster and Richard Fairbanks appointed to nurture the cows on the Common, how John Samson had been set in the stocks for trucking with the Indians, and how Prudence—the hussy—wore her scarlet "A" with quite an air of pride. The Great Spring dried up after two hundred years, but the stream of puerile and malicious gossip continues to flow. It changes its location and direction from time to time but never diminishes.

At one side of the spring was the house of the Governor and near the other side was the home of William Hibbins, a merchant, at one time agent of the colony in England. Through no fault of his own he failed in his business and died in extreme poverty.

His widow, unable to endure her hard lot with patience, became a common scold and general nuisance to her neighbors. Despite her poverty, she had retained ownership of her home so there seemed no way of getting rid of her. The neighbors, however, knew the proper procedure. They preferred charges that she was a witch. The jury, most of whom had suffered from her sharp tongue, brought in a verdict of guilty; but the presiding judge, being a just and honest man—and living at some distance from the spring—reversed the decision and the virago was set free.

But not for long, for the House of Representatives reviewed the case and reversed the reversal of the honorable judge. Poor old Ann Hibbins was hanged, on Boston Common in 1656, her only crime being that she talked too freely, too pointedly, and to the wrong people at the Town Pump.

Just north of the spring was the residence of Elder Thomas Oliver, one of the deacons of the First Church. Elder Oliver was as popular with his neighbors as the unfortunate Ann had been unpopular. The residents of the little lane knew how to punish Ann for her shrewish ways and they also knew how to reward the good deacon for his many virtues. When, in 1646, all horses were forbidden to graze on the Common, there was one exception. The horse of Elder Oliver was, by special act of legislature, permitted to remain.

There was another town pump which probably drew water from the same underground river as the one in Spring Lane. This was on Milk Street, near Congress. In 1827 a petition was presented to the General Court requesting that a watchman be appointed to guard the pump against thieves who were diverting the stream.

Water was being stolen on Milk Street!

III. What's in a Name?

MULTUM IN PARVO

There is a fascination about the street names of Boston. They convey so much in a single word. A new concept of government is indicated by Federal Street, and the Continental Congress is remembered by Congress Street. Liberty Square is named to commemorate French—not American—liberty, but Union Street celebrates the union of the United States.

Almost forgotten battles are kept in mind by the names of Derne Street and Louisburg Square. A far-flung commercial venture is honored by India Street; regard for the original owners of the land by Shawmut Avenue and Sachem and Sagamore Streets; and the nostalgic love that the residents felt for the old country by Fleet, Oxford, and Wapping Streets.

In the early days of the struggling colony, folks were too busy to bother with names. Their paths and roadways were simply designated as "The Way to the Mylne" (Summer Street), "The Path to the Fort" (Batterymarch), or "The Way to the Poorhouse" (Beacon Street). Later, as these pathways became definite streets, more permanent and dignified names were found for them.

In 1701 the first list of streets, 110 of them, was published. Some of the names were descriptive of the streets themselves: Short Street, Blind Lane, Crooked Alley, Long Lane, Turnagain Alley, and Elbow Lane. Other names indicated the location of the highway: Beach, Pond, Spring, Creek, and Marsh.

Noted residents were honored by Winthrop Square, Rainsford Lane, Rawson's Lane, Oliver and Belcher Streets. Other inhabitants, just as important, perhaps, were indicated by Frogg Lane, Hog Alley, and Cow Lane.

The town's chief industry was remembered by Fish Street,

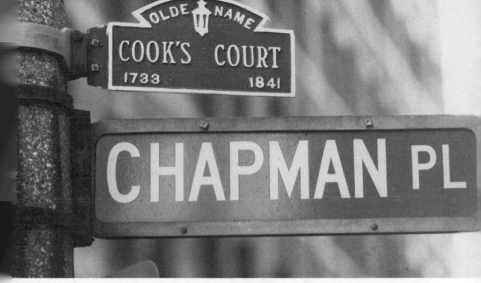

"What's in a Name?"

Flounder Lane, Mackeril Lane, and Crab Alley, while trades were represented by Cooper Alley, Corn Court, Lime Alley, and Tanner's Lane. Streets named King, Queen, Prince, and Hanover showed that the colonists did not forget their duty to their rulers. Wistful memories of old London were found in the names of Pudding Lane, Beer Lane, Sun Court, and Whitebread Alley.

Few of these old names endure. Boston streets seem to change their names with the ease and frequency of movie stars. Of the 312 streets in Boston proper approximately half retain their original appellations.

Some, like Congress Street, have had as many as eight different names. This is unfortunate. None can deny that Winter Street sounds better than Blott's Lane, and one would rather live on Tremont Street than Slough Street. Yet Boston lost something when Black Horse Lane became Prince Street, Green Dragon Lane changed to Union Street, and Seven Star Lane was renamed Summer. The color and flavor of the old city would be greatly enhanced had we not, in the interests of a spurious refinement, abandoned such names as Fiddler's Lane, Distill House Square,

Gay Alley, Black Jack Alley, Lobster Lane, Cobblers Court, and Ding Dong Alley.

As might be expected, over a third of the streets of modern Boston are named for persons. However, the city has avoided the common error of using the names of people of minor or temporary importance. The city street directory has a list of names worthy of inclusion in Boston's Hall of Fame. Great statesmen are represented: Franklin, Ashburton, Hamilton, and Pinckney; esteemed ministers: Cotton, Stillman, Chauncy, and Mather. Heroes of the Revolution are remembered: Adams, La Fayette, Hancock, Otis, and Revere. Artists Allston, Bulfinch, Greenough, and Copley are chosen, as are the great philanthropists Parkman, Devonshire, and Kilby. Even famous persons of the Old World are not entirely neglected. Columbus, Cortes, and Isabella make the list. Incidentally, Isabella runs from Columbus—which is something that the lady of the same name never did.

Long-vanished buildings and topographical features are brought before the mind's eye by Arch, Beacon, Canal, Causeway, and Church Streets. There is no dock at Dock Square, neither hill nor fort at Fort Hill Square, no school on School Street, no temple in Temple Place, and perhaps not one Quaker in Quaker Lane, but all these things were once in the places indicated.

The sinuosities of Boston streets save the city from the banality of calling its highways A, B, C, and so on—like so many vitamins. The only place where this would be possible is in a small section of the Back Bay. Here the city has used the highly functional A, B, C system, while losing nothing of the true Boston flavor. We have Arlington, Berkeley, Clarendon, Dartmouth, and so on even to Hereford. Unfortunately the parallel ways end at this point so there is no Yolander or Zilch Street.

Possibly the oddest feature of Boston's nomenclature is in its little "avenues." Webster defines avenue as "A broad passageway bordered by trees." This is not at all the Boston definition. City Hall Avenue and Franklin Avenue would be alleys in a less polite city, and Primus Avenue is a flight of steps.

City Hall Avenue

BOTOLPH BECOMES BOSTON

About the time that the Knights of the Round Table lived, loved, battled, and banqueted for the glory of King Arthur and their Ladies Fair, there lived by tne shores of Lincolnshire in England a Saxon monk who cared for none of these things. He spent his time in prayer, asking divine help for the simple sailor and fisher folk among whom he lived.

The sailors of that day were men of vigor and skill, but their boats were crude and the sea was cruel. There were more widows than wives in Lincolnshire, and the prayers of the good monk were deeply appreciated by the afflicted people, who called him "The Boat Helper." In the Anglo-Saxon this was pronounced "Bot-holph."

The saintly monk died and in due time became a saint in good earnest, being canonized and admitted to the calendar as Saint Botolph. A church was built in his honor and around it grew a village which bore the name of Saint Botolph's Town.

Through the centuries, the careless pronunciation for which the English are notorious did strange things to the name of Saint Botolph's Town. In less than fifty years it became Botolphs Town. Later it had changed to Bottleston, Botolston, Bottston, Buston, and finally Boston—Boston, Lincolnshire, England.

Many of the little band of exiles who came to our shores in 1630 were from Saint Botolph's old town; and, at a court held in Charlestown on September 7, 1630, they voted "that Trimountain be called Boston." It was easier for them to face the brutal winter that lay in wait for them if their new habitation bore the name of the beloved little town where their childhood memories were enshrined.

Trimountain was the name that the settlers had given to the peninsula when they had first seen it because the most prominent feature of the landscape was the three tall peaks at that time forming the top of Beacon Hill.

The Indian name for the region was Shawmut, which has been variously translated as "Living Fountains," "Place where boats land," "Unclaimed land," or "Place near the neck," according to the taste and fancy of the translator. The sober truth is that no one now knows what Shawmut did mean.

Much may be forgotten in fifteen long centuries, but the Saxon saint of seafaring men is still remembered in this newer Boston. We have named a street and a club in his memory. Shawmut Avenue and Tremont Street recall the earlier names of the town.

The good Saint Botolph would be considerably astonished could he visit the street named in his honor. He might not wholly approve of some of the events which have taken place on "his" highway. However, he was no mollycoddle, and he would have enjoyed the clean sportsmanship which, for many years, was a tradition of the old Arena, so long the home of local sportsmen.

Many colorful nights have been enjoyed at the Arena—not all of them connected with athletics. When Al Smith spoke there in 1928, every seat and every inch of standing room was occupied before noon, although the affair was not to begin until eight o'clock. The concessionaires, unable to reach the doors, were obliged to haul their supplies up through the windows by ropes.

Lindbergh was welcomed home from his historic flight by a tremendous ovation from a crowd which would have filled the building several times. The whole street was jumping that night!

Other famous speakers whose mere presence attracted

28

tremendous crowds to the Arena included Admiral Byrd and Presidents Calvin Coolidge, Herbert Hoover, and Franklin D. Roosevelt. Yes, the vigorous, understanding, human old Saint would have loved it all.

The feast day of Saint Botolph is on the seventeenth of June, which, by a happy coincidence, is also the anniversary date of the Battle of Bunker Hill. It is a day when different people celebrate in different ways. The members of the staid old Saint Botolph Club meet to honor the two Bostons and to drink a toast to the beloved Saint from the silver-gilt loving cup which was presented to them by the Corporation of the older town. Those who live in the shadow of Bunker Hill Monument and to whom Saint Patrick is a more familiar name than Saint Botolph hold a riotous parade followed by banquets and dancing in the streets.

Some of our Puritan ancestors were given a rather rough time in the older Boston. Before the bar of so-called justice in the Guildhall they stood trial for their religious beliefs and heard harsh sentences pronounced against them. Under the Church of England they were obliged to listen to a creed of which they could not wholly approve. However, they still loved the old town well enough to perpetuate its name in their new habitation and the most cordial relations have always been maintained between the two Bostons.

JOY

Joy Street on Beacon Hill has no connection with nor similarity to Les Rues de Joie of Paris.

Here are probably more societies, leagues, bureaus, and guilds organized for religious and social betterment than could be found on any other street in this or in any other city. That there is joy in such service no one will deny, but the street does not derive its name from this source nor does it come, as some have maintained, from the happy shouts of the Negro children who, in the early nineteenth century, lived at the lower end of the street.

Dr. John Joy, a Boston apothecary, decided, in 1791, to move out "into the country" and he accordingly bought two acres of land on Beacon Hill where he built his home. The street where Dr. Joy built was one of the oldest thoroughfares in the town. A cow path in 1661, it became Belknap Lane in 1734, for the very good reason that it ran through the land of Joseph Belknap.

After Dr. Joy's arrival, the street quickly became both popular and populous, with the altitude of the house plots becoming a direct indication of the social eminence of the people who lived there.

Joy Street rises quite steeply from Cambridge Street to Beacon, and the wealthy "first family" Bostonians settled at the top of the hill, the middle-class folk halfway down, and the people of poverty and obscurity at the lower end. This social stratification was emphasized by the fact that the street even had different names for the three sections: Joy Street at the top, Clapboard Street in the middle, and Belknap Street at the bottom. As soon as the residents of the lower social and topographical levels realized this invidious distinction, they petitioned, successfully, to have the entire highway under one name—Joy Street.

It was during the period when the "socially immaculate" dwelt at the upper end of Joy Street that James Fiske, the notorious and wealthy stock manipulator, had a door slammed in his face. Fiske himself would have been welcomed, but the prospective hostess felt that his equipage was a bit too ostentatious to be permitted to stand in front of her home. It was drawn by a pair of horses, one coal black, one pure white. The white horse was equipped with black harness, while the black had gleaming white trappings. The chariot was attended by a white driver dressed entirely in black and by a black footman clothed in spotless white. It *was* a bit theatrical for staid and proper Joy Street.

Some of the attractiveness of this old-time thoroughfare remains. The houses numbered 1 to 4 were built by the famous architect Cornelius Coolidge in 1833. The land on which they stood was sold by Thomas Perkins with the stipulation that each house must be set back fifteen feet from the street, thus permitting him to keep an eye on his cows on the Common.

For many years the old Tudor apartment house, which stands on the former site of Dr. Joy's house, was unique in that it had no street number. It could not be number 1, for that is the Diocesan House. For years it was listed in the telephone book with a blank space instead of an address. Later it was listed as "The Tudor— Beacon Hill," and still later as being at "Beacon & Joy." Now owned by the Family Service Association of Greater Boston, the building has joined the rank of its more common neighbors, and, though its entrance is on Joy, is listed at 34½ Beacon Street.

This house of much debated address has a bay window above the service entrance which is required by court decree to be high enough to permit "a boy with a basket on his head to pass under it." It is just one of those little oddities which makes Beacon Hill different.

BY RIGHT OF PURCHASE

Belcher Lane is one of Boston's older streets, laid out when the colony was only thirty years old. It ran through the land of John Harrison and was free for public use "except such time as he shall be making ropes."

Harrison was the only ropemaker in town and, with the need for rigging for all the ships and a new rope every time an Indian was hanged, the demand was heavy. John seemed to be making rope all the time, and Belcher Lane was closed more often than it was open.

The town urged Harrison to move his ropewalk to a different location so that the street might be free at all times. John, a thorough businessman, realizing that he had the town roped and tied, agreed to move— if he were well paid for it. This was an unheard-of situation—a citizen expecting his neighbors to pay for the right to cross his land—but John was adamant. The town would purchase his land or he would continue to stretch his ropes across it, as was his legal right.

After much debate and some angry words, the Town

Fathers, realizing that a right of way across the Harrison land was a civic necessity, did purchase the strip needed for the passageway. They named it "Purchase Street" but whether in derision of Harrison's churlishness or in admiration for his business acumen it would be difficult to say. So Belcher Lane became, and still is, Purchase Street.

Living in or near the lane which was named in his honor was Andrew Belcher, a rich merchant of the late seventeenth century. Andrew owned two warehouses, which are helpfully described in the ancient records as "the one larger and the other less."

Andrew's son Jonathan was sent to England as representative or agent of the colony. His duties brought him in contact with the King, George I, and he made such a favorable impression on His Majesty that he was appointed governor of the province. It was because of his influence while serving in this capacity that King George II was graciously moved to present the silver communion service to Christ Church. This priceless example of the silversmith's art is still one of Boston's treasured historical possessions.

Unpopular with the people, as were all of the royal governors, Jonathan Belcher has left little by which he is remembered, save his name on a tombstone in the Old Granary Burying Ground.

THE BEACON AND THE HILL

In early Colonial days, Beacon Hill was a small mountain having an outline somewhat resembling the head and shoulders of a man. The Puritans gave this three-peaked hill the name of Trimountain, variously spelled Trimount, Treamount, or Tramount.

The earliest maps not only gave the name Trimountain to the hill but also gave individual names to the separate peaks. The easterly peak was Pemberton or Cotton Hill. Centry or Beacon Hill was the highest and central peak, and to the west of

Trimountain from Charlestown

it was Mount Vernon—also known, with regrettable indelicacy, as Mount Whoredom, Hoardam, or Horam.

Between the years 1804 and 1845 these three peaks were gradually cut down to meet the growing need for more land for residential use. All that remains of Trimountain today is what we now know as Beacon Hill.

On the top of the highest central peak the colonists erected a mast holding an iron bucket of tar ready to be set on fire as a signal to warn the town of enemy approach. Fortunately no foe worthy of a pyrotechnic display ever threatened the town, and the beacon was never lighted. As soon as harbor and land defenses were sufficiently strong, the beacon was no longer needed and the "centry" was withdrawn.

In the tense days of 1768, however, the Sons of Liberty rebuilt the beacon and prepared a barrel of tar ready for instant lighting if the British, already quartered in Boston, should show hostile intent. If this was done, as it probably was, merely to annoy the royal governor, Sir Francis Bernard, it was a complete success. His Excellency was definitely vexed. "Matters now," he wrote to the King, "exceed all former exceedings."

Hauling stone and brick up the precipitous slope must have been a backbreaking job; but in 1790 a monument was erected on the spot previously occupied by the beacon. A little park surrounded it. This was provided with benches where the visitor could enjoy the magnificent view while he rested after a climb that even our hardy ancestors must have found exhausting.

The approach to the summit was by way of a road named, for obvious reasons, Hill Street. This street ran only partway up the hill and then turned into a flight of steps which ended several yards from the summit. The rest of the way was by a path so steep that it required expert mountaineering to negotiate it.

When Beacon Hill, the central peak, was cut down to its present level in 1811, a duplicate of the monument was placed on the grounds of the State House very near the location of the original shaft. It is claimed that the bronze eagle atop this monument is at exactly the same level as the top of the original peak.

Hill Street remains, but with a different name. For the derivation of its new name we must travel four thousand miles in distance and a hundred and seventy years or more in time.

Around 1800 the United States determined to end, by force of arms, the humiliation of paying tribute to the pirates of the Barbary States. Captain William Eaton, who was United States Consul at Tunis, decided to help. Without much of any authority he raised a private army with the objective of restoring the exiled Pasha, Hamet, to the throne of Tripoli.

Hamet was favorable to the United States and had no love for the marauding pirates. Captain Eaton accomplished his objective by an intrepid and brilliant attack which resulted in the capture of the city of Derne, the principal seaport of Tripoli.

Stupid diplomacy made Captain Eaton's achievement useless, but at least one Bostonian, Mr. Samuel Burrell, a resident of Hill Street, felt that a memorial of the event was in order, so he removed the marker which read "Hill Street" and nailed up a homemade sign reading "Derne Street." Derne Street it has remained ever since.

The easterly eminence, Cotton Hill or Pemberton Hill, was the chosen site for the homes of some of Boston's most outstanding and wealthy citizens. On the very top of Pemberton Hill was the mansion of Governor Endicott, who succeeded Governor Winthrop in 1644 and again in 1649. The estate of the Rev. John Cotton occupied a considerable part of the rest of the hill. By far the most valuable gift from the Mother Boston to her namesake was this Puritan clergyman who was Vicar of Saint Botolph's Church in Lincolnshire from 1612 to 1633, when he emigrated to

*"Beacon Hill from Derne Street," lithograph by
Bufford (1858) after drawing by J. R. Smith (1811–1812)*

the new colony to become teacher in the First Church here.

It is a pity that these two neighbors should have quarreled, but quarrel they did, and that right bitterly, for a momentous moral principle was involved. Cotton believed—and preached—that women should not wear veils. Endicott believed that they should. Neither man was of the retiring type. Both were highly vocal, earnest, and dedicated to the cause which each espoused. The debate was long and acrimonious. Meanwhile, the women did, as they always have done, exactly as they pleased.

When Sir Harry Vane, the Boy Governor, arrived in 1635, he occupied the Cotton mansion during his brief stay. Only twenty-four years old and totally inexperienced in affairs of state, he found the problems of the Pequot War and the complexities of the religious controversy introduced by the minister-baiting Mrs. Hutchinson beyond the scope of his ability. He returned to England after a stay of only two years. If he was as handsome and dashing a figure as his statue in the lobby of the Boston Public Library would indicate, he left many palpitating female hearts behind him.

About 1733, the entire hill was purchased by one of Boston's wealthiest citizens, Gardiner Greene. He laid out the property in terraces and built what was perhaps the most palatial mansion that the town had ever seen up to that time. There were magnificent orchards, beautiful gardens, and the first greenhouses ever · constructed in Boston.

During the early part of the Revolution, the Gardiner Greene mansion was occupied by the British officer Lord Percy, who rescued the royal troops at Lexington. This country owes much to the bungling ineptitude of most of the military leaders on the British side. Had they all been of the caliber of Lord Percy, we might be singing "God Save the Queen" instead of "God Bless America."

In 1835, Pemberton Hill was cut down to its present level, and Pemberton Square was discovered under the hill. The job of removal required the work of 190 pick and shovel men and sixty yoke of oxen. The contract price for the removal of the earth was twenty-seven cents per cubic yard; but even so the contractors did very well and were entirely satisfied with their bargain.

If you have ever been entangled in the meshes of the law (which Heaven forbid) it is probable that you have visited Pemberton Square, for here is a veritable nest of lawyers, constables, prison officers, court stenographers, and other gentry who make their living by alleviating—or augmenting—the misery of others. The square (behind Center Plaza) leads directly to the old courthouse and is adjacent to the new one.

Mount Vernon was the first of the three peaks of the Trimountain to be shorn. In 1795, the Mount Vernon Proprietors, a syndicate which included such notable Bostonians as Harrison Gray Otis, Jonathan Mason, Charles Bulfinch, Mrs. Hepsibah Swan, and William Scollay, purchased a large tract of farm land on the southwest slope of Beacon Hill from the artist John Singleton Copley, and proceeded to develop Mount Vernon for residential use. In 1803, the digging began, and what is believed to be the country's first gravity railroad was put to use for this extraordinary venture. Empty cars moved up the hill while cars filled

Courthouse: Pemberton Square

with Mount Vernon dirt descended and dumped their loads along the Charles River, thus creating the foundation for Charles Street.

The memory of Trimountain's westerly hill has been perpetuated by a street of the same name which is one of the most pleasing of the many delightful streets of the region.

Wherein lies the charm of these Beacon Hill streets? Is it in the evidence of antiquity, the suggestion of gracious living, historical associations, interesting architecture, indications of social progress, or houses made noteworthy as the homes of famous people of the past or present? Almost any of our highways can offer the visitor one or more of these attractions, but the streets that can produce them all are few indeed. Among the best of these is Mt. Vernon Street.

Evidences of a mild antiquity are everywhere. Iron shoescrapers at nearly every door recall the days before the "modern" brick sidewalks were installed. The round cobblestones still seen in the driveways gave a firm footing for the horses that are no more. Gas streetlights punctuate the way; they will doubtless still be there when the light is furnished by atomic power. Boston is like that.

The houses are, for the most part, of red brick laid in the Flemish bond which dates them from the early 1800s. The hungry tooth of time has gnawed away at the sandstone columns and pediments of the entrances, but the gnawing has been gracefully done and the result is entirely pleasing.

Architecturally, Mt. Vernon Street is Boston's "conversation piece." The majority of the houses are of Federal and Greek Revival style. Many show the keystoned window lintels, the band courses of stone, and the recessed window arches that mark them as the work of the incomparable Bulfinch. Some are by Asher Benjamin; others are the work of such men as Upjohn and Dexter, whose skill proves them to have been artists of merit although they used only the modest title of housewright.

The buildings on Mt. Vernon Street are in actual physical contact, but such is their individuality that each conveys a feeling of exclusiveness and privacy. Much wrought iron is to be seen in fences, window guards, balconies, and railings. A little of it is plain and heavy in the Colonial tradition, but most of it is as light, fanciful, and delicate as the famed balconies of Seville. Why should it not be? Most of it came from Spain as ballast in the sailing ships. Black lace is definitely the proper wear for this type of house.

Oddities? Oh, yes, Mt. Vernon Street has its oddities. There is a most attractive group of one-story houses, once stables, at numbers 50, 56, and 60. The original deed for the houses read: "The roof of the aforesaid stable shall never be raised more than thirteen feet above Olive Street." Olive Street was one of the several earlier names of Mt. Vernon; perhaps the owner of the stables, who lived at 13, 15, and 17 Chestnut, set this stipulation out of kindness for her neighbors on Olive Street who wanted to keep an eye on their cattle grazing on the Common. The deed also requires the proprietors "to maintain a passageway through the house large enough for a cow to pass through."

The houses from number 57 to 89 are set well back from the street. In the early 1800s, Jonathan Mason and Harrison Gray Otis, two of the Mount Vernon Proprietors, purchased land and built for themselves imposing mansions. Mr. Mason's lot com-

Black Lace: 57 Mt. Vernon Street

prised what we know as numbers 59 to 67 Mt. Vernon, and Mr. Otis built his beautiful home at number 85, which fortunately still stands today. In 1801, these gentlemen agreed that no structures could be built upon the property (now numbers 57 to 89) closer to Olive Street than the façades of their homes—or thirty feet from the street. In 1820 this gentlemen's agreement was made a law. It's still in force.

Even the street itself is a little different from the others. One could not justly call it crooked nor is it quite straight. There are slight, unexpected curves and bends hardly noticeable until one looks for them. It is rather like a candle which has been bent in the heat and then straightened by hand.

Thirteen-foot House: 50, 56, and 60 Mt. Vernon Street

It is in no way surprising that the flavor of Mt. Vernon Street should be attractive to men and women of discernment and culture. A list of the residents during the nineteenth century would contain many famous names. Here lived such literary lights as Julia Ward Howe, Thomas Bailey Aldrich, and Margaret Deland; statesmen Charles Francis Adams, Governor Chaflin, Henry Cabot Lodge, and Governor Long; the philanthropist Cornelia Warren; the famous theologian William Ellery Channing, minister of the Federal Street Church, and his son William,

Beacon Street from the Common

inventor of the electric fire alarm; the sculptress Ann Whitney; and many others of only slightly lesser note.

"Poor House Lane" was not considered a particularly felicitous address in the eighteenth century. In 1708 the name was changed to Beacon Street, which is a very good address indeed. The name, of course, derives from the hill, which still earlier got its name from the signal mast.

William Stoughton, one of the early Puritans, wrote that "God sifted a whole nation that he might send choice seed into the wilderness." Many years later Oliver Wendell Holmes, himself living on Beacon Street, referred to it as "the sunny street that holds the sifted few." As a result of this double screening there has been a choice selection of Boston's best—in culture, ability, and wealth—along Beacon Street.

It would be difficult to mention any name famous in the annals of the city which could not be found on this famous thoroughfare in the past or the present. The mesh of the sieve is, admittedly, a little coarser than it used to be, but "Beacon Street, Boston" at the head of a letter still commands respect.

Hancock House

Until the beginning of the nineteenth century, land on Beacon Hill was of little value. Dr. Jerome Van Crowninshield Smith, who was mayor of Boston in 1854, used to tell of a carpenter who was hired to fence in a pasture (mostly huckleberries) just west of the State House. The owner felt that the bill was excessive and offered the land in payment for the fence. Mr. Ingersoll, the carpenter, indignantly refused the offer. A tender of a million dollars today would be refused with equal indignation.

One of the earliest houses to be built on Beacon Street was the John Hancock residence (a plaque near the home of the Unitarian Universalist Association indicates the site). It is a great pity that this magnificent mansion was not preserved for posterity. It very nearly was.

Hancock had a deed of gift prepared presenting the mansion to the State as a memorial, but he died before he could sign it. The John Hancock signature was no job to be undertaken by a sick man. The Hancock heirs offered to sell the building to the State at a very reasonable figure. Had only three legislators voted differently we would be saying "Here it is" instead of "There it was."

Athenaeum: 10½ Beacon Street

At 10½ is the Athenaeum, a private library reserved for its shareholders. One of the older libraries of its kind in the country, having been founded in 1807, it contains the greater part of George Washington's personal collection of books—each enriched by his autograph and book plate. Here also are two hundred volumes presented by King William III to King's Chapel. They are sermons for the most part, and the uncut leaves indicate that they have never been read. The Athenaeum may be relied upon to see that they shall not be so desecrated.

There is one book at the Athenaeum which, we may hope, is unique. This is *The Life of a Highwayman*, published in 1837. It is the autobiography of James Allen, alias George Walton, alias James Pierce, alias James Yorry, alias Burley Grove. This man of many names wrote the book while he was in the Massachusetts State Prison awaiting execution for highway robbery. The volume is bound in leather made from his own skin!

Just down the street from the very important library is a building that has sufficient frontage to entitle it to a full number of its own. The wide and impressive Athenaeum is numbered 10½ and the taller bulkier office building is 14A. What fine distinction lies between the ½ and the A?

The attractive building, formerly the Judge Baker Guidance Center, at the corner of Walnut and Beacon was the birthplace of Wendell Phillips.

The two houses at numbers 39 and 40, now the home of the Women's City Club, are attributed to Bulfinch and were built to replace some houses that had belonged to the artist Copley. It was in one of these that Longfellow courted the beautiful Miss Fanny Appleton. Here, as well as at numbers 63 and 64, are windowpanes of the famous violet-tinted glass which are found in only a very few of the houses on "The Hill."

Much nonsense has been written about these violet panes. It has even been stated that there is a law forbidding any but direct descendants of the Puritans to use this glass. The simple, unromantic truth is that a shipment of glass was received from England in 1818. This, by accident, contained some chemical which, after long exposure to sunlight, turned a delicate violet hue. That is all there is to it; but, to paraphrase Diamond Jim Brady, "Them that has 'em loves 'em."

In 1825, Cornelius Coolidge built a number of houses on and near Beacon Street. Close by were a number of outhouses, the only sanitary convenience connected with the State House at that time. In order to rid his property of this nearby annoyance, Coolidge offered to install water-closets in the State House at his own expense.

The Governor's Council hesitated. After long deliberation, their reply to his generous offer was: "Although such closets may be much approved in private dwellings, it admits of doubt at least whether all of these advantages can be expected and realized in so public a place as the State House, where visits to them must of necessity be frequent and by persons unaccustomed to their use."

Coolidge was finally allowed to install the improvements, but only after he had posted a bond of five thousand dollars with an agreement to remove the closets and restore the vaults if, after three years, the closets proved "inadequate." Evidently the public was brighter than the Governor's Council had anticipated, for the bond was not forfeited.

If Boston is the Hub of the Universe, then Beacon Hill is the

Louisburg Square and Aristides

Hub Cap and the sacrosanct little private park known as Louisburg Square is the medallion on the cap. This tiny street with its central park is so exclusive that only cars of the Proprietors and of those to whom they have issued "guest cards" are permitted to park there.

At one end of the park is a small statue of Columbus gazing inquiringly into the windows of an apartment house across Pinckney Street. At the other end stands Aristides the Just with a faraway unseeing stare which seems to be directed at nothing—evidently this gentleman is of the introspective type.

These were the first outdoor statues to be placed in Boston, and many persons as well as a few books will tell you that no one knows how or when they were placed there. A very little research, however, discloses the fact that they were the gift of Mr. Joseph Iasigi, a resident at number 3 in 1849.

Boston has many sights and sounds that arouse the emotions and remain in the memory, but the most soul-stirring and heartwarming of all is Christmas Eve on Beacon Hill. There is a semi-religious, semi-carnival spirit in the air that profoundly affects the observer and remains as a fragrant memory throughout the year.

Ligted candles appear in every window; shades are drawn back so that gracious interiors, Copley paintings, Bulfinch stairways, and rich brocades may be glimpsed.

Automobile traffic is severely frowned upon after eight o'clock, and hundreds of visitors overflow the streets. Groups of carol singers under experienced leadership go from house to house singing the ancient and well-remembered carols. A band of remarkably skillful bell ringers makes its rounds. Some of the singers are dressed in the costumes of the Puritans, and many Colonial lanterns and shepherd's crooks may be seen.

Hospitable bowls of punch, wassail, and champagne-cup are in evidence where the residents are having open house for their friends, and on Christmas Eve friends are more easily made—even on conventional Beacon Hill.

Allen Chamberlain records that Boston's first holy candle shone from the window of Mr. Nicholas Reggio's Commonwealth Avenue home. It is fairly well established that the first gracious candle to send its cheering message on "The Hill" was from the window of the Unitarian minister, the Rev. Alfred Shurtleff, at 9 West Cedar Street. To the horror of the fire department and to the annoyance of the electric company, "The Hill" still favors the single *real* candle rather than the garish display of multiple electric lights seen in other parts of the city.

In 1895, another Unitarian minister, the Rev. Christopher R. Eliot, moved to West Cedar Street and became, if not the originator, at least one of the earlier organizers of the Christmas Eve carol singing which has become a most delightful and cherished tradition of Beacon Hill.

iv. Little Lanes and Hidden Homes

AS IT WAS IN THE BEGINNING

Occasionally it becomes a civic duty to dazzle the blasé visitor from the hinterlands with a demonstration of the "Boston-ness" of Boston. Otherwise he would begin to think of us as "just another city"—which would be unfortunate.

When such a tour de force is needed, it is well to invite the guest to a luncheon at Ye Old Union Oyster House on Union Street. First, to set the mood, one should walk through the flower and vegetable markets around Faneuil Hall, a new experience for most visitors, and one that will help produce a fitting frame of mind to appreciate the old restaurant with its ancient mahogany bar and its little booths, so like a ship's cabin. These have been practically unchanged since the founding of the restaurant in 1826.

The building was old before it became a restaurant. When new, about 1750, it was the store of Hopestill Capin, who, at the Sign of the Cornfields, sold silks and fancy dress goods. Here also Benjamin Thompson, the scientist, later Count Rumford, was apprenticed.

On the second floor lived Louis Philippe, who was destined to become King of France. During a part of his exile he taught the French language to a select group of Boston merchants. After he had acquired sufficient funds in this way, he moved to more congenial quarters in a nearby tavern.

On the third floor, Isaiah Thomas published one of the early newspapers, *The Massachusetts Spy*, whose motto, "Open to all parties, but influenced by none," was followed as strictly as such mottoes usually are. The *Spy* had definite and pronounced leanings toward the Whig party.

Back of the Oyster House lies a labyrinth of crooked, tangled, narrow, dark, and dirty little alleys, twisted and interlaced in as meaningless a maze as one could hope to find even in this city of sinuous streets. Cow paths? Hardly, unless the cows were drunk. Besides, one of the lanes is so constricted that only a very narrow cow, however sober, could negotiate it.

Originally this region was a salt marsh with a small creek running into it. Its margin was, at one time, bordered by shops which have long since disappeared. But the names Marsh Lane, Salt Lane, and Creek Square still remain to intrigue us. The marsh itself had belonged at first to a Captain Joshua Scottow, so one of the lanes, the narrowest, was named Scottow Alley, now shortened to Scott Alley.

On Creek Square still stands part of a worn brick structure which is the last remnant of a row of brick warehouses long known as Hancock Row. These were Boston's first W.P.A. project. Times were bitter after the Revolution, and Hancock built these warehouses to give employment to the needy veterans. We may rest assured that this charitable action also made a neat profit for John Hancock, his heirs and assigns.

There is a triangular piece of land where Creek Square, Marsh Lane, and Salt Lane more or less come together. From the beginning of the town this was actually a "no man's land." It was listed in the tax books as "owner unknown." A few decades ago this was declared to be city property and, as such, sold to a private concern.

Thomas Marshall was a shoemaker, selectman, deacon, and both captain and crew of the first ferry "from Mylne Point to Charlestown." He gave the town a right of way through his land as a convenient short cut "to the swing bridge on Mill Creek." Probably the shortest and narrowest two-way street in Boston, Marshall Street is now a convenient short cut from Union to Blackstone.

You could walk the entire length of Marshall Street in less than a minute, but take a little longer and look about you. Note

Marshall Street

the thirty-inch spherical granite stone imbedded in the brick wall of the building at the corner of Creek Square.

This stone was brought from England about 1700 to be used as a grinder for paint. It was so used for many years. Then it dropped from sight but was rediscovered in digging the foundations for the present building in 1836. It was placed in the wall resting on a fragment of the granite trough with which it had been used. This is the Boston Stone.

Many people believed that it was placed in the wall to mark the exact spot which was then the center of the town and that it was used as a fixed point from which distances were measured in Boston and surrounding areas. Certainly it was used to locate some of the nearby buildings, for in the early newspapers we find houses and shops noted as "near the Boston Stone," "just west of Boston Stone," and the like.

Examine the three-story structure directly across the street, which is said by some to be Boston's oldest brick building. Take note of the little hand-made bricks imported from England, the original hand-wrought iron door hinges, latches, and window brackets. Also observe the immense ax-hewn beams. The original owner, William Courser, occupied this building in 1660. It was from this house that he would start out on his nightly excursions to "observe, inquire and admonish"—for William was one of the Town Watch.

In 1737, in this house lived James Davenport, brother-in-law of Benjamin Franklin. From 1764 to 1785, it was owned by John Hancock, although it was occupied by his brother Ebenezer, paymaster of the Continental Army. As paymaster, Ebenezer had little enough to do until, in 1778, Count d'Estaing arrived, bringing a huge supply of "lend lease" crowns from France, making it possible for the long-unpaid army personnel to again enjoy the luxury of having a few crowns in their pockets. All of this vast treasure was disbursed from Ebenezer Hancock's office in the building.

The pay-off man is always well received; and, as may be supposed, Count d'Estaing and his officers were given a royal welcome in Boston. About forty of the officers dined every day with the lavish Governor Hancock. It was at one of these dinners that an often recounted incident occurred. The milk supply ran short. Not much of a tragedy, one might think, but that would be because he did not know the popularity of the Governor's milk punch, which, although it was mostly rum and spices, did require some milk. Mrs. Hancock met the situation by sending some of the servants to milk all of the cows on the Common, regardless of ownership. The fact that there were no complaints attested the popularity of d'Estaing or Hancock or both.

A state banquet tendered to the officers of the Count's fleet proved somewhat of a shock to the diners. The head cook, having been misinformed as to the favorite dish of the French, served a soup with a whole boiled frog in each plate. Astonishment overcame the traditional French politeness when the Count, holding his frog aloft by one leg, exclaimed in horror, *"Mon Dieu, une grenouille!"*

After the Revolution, Hancock sold this historic old house to a china-and-glass merchant who, in turn, sold it, in 1798, to a boot-and-shoe dealer. A shoe store it remained for more than 150 years, until it was taken over by the East India Trading Company.

The Ancient Cobbles of Acorn Street

It is doubtful that any other spot in this city can give one as accurate a picture of what the old town looked like in the late seventeenth century as does Marshall Street and its environs. Ignore the electric lights in the shops—they are rather dim as it is—and you are back in the Boston of the old days. One generation passeth away and another generation cometh, but the little area back of Ye Old Oyster House changeth not.

There are a very few other spots in the city which time and change have touched with a light and reluctant hand. In 1699 a roving reporter for the newspaper *The London Spy* visited Boston and wrote a series of spicy stories about the town. In the first of these he said: "Their buildings, like their women, are Neat and Handsome. And their streets are like the Hearts of the Male Inhabitants, paved with pebble." The "pebble" were round or egg-shaped stones from the beaches, very smooth and polished by the waves. They varied in size from that of a small egg to that of a large grapefruit.

Few of the streets of the city retain this type of paving. Acorn Street is the only example on "The Hill." The ancient cobblestones, the brick and tile sidewalk, and the old-style street lamps give a charming flavor of venerable antiquity to this little highway, the narrowest of all the narrow little streets on Beacon Hill. The row of century-old houses, all on one side of the street, add to the attractive effect with their interestingly framed doors, each with its brass knocker and each with its little grated peek-hole—round, square, or oblong. The houses numbered 1 to 5, and probably some of the others, were designed and built by Cornelius Coolidge, the inspired architect and builder of more than fifty of the Beacon Hill houses. Most of those on Acorn Street were the homes of coachmen who served families living on nearby Chestnut Street.

One of the most picturesque bits of old Boston which has remained to delight the explorer of the present is the so-called Province Steps. This is a short stairway of granite with twisted iron side rails. It is covered by a cunningly wrought arch of iron which supports a hanging lantern obviously dating from Colonial days. Why the steps were built or by whom are questions that will probably never be answered; but it is a reasonable guess that this was a feature of the garden of the Province House in the days of its royal magnificence.

The present Province Street was, in 1658, named Governor's Alley and was described as "a lane behind the governor's house." Later, renamed Province Street, it led to the stables and gardens of the Province House, the official abode of the royal governors. Politics and politicians were no different in the early days from the way they are today, so it is probable that the retired way to the secluded back doors saw fully as many important people passing in and out as did the imposing but more public front entrance.

In 1679 Peter Sargeant, an extremely wealthy merchant, decided to build the most imposing mansion in town. He chose to place it on Marlborough Street (now Washington) about opposite Milk Street. In order that the grandeur of his residence might be fully appreciated, Peter built so far back from the highway that the house itself was practically on Province Street. A velvety, tree-studded lawn stretched from the front of the building to Marlborough Street. The appropriately named Province Building at 333 Washington Street now occupies the site of this lawn.

The mansion house fully realized all of Mr. Sargeant's anticipations. It was commodious and convenient as well as being a

Province House

magnificent structure. Built of bricks imported from Holland, it rose three stories in height with a tall roof and lofty cupola. A long flight of massive red freestone steps led to the spacious entrance, over which was a skillfully wrought iron balustrade, with the date and the initials of the owner interwoven in the design. The interior of the house was paneled with rare and beautiful woods enriched by curious carvings, choice paintings, and luxurious hangings.

Mr. Sargeant's marital affairs, while strictly legal and eminently proper, were curious. He had three wives, the second having been twice a widow, and the third, three times widowed before marrying Peter, ultimately becoming his widow. After a suitable mourning period of two years, this experienced lady became the third wife of a Simeon Stoddard, Esq.

Since Mr. Stoddard had an attractive mansion of his own, the Sargeant estate was offered for sale. It was at about this time that the colony of Boston became a royal province and a commodious and dignified residence for the royal governors was needed. The centrally located home of Mr. Sargeant was exactly right for the purpose; and on April 12, 1716, the house with its ample grounds became public property under the name of the Province House.

Here the royal governors governed, or tried to, without any noteworthy success. The people of Boston had very definite and ingrained ideas of personal liberty even in the early 1700s. Although loyal to the King, they resented the advent of the royal governors, and, it must be admitted, few of these officials did much to alleviate the bitterness of their subjects.

The people possessed one of the oldest and most effective weapons against the authority of the governors. It was their privilege and duty to pay the salaries of these officials—and to fix the amount. They resolutely refused to pay any salaries but instead would give the governors an occasional present of money, the amount carefully scaled according to the actions of the ruler.

Altogether there were ten governors who successively occupied the Province House. None of them had what could honestly be described as a happy time. Relations were strained from the first, and when the ill-advised Governor Bernard introduced the British troops into Boston, all sensible persons realized that an open rupture could not be long delayed.

Bernard was succeeded in office by General Gage, who by his weakness and indecision probably helped the patriots more than he would have done had he been on their side. Gage, the last of the governors, occupied the Province House during the siege of Boston.

For a short time after the Revolution the historic house was used as an office building for the newly created state officials. Renamed the Government House, it was, in effect, what now would be designated as the State House.

In 1811 the Province House, no longer needed for purposes of state, was given to the newly incorporated Massachusetts General Hospital and by them leased for business purposes. Its deterioration was rapid and complete. First it was a tavern, then a theater of a rather low order. Finally the old building, except for parts of two walls, was destroyed by fire in 1864, having run the gamut from the highest and most dignified position to the lowest condition of no dignity at all.

Portions of the walls have been built into existing structures, but nothing else remains of the important old estate save the iron archway and the granite steps, which probably led to the stables or the garden. At present these steps serve the useful purpose of uniting Province with the higher levels of Bosworth Street.

On the building at the top of these picturesque steps is a bronze plaque noting the birthplace of Amasa Walker, who was third president of the Massachusetts Institute of Technology. The same site was the childhood home of Oliver Wendell Holmes.

Bosworth Street, running from the top of the steps to Tremont Street, has every appearance of being a public way but a part of it is privately owned. Once a year it is roped off and formally closed to traffic for twenty-four hours so that the owner may retain title. For the rest of the year it is yours to use as you wish.

Walking up Bosworth Street from the steps one is afforded a splendid view of a graveyard. This is considered a great asset in Boston.

STREETS TO NOWHERE

The Hub is full of little "places," "courts," and back streets that go nowhere. What were they for? Where did they go? What purpose did they serve before the advent of the automobile? Today they are used for parking, and most of them seem to have no other function. Some of them have actually turned into parking lots and have ceased to have any appearance at all of being streets.

A few of these converted roadways make a feeble protest against the encroachment which is evidenced by numerous "No Parking" signs. No attention is paid to them, of course. There are a few "places" which submit to the daily occupation but— for some unexplained reason—have chains and padlocks ready to stretch across the entrance so that the street may be put to bed at night after the transients have left.

The Battle of Winter Street

Not all of these ad hoc parking lots are minor thoroughfares. Winter Street, one of the most heavily traveled and congested streets in Boston, is a prime example. Daily confrontations occur between cars and pedestrians, and with the added annoyance of those drivers who can't decide whether to plant their cars on the sidewalk or on the street of the "No Parking Zone," the area resembles a battleground.

In many of the smaller streets-turned-parking-lots the cars stand bumper to bumper. How do these get out of their narrow confines? No car in the line can move until the one ahead has left. The last arrival is like the cork in a bottle. Nothing can get out until the cork is removed.

What happens if the owner of car number one stops after work for a quick one and the quick one is followed—as it so often is—by a long series of slow ones? Do the others in line wait patiently? Do they join owner number one in his bibulous interlude, or do they search the neighboring bistros until they find the obstructionist and drag him out to remove the stopper from the bottleneck? At times it must present a real problem.

Some of the parking lots which are still listed as public streets have all the trimmings: attendants, fixed charges, cash registers, and even little sentry boxes for rainy days.

A few of them seem to have been overlooked by questing parkers. Into these, fruit and vegetable peddlers wheel their pushcarts and set up shop. But they are a nomadic fraternity and move frequently from place to place as the exigencies of business or the whim of the policeman may dictate.

There is, however, one exception. Many years ago a florist set up his fragrant stand in Jackson Place near the Winter Street subway exit and has there remained. His "shop" is as well known and has the same air of permanency as any of the great department stores nearby. He may be rated as a public benefactor for, after the arduous climb from the regions below, the sudden glimpse of gorgeous color is like a breath of spring.

"A Breath of Spring": Jackson Place

TUNNELS AND SHORT CUTS

By and large, the Bostonian is a placid and sedate individual. One rarely sees in Boston streets that mad rushing and scrambling that characterizes New York and many other large cities, although at certain hours of the day the subway and elevated stations can give a reasonable facsimile thereof. On the other hand, the Bostonian never disdains to save a few minutes or a few steps by using a short cut if there is one available. There usually is.

Beverley Nichol's book *Crazy Pavements* was banned in Boston, but the city has placed no ban on crazy pavements in actuality. Connecting the financial and retail districts are a number of little streets used by hundreds of persons who work by day, shop by lunch, and commute by evening. Of these hundreds, it is doubtful if any could tell unerringly the names of the highways over which they pass.

In the neighborhood of Federal Street, one might pass through the parking lot across from 100 Federal, meander through Winthrop Square and its mini park, mosey along Snow Place to Hawley, shop in a department store or two, and return in half the time it would take by a more conventional route—and still have a minute to study the merchandise on display at the Snow Place flower vendor's.

In turn, those employed in the region of Government Center might take Franklin Avenue (Brattle Street Mall) to Court Square and walk down City Hall Avenue to School Street and on to Washington.

And for those who are in a hurry to get from the financial district to South Station, there's Matthews Street, named for Nathan Matthews, who bought and sold Boston real estate at such a rapid rate that it was jokingly recommended that he be jailed in order to give the Registrar of Deeds some much needed rest. It is a narrow way with many angles. A short distance from Congress it widens into a small court called High Street Place, then narrows and becomes Matthews again.

One of the better known short cuts in the city of Boston is

Winter Place, home of the noted Locke-Ober's. Often quite awkward to navigate, especially after a sumptuous meal, this little alley, at times three feet wide, connects Winter Street to Temple Place.

Most of these thoroughfares are alike in their general character. While the reality of their worth as short cuts is debatable in some cases, they do produce some psychological benefit by making the pedestrian think he is "getting there" faster. They are dark streets, often dirty streets, streets where unexpected air currents swirl the dust into one's hair and eyes, streets of noise and of unexpected blockades by loading trucks. They are the last places in the world where one would expect to find the prosperous, the clean, the dainty, and the beautiful; yet daily these alleys pulsate with pulchritude.

Many of the streets of the Back Bay and the South End are laid out in careful rectangles. This is pleasing to the outlander, but the true Bostonian rejoices in the tangled sinuosities of the Central Business District and the North End. He likes them that way.

The Puritans never heard of city planning. Each settler simply chose the situation that pleased him and built a house there. Those interested in fishing and maritime pursuits built their homes near the town dock at Dock Square, now almost a half mile from the nearest salt water; those whose tastes were for farming made their homes in the hinterlands around Beacon Hill; and the merchants chose the region which gave promise of becoming the most thickly populated—along what is now Washington Street.

Houses were built wherever there appeared to be a good site for a house, without thought as to their relation with one another. Later when paths and roads connected these houses they had to be laid out at odd angles.

The old question "Which came first, the hen or the egg?" has its parallel in cities: "Which came first, the houses or the streets?" In the newer sections of the city where land has been made by filling in bays and coves, the streets came first and are arranged in orderly fashion; but in the older part of the city, the houses came first and the streets uniting them are narrow, crooked, and never parallel.

As the population increased and buildings became more numerous and closer together, this haphazard arrangement of streets led to some odd and legally difficult situations. A happy solution to a few of these problems was found to be tunnels— tunnels even through private houses and public buildings.

Possibly the earliest example of this mole-like device of the architect appeared in 1793. A large block of apartments was built on Franklin Street. A well-established right of way passed through the exact center of the proposed location. Nothing daunted, the builders provided a passage for the highway through an arched tunnel which pierced the first story of the structure.

There are a number of tunnels on Cedar Lane Way, a few on Myrtle Street, several on Walnut and West Cedar, but the most interesting are to be found in Pinckney Street. Some lead merely to utilitarian ash barrels and necessary garbage pails, but others take the visitor to charming little gardens and hidden houses. Number 9½ Pinckney is one of these. A cunningly wrought iron gate gives access to a tunnel through a house and into a quaint courtyard where a miniature garden is bordered by three Old World houses, one with an outside stairway curving up to the second floor.

Under number 74 is a narrow passageway which leads directly to number 74½, "the hidden house of Beacon Hill." Here is seclusion indeed!

Not all of the architectural oddities of Pinckney Street are hidden. Each of the windows of the house numbered 24 is different from all of the others, either in shape or in size. This house was built to the design of W. R. Emerson, the nephew of Ralph Waldo Emerson, for Thomas Bailey Aldrich. The reason for the odd windows was that he liked them that way. He was a Bostonian

The façade of number 56 with its large bay window appears perfectly normal as it fronts on Pinckney Street; but in the rear the building tapers to a point exactly like a slice of pie. The construction is as carefully done as that of a fine piece of furniture.

9½ Pinckney Street

House of Odd Windows: 24 Pinckney Street

Charles E. Pinckney, for whom this charming street was named, is best remembered, perhaps, for his reply to the suggestion that Talleyrand be offered a bribe to receive the American ministers. Said Pinckney, "Millions for defence, but not one cent for tribute." Actually he said, "Not one damn Penny" but his comment was slightly purified for local school consumption— the Watch and Ward on guard as always. Pinckney was one of the framers of the Constitution and it was he who insisted that no religious test be required for political officeholders. His suggestion that senators serve without pay was received with less applause—at least from the senators.

Pinckney Street runs from Joy to the Charles along the westerly ridge of Beacon Hill. In the days when society was spelled with a capital "S" it was the dividing line between those who "were" and those who "were not." The houses are all of brick and are all joined, but there is no monotony, since the buildings vary in height, size, and design. The doors, too, are different—strikingly different. Doors of red, white, green, brown, yellow, and natural wood. Paneled doors, carved doors, plain doors, and some with sly little windows giving a surreptitious preview of the visitor.

Looking down Pinckney Street is an adventure in loveliness. The steepness of the hill gives a piquancy to the converging perspective of mellow brick houses. They vary in stature, in the position of the many oriel windows, and in the unexpected slants of the Londonesque chimney pots. At the end of the vista is the sparkling river with the panorama of Cambridge beyond.

Not all of the tunnels which bore and burrow under the pavements are for pedestrian use. Like every city, Boston has a labyrinth of hidden excavations honeycombing the earth beneath. The vast network of pipes and wires necessary for the health and comfort of over a million people run through these subways, but most of us take such services for granted.

Probably no one person knows the ramifications of these underground ways. Occasionally we see some troglodyte entering or emerging from a manhole and give a fleeting thought to Boston's underworld; but for the most part we completely ignore

Down Pinckney Street to the Charles

the highways that lie under our surface streets. Visitors are un-welcome and it is doubtful if anyone unconnected with the work ever has explored or ever will explore these tunnels.

There is one system of subways, however, which is traveled daily by thousands: the "elevated," which, in spite of its name, runs underground for a considerable part of its journey. This is not the only peculiarity of the Massachusetts Bay Transportation Authority's railway, once known as the Metropolitan Transit Authority:

> When you go to town for work or play
> You will probably ride on the M.T.A.
> So, to help you reach your destination,
> They publish a booklet of information.
> How to get from the Navy Yard to Scollay—
> How to get on the track of the trackless-trolley.
> "To get to the subway," it's solemnly stated,
> "Take a surface car marked 'Elevated.' "
> *Over* the Charles the subway trains thunder
> From Harvard Square to Park Street Under.
> Beneath the city, deep underground,
> The elevated trains are found.
> *Down* to the El. and *up* to the subway
> Is just an old, accepted Hub way.

HIDDEN NOOKS

"Let's get away from it all!" How we hate the city at times —the crowds, the confusion, and the noise! How desirable seem the peace, the quiet, and the seclusion of the country! But after a week or two of retirement how good it seems to return to the strife and turmoil! It is a strange contradiction of the human mind. We want the pleasures and excitement of the city and we demand the peace and quiet of the country at the same time. It is as though one insisted that his drink be piping hot and icy cold at the same time. Yet a few fortunate Bostonians have achieved this seeming impossibility.

Lyndeboro Place

In the very heart of the city there are a few retired and hidden little nooks where time stands still. There the city's clamor is reduced to a soothing murmur, and tranquil and serene living is possible.

One of the more curious and delightful of these nooks is Lyndeboro Place in Bay Village. If one is tempted to take a look, he will find that Lyndeboro Place is a short street, some eighty feet long, ending in a wooden fence gaily decorated with a pastoral scene. There is even something of a country atmosphere, for benches, tables, and plants have transformed the little street itself into an outdoor sitting room. Five apartments have their entrances on this small courtyard, and their interiors echo the quiet graciousness of the place. There are fireplaces of brick and of marble, balconies of grillwork open from the upper floors, and traces of ivy overhanging from the roof gardens above. In an area once slated for complete demolition and rebuilding by the Boston Redevelopment Authority, Lyndeboro Place now stands alone amidst rubble, awaiting the construction of a neighboring park.

In quite a different part of the city is another charming Old World courtyard—Primus Avenue. Cut off from Phillips Street by a gate of lacy grillwork, this "avenue" consists of a series of shallow steps connected by platforms of brick and tile. It is bordered by trees of the species that grew in Brooklyn—the ubiquitous ailanthus—growing out of stone pots.

On one side is a little park in the form of a half-circle equipped with benches. Here lilacs bloom. A lion's-head fountain after the Italian manner adorns the side wall. The street itself ends in another wall of brick sheltering an odd plant stand holding an ambitious ivy. The doorways of two apartment houses open into the court from the side opposite the park.

Around 1830 this "avenue" was named Wilberforce Place. A dark, dirty, and dismal place it was then—truly a slum—with three cold-water tenements housing a horde of the city's dregs. In the 1920s Elliott Henderson, a real-estate man with a vision, took over the job of slum clearance, although it was not so called in those days. In an amazingly short time he had transformed the noisome alley into a delightful bit of old Europe. Why the name "Primus" was chosen we do not know. Perhaps Mr. Henderson contemplated building a Secundus and a Tertius. It would have improved the city had he done so.

Lindall Place is a short, dead-end way running from Cambridge Street. To enter, one must pass under the "el," which at this point is so low that a tall man feels like crying "Low bridge" as he goes in. This has the effect of shutting off the rest of the street and gives a feeling of remoteness and seclusion. The impression is enhanced by the presence of old-type street lamps, and potted plants spread colorful blooms here and there along the street.

One cannot fail to like these withdrawn, almost hidden courts. They have the charm of exclusiveness. Happy family life is not confined to the houses; it spills joyously out into the street where it may be shared by the neighbors and the chance passerby. The householders, removed in a way from the busy thoroughfares, find time and inclination for some personal decoration of their own highway. The streets seem to belong to the residents in an intimate and personal way which is never found in the busier and better-known localities.

These retired nooks are a constant reminder that real joy in living is not necessarily a matter of large estates and proud houses. The serenity which is to be found in a few of the hidden squares and courtyards of Boston is a delight equally to the residents and to the visitor.

Two of the more charming of these placid residential squares are to be found between Charles Street on the east and the Embankment on the west. Charles River Square and West Hill Place are the essence of an affable era long past. Even the bricks of the houses are of the small hand-made type which evoke memories of a former day, and they are laid in the old Flemish bond which was the accepted technique of the late seventeenth century.

Charles River Square is oval in shape with a little forest of evergreen trees dividing the two sides. An iron lantern of Colonial design at each end of the garden completes the picture.

West Hill Place is shaped like a keyhole with venerable ivy climbing over the walls of the houses. Otherwise, the two squares are quite similar. In both, the houses are of brick, each house of three stories and each connected to its neighbor. Here one finds granite steps, with doorways having granite keystones after the Bulfinch manner. Wrought-iron balconies are interestingly placed at the upper windows of many of the houses, and delicate fanlights are over the Georgian doors. In the true Boston spirit, the squares are accessible by tunnels through houses; and in the case of West Hill Place, also through a garage.

These secluded places seem even more attractive than the much-better-known Louisburg Square. The difference is that Louisburg Square is really old, but the others are not. Here, appearance of great antiquity is deliberate and intentional. The little squares were designed and built in 1910. Both are reproductions of old London places, and the reproduction has been done with great skill and with careful attention to detail.

One of the most noteworthy of the many outstanding women who have graced the society of Boston was Mrs. Annie Fields, whose cultural background, executive ability, and sympathetic

personality made her the perfect hostess. As the wife of James T. Fields, editor, publisher, and proprietor of The Old Corner Bookstore, Mrs. Fields met and entertained the leading literary lights of her day, including Willa Cather and Sarah Orne Jewett. Even the censorious Charles Dickens, highly critical of all else in the United States, spoke of her personal kindliness, hospitality, and mental ability in terms of warmest praise.

The re-creation of these bits of old London in the midst of busy Boston was an idea which originated with Mrs. Fields and was carried out under her supervision, using the land between her home and the Embankment.

The Fields family lived in a roomy house at 148 Charles Street (now the site of a garage!) with a considerable garden in the rear which was, for many years and in a very personal way, Mrs. Fields' own domain. She took great pleasure in its cultivation, and in her will she left it to the residents of Charles River Square, for the use of their children. The little park reverted to the City of Boston for taxes but was soon repurchased by the Proprietors of the two Squares and is again kept as a private park which can be reached through an archway from West Hill

Place. It is a happy coincidence that this park, dedicated as it is to the pleasures of childhood, should contain several flowering shrubs which were planted there by the "children's poet," Henry W. Longfellow.

When the southerly of these squares was opened, it was given the name of Parkway Square by the street commissioners, but the name was promptly changed to Charles River Square at the request of the abutting owners.

The name of West Hill Place derives from a high bluff which was in the locality when the Puritans arrived. Lying just west of the garden of Mr. Blackstone, the first settler, it was at first called Blackstone's Point but in 1722 was given the name of West Hill, which has been perpetuated by this residential court.

Rollins Place is a short court running from Revere Street. It is wide enough to accommodate an automobile, but it is unaccommodating enough to have a granite post in the center of the street at the entrance. This is the only "no parking" device which seems to be effective in Boston. The post must, however, have been placed long before the advent of the automobile. Perhaps the chaises, coaches, and herdics presented their problem in an earlier day.

The rough brick floor of the passageway is divided down the middle by a row of granite slabs. The brick walls of old residences line both sides. The apartments are not large, but they are altogether delightful. Numbers 3 and 6 are some of the few homes in the city that have fireplaces in the bathrooms. The coachmen who served the wealthy residents of the nearby streets were the original inhabitants of Rollins Place. The odor of the stables has long since been replaced by the odor of antiquity, and the remodeling has been done with taste and restraint.

This street runs directly into the front of a most attractive house—which isn't a house at all. Three steps lead up to a spacious piazza and to an imposing front door with its mat and brass knocker. The steps are flanked by large stone urns of pleasing design. The front of the house is enriched by a pair of Ionic columns which support the second floor, while a second pair support the roof. The façade is of white painted wood with black

The House That Isn't a House: Rollins Place

shutters at the windows. It suggests a small reproduction of one of the nicer mansions of the deep South.

The visitor, looking at this engaging entrance, finds himself envisioning a warm, hospitable interior—also a thoughtful hostess, entertaining, tactful, and witty, with just a hint of the grande dame in her manner. And assuredly there is a courtly host; a little brusque, possibly, but solicitous that the sherry be at exactly the proper temperature.

It is all illusion, mirage, of the mind only. The dream-invoking façade has no substance behind it. The charming house front is merely a wooden facing to a brick wall. Its humane but prosaic purpose is to keep the wandering wayfarer from carelessly walking off the forty-foot cliff that lies behind it.

In earlier days the short street known as Van Rensselaer Place was not as retiring as it now is. It was, in fact, one of the gay spots in a rather drab town which the Puritans founded and strove so fervently and uncompromisingly to keep pure.

The Puritans came to Boston in 1630 to escape from religious persecution in England. The French Huguenots came in 1685 to escape the religious persecution which followed the revocation of the Edict of Nantes. Both groups had a fierce and burning desire to worship God in their own way, and their ways were not dissimilar, but they were alike in nothing else.

The Puritans, dour, introspective, and austere, looked with suspicion on any activity that gave pleasure to the participants. Their laws forbade dancing, "play acting," games, music, and all forms of public entertainment. Men were fined for "playing at bowles"; jailed for card playing; and put in the stocks for kissing their wives in public on Sunday, which, if the portraits that have come down to us are accurate, might have been classed as a penance rather than as a dissipation. The Puritans dressed as sadly as they lived, and any attractiveness or originality was sternly suppressed.

The Huguenots were everything that the Puritans were not. They were merry, buoyant, and cheerful. They loved music, dancing, theatricals, and entertainment. They gaily kissed their wives —or other men's wives—on Sunday or any other day. They dressed to please themselves and their neighbors, in bright and attractive colors.

The influence of the French way of life on the Puritans was slow but pronounced. By the middle of the nineteenth century Boston society had become almost sprightly. One of the greatest changes wrought by the influx of the Huguenots was in the eating habits of the Bostonians. The plain but substantial fare of the eighteenth century was, to a considerable degree, supplanted by the artistry of the French cooking with its rich sauces, alluring flavors, and appealing garnishments.

In the late 1800s there were a number of little French restaurants clustered in Van Rensselaer Place which attained great popularity. Here the citizens of the young Republic learned to enjoy the pleasures of dining in an atmosphere of genial good fellowship. The food, prepared in the French manner, was superb, the decor attractive, and the service excellent.

Occasional dining in Van Rensselaer Place became an accepted rite of people "in society." For congenial groups of artists, writers, and professional men it became a pleasant daily habit. Like the taverns of an earlier day, these restaurants were, in a way, unofficial clubs where the banter and sparkling conversation of the "members" was not the least of their attractiveness.

When the Majestic and the Colonial Theatres were built, their stage doors opened into Van Rensselaer Place and the character of the little street underwent a sudden and drastic change. Actors, musicians, and stage hands took over the alley as their own, and it became a rendezvous for people of the theater. Even the name was changed, although never officially, and, as Majestic Alley, it became a sort of outdoor clubroom for those in "the profession."

Such great artists as Maude Adams, Julia Marlowe, Joe Jefferson, Richard Mansfield, and Ethel Barrymore have chatted here between scenes. An elderly stage hand in a reminiscent mood used to tell of seeing Elsie Janis running a race with an orchestra leader down the length of the alley, and of his keeping score in a horseshoe pitching contest in which Madame Schumann-Heink was the winner.

Allen's Alley

The glory of Van Rensselaer Place and its aristocratic name have departed, although from time to time a dine-and-dance spot still strives valiantly to introduce a note of gaiety into the now gloomy Allen's Alley.

HE MARRIED HIMSELF

Bellingham Place is a short dead-end street running from 85 Revere Street. There are only four houses on the street and, as in Rollins Place, a post, this time of iron, is set squarely in the middle of the entrance to ensure privacy. The residents are protected from the annoyance of automobiles, although, of course, when the post was set in place there were none of these monsters. The paving is of brick and the houses are of brick—time mellowed and ivy grown. There is an air of peace and tranquillity about the spot.

This explorer, chancing on the little highway for the first time, had a persistent feeling that he had visited the place before —long ago and in a dream. The haunting idea that the scene was out of his past experience remained as an annoying, unsatisfied question in the back of his mind.

Following the mysterious laws which govern human thought, the subconscious dutifully came up with the answer in good time. The picture came into focus: A small boy lying on a rug in his father's library, finding delight in the Cruikshank illustrations of a volume of Dickens' stories. This is Bellingham Place. It is London, the London of Dickens and Cruikshank—a London that never existed, perhaps, save in the minds of authors and artists, but very real to those who enjoy the English writers of a century ago. It is a delight to find a bit of this London in Boston City. There are several such places on "The Hill."

Like so many of the Boston streets, this little court has had a variety of names. When it was laid out, in 1847, it was Sherman Place. Two years later it was May Street Court, then, in 1867, Hill Street, and finally Bellingham Place in 1885.

Richard Bellingham, for whom this tranquil retreat was named, was an odd character, even for Boston; but he had what it took to get out the vote. He was four times elected deputy governor and three times governor.

Coming to these shores in the same ship that brought Governors Winthrop and Bellingham was a personable young man named Herbert Pelham. Herbert liked his new environment and

A Little Bit of Dickens: Bellingham Place

wrote home such glowing accounts of his life here that his sister, Penelope, decided to join him and share the great adventure. She arrived in Boston some five years after her brother and assumed the duties of housekeeper for him.

A young man who was living as a boarder in Governor Bellingham's house met the charming Penelope. They found each other mutually attractive and love soon followed. They became engaged to marry, the banns were published, and the marriage contract was about to be signed when the Governor decided that such unusual charms and such striking beauty should really grace the gubernatorial mansion.

Penelope was twenty; the Governor was fifty. Penelope was engaged to marry an eligible young man of her own age whom she presumably loved. But Bellingham must have practiced some of those wiles which brought him the vote year after year, because the fair—but fickle—maiden promptly jilted her fiancé and transferred her affections to His Excellency. Possibly the temptation to be one of the first First Ladies of Massachusetts was too strong for her.

In the early days of the colony it was illegal for a clergyman to perform a marriage ceremony. Marriage was a civil contract and, as such, must be conducted by a magistrate. Happily, Bellingham was a magistrate; so, in this capacity, he speedily performed the ceremony which united him in the bonds of matrimony with his Penelope. In other words, he married himself.

Although there was some question as to the legality of this marriage, there was no doubt at all that the Governor had done an illegal act in not having the contract "published where he dwelt" as required by law.

The bridegroom was indicted and summoned to appear before the court. When it was learned that Bellingham refused to leave the bench, and that he would preside as judge at his own trial, the whole matter was quietly dropped.

PIE OR PI

The average Bostonian is a kindly soul and will help you if possible. And if you ask to be directed to Pie Alley, nine out of ten persons will be able to locate it for you. Pie Alley, formerly Williams Court, represents a case perhaps unique in Boston, in which city officials, most likely frustrated by the habits of its citizens, yielded to popular usage and adopted the nickname of a street.

In the old days, about 1730, Williams Court, then known as Savages Court, was a residential street of the better sort and so it remained until the early 1800s. Its name was then changed to Williams Court in honor of Deacon Williams, who owned considerable property thereabouts.

The street gradually deteriorated, becoming first a semi-slum, later a haven for cheap restaurants, then a back-door entrance to mercantile establishments. Today it is used as a convenient passageway connecting Washington Street to City Hall Avenue and Court Square.

Regarding the spelling of the nickname—whether it be Pie Alley or Pi Alley—there are two schools of thought; and the debate between them is always acrimonious, sometimes bitter, and often profane. Without heat and without rancor we shall present both sides, and the reader may call the decision as he sees it.

The Case for Pie Alley

For many years the Gridley Restaurant was on the corner of Washington Street. It served pie. It was succeeded by the justly famous Thompson's Spa. It serves pie—though in a different location. The bakehouse of George Bray, which was located in the alley, was burned in 1762 with the loss of 150 pounds of flour and about a hundred pies.

Half a century ago there were a number of little "Coffee and" places in the alley. More often than not the "and" was a slab of pie. Most famous of all of these eateries was Henry's Hole in the

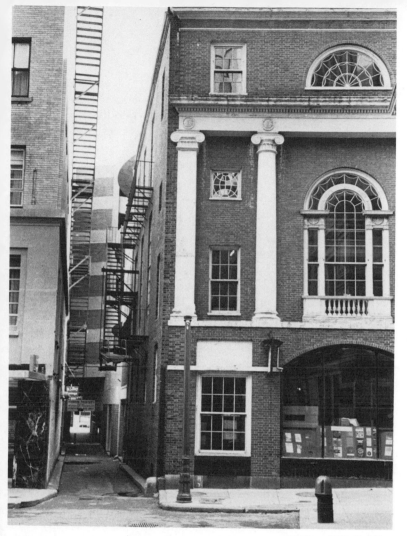

"Pi" or "Pie" Alley

Wall where the specialty of the house was a savory meat pie which sold for ten cents. This was a great favorite with impecunious newsboys and shop clerks. It was generally ordered under the colorful and descriptive name of "Cat Pie." Another favorite was beans and coffee for six cents. Henry could slide a plate of beans and a full cup of coffee the length of the ten-foot counter yet never spill a bean or a drop.

The name of Pie Alley was used, it is claimed, for years before there was a newspaper in the neighborhood.

The Public Works Department of the City of Boston lists Pie but not Pi as the name for the street.

Pie is, therefore, the correct spelling.

The Case for Pi Alley

For many years there was, in this alley, a pleasant tavern called the Bell in Hand. It was a favorite resort for the horde of printers and typesetters who worked in the nearby newspaper plants. It frequently happens in a printing plant that a considerable amount of loose type, often of different styles and sizes, will become thoroughly mixed up. In the printer's argot this loose type is called "pi."

Probably the most disagreeable and time-consuming task that a compositor has to face is to sort out this "pi" and return it to its proper boxes. How much easier it was to put the loose type in a pocket and, on the way to the Bell in Hand, scatter it along the dark alley. It was said that at times the little passageway was practically paved with "pi."

Pi is, therefore, the correct spelling.

James Wilson, the last of the official town criers in Boston, retired in 1795 and opened the Bell in Hand tavern. It became the most famous of the alehouses in a town which has never been deficient in these cheering institutions. Mr. Wilson chose as his sign a wooden arm holding a wooden bell. This was a copy of the bell which he had carried when, as Town Crier, he had had the duty and pleasure of awakening the citizens every hour—on the hour—in order to assure them that all was well.

Anyone who is interested in inspecting the original Arm and Bell sign will find it on display at the Old State House. He may see it also at the newer Bell in Hand tavern, which is now on Union Street. Certainly, Mr. Wilson had two arms and he may have had two bells and two signs. Doubtless both are authentic; the museum of the Old State House is meticulous about its exhibits, and the Bell in Hand on Union Street is a direct descendant of the original one. Many memorabilia of the older tavern are lovingly preserved there.

A favorite resort of Harvard students—and professors— was the old Bell in Hand. Many a learned dissertation was given there over mugs of good ale served with crackers and cheese. Many an old-timer remembers that ale. It was Smith's Philadelphia Cream Ale; the Bell in Hand served nothing else. This was a brew so lively that a standard ten-cent mug would have almost as much "head" or froth as it had ale. The regular patrons would invariably order two "arves" (colloquial for "half") at five cents each and would receive two mugs supposedly half full. Careful and prolonged research indicated that there was nearly as much ale in an "arve" as in a full mug.

While to some, Pie/Pi Alley may be no more than the name of a theater complex, it remains as a fragrant memory in the minds of older residents.

v. City Ways

THE MAIN STEM

Our main stem, Washington Street, was also the chief thoroughfare of the colonists, but they didn't call it Washington—George had not even been born at that time.

The highway was so long that the early residents found it convenient to name it in sections. The part which once ran between Dock Square and School Street was called Cornhill, a nostalgic tribute to a well-remembered London road. From School to Summer it was Marlborough Street, after the Earl of the same name. From Summer to Essex it was known as Newbury Street, and the dismal pathway across "The Neck" was named Orange Street as a delicate tribute to the Prince of Orange.

When George Washington, in 1789, visited Boston, which he had liberated thirteen years earlier, he was met at the edge of the town, on Orange Street, by the Governor's suite. But the Governor himself was conspicuously absent. John Hancock, who occasionally suffered from delusions of grandeur, believed that the chief executive of such a state as Massachusetts was, within his own jurisdiction, more important than the President, so he waited for the General to call upon him. Washington felt otherwise and it was only after a long delay that he was finally persuaded to enter the town.

The first President of the United States made an impressive picture as, dressed in his old Continental uniform and mounted on his white charger—gift of Charles IV of Spain—he rode down Orange, Newbury, Marlborough, and Cornhill Streets to the Old State House. Deeply offended by the nonappearance of the Governor, the President did not return the salutes of the crowd which lined the way, making what amends they could for the churlishness of their local chief executive. Hancock finally realized his

George Washington: The Public Garden

error and, with his legs swathed in bandages, had himself carried into Washington's presence, pleading an excruciating, though not too convincing, attack of gout as the reason for his failure to meet the General. Washington graciously pretended to believe the Governor, and the breach was healed. Mrs. Hancock, as long as she lived, stoutly maintained that the attack of gout was very real and that John was physically unable to welcome the President in person. She was a good wife.

The man who had driven the British out of Boston was given a hero's welcome by the people and, as a mark of their appreciation, they renamed a section of their chief highway Washington Street.

When the Marquis de La Fayette visited Boston in 1824, an emotional populace began naming streets in his honor also. An avenue, a court, and a place were named Fayette; an avenue, a street, a mall, a square, and a park were named La Fayette. They even named a street La Grange after his summer residence in France.

During this orgy of street naming it occurred to someone that a greater hero than the Marquis was being neglected. As a result, all of the sectional names of the main stem were dropped and it was called Washington all the way from Dock Square to Roxbury. Washington Street, in fact, does not stop at the Boston line but continues under the same name throughout the way to Providence. It is the longest street under one name in New England.

Like many of Boston's thoroughfares, Washington Street is a bit devious. It is customary to attribute this to the cows but the real reason is not bovine. Originally starting at Dock Square, it was necessary to curve around a cluster of houses near the dock as well as to pass the water itself. The Great Spring at Spring Lane had to be avoided, and a swing to the west skirted Governor Winthrop's estate. To get around a swamp at Franklin Street required another bend, and a pond at what is now Bedford caused still another curve. At Beach Street began the narrow neck of land which connected Boston with Roxbury. Along this stretch the future Washington Street naturally followed the contour of the shore line. Most of the ancient deviations still exist and furnish an interesting clue to the early topography of the town.

The most thickly settled part of Boston in the very earliest days was the unpaved cart road from the dock as far southward as School Street.

"Rank hath its privileges," and Winthrop, being the governor, had first choice of land for his home. He selected the site next to the "Great Spring." His fellow shipmates chose, or had assigned to them, other lots of land for their homes and gardens. The more important members of the group were located nearby. Elder Thomas Oliver, being elderly as well as an elder, was permitted to be next to the spring, on the other side from the governor.

The south corner of Brattle Street (now replaced by Government Center) was the lot of Richard Bellingham, the several times governor whose somewhat irregular marriage is noted in the previous chapter.

Henry Dunster owned the north corner of Court Street but removed to Cambridge when he became president of Harvard College. The lot on the south corner of the same street was the property of John Leverett, who became governor in 1673 and was re-elected annually until his death in 1678. His son, born in 1662, became another president of Harvard. There are very few neighborhoods that have produced two governors and two college presidents.

On the lot next to that owned by Leverett was built the first church of the Puritans and beside it was the home of the pastor, the Rev. John Wilson. According to an ancient document, Pastor Wilson "came hither to avoid persecution and to have freedom to think and speak as he chose. He left his wife in England."

The land at the corner of Cornhill (Washington) and School Streets was assigned to "Mr. William Hutchinson with his wife Anne." This was the last time that the couple were mentioned in that order. The early records of the colony are filled with discussions about the redoubtable Anne, but the retiring William, on the rare occasions when he is referred to at all, is merely mentioned as "and her husband."

"A Woman of Piety": Anne Hutchinson

Anne Hutchinson was described as "a woman of piety, ready talents and flow of speech." This description was right on all three counts, especially the last. She was a fluent talker, but her ready flow of conversation had a firm background of common sense and deep thinking.

Mrs. Hutchinson organized the women of the colony for the purpose of reviewing and debating the sermons of the Rev. Mr. Cotton. This was innocent enough—even laudable—but Anne soon began to introduce her own ideas and theories into the discussions. She was an Antinomian, believing in a "covenant of grace" rather than a "covenant of works." These phrases, almost meaningless today, were real and dangerous heresies to our ancestors in the 1600s. The Puritan community was deeply agitated. The affair soon resolved itself into a contest, the clergy leading one faction and Anne at the head of the opposing group.

It is a great tribute to the ability and erudition of Mrs. Hutchinson that nearly half of the community, including the youthful governor, Sir Harry Vane, were on her side. Unfortunately for her, however, the opposition included, not only the all-powerful clergy, but the influential ex-Governor Winthrop as well. Anne, whose only crime was thinking in advance of her time, was banished. Governor Winthrop pronounced the sentence: "You are banished from out this jurisdiction, as being a woman unfit for our society; and you are to be imprisoned until the court send you away."

Seventy-six men (over a fourth of the businessmen of the town) were convicted of being her followers and, as a punishment, were obliged to turn their arms and ammunition over to the town. This entailed considerable hardship as well as being a serious disgrace. Winthrop was elected governor in place of her follower, Sir Harry Vane, and a number of lesser officials also lost their positions through having adopted her "dangerous" doctrines.

A more tolerant age, recognizing the merits of this much misunderstood woman, placed her statue on the lawn in front of our State House—one of the few statues of a woman in Boston. The memorial was erected in 1915, but it was not until 1945,

Old Corner Bookstore Building

three hundred years too late, that the Great and General Court of Massachusetts formally revoked the edict of banishment against this enlightened feminist.

The Hutchinson land passed through various hands and, in 1707, became the property of Thomas Cresse, an apothecary, who built thereon a combination shop and home which is still standing—without doubt another of the oldest brick buildings in the city. In 1828, this building was occupied by a firm of publishers and booksellers. As a bookstore it continued until 1903, when the company removed to Bromfield Street. Although no longer on a corner and in a new building they have retained the honored name of the Old Corner Bookstore. Apart from its antiquity, the Old Corner Bookstore is interesting for its association with famous writers. In the golden age of Boston's literary activity—the latter part of the nineteenth century—it served as a meeting place, almost a club, for a group who could be considered the first of the truly great American authors. Longfellow, Emerson, Hawthorne, Holmes, Whittier, Julia Ward Howe, and Harriet Beecher Stowe would gather here for discussions and conversations which must have been a delight to their only auditor, the genial and erudite publisher, James T. Fields, who brought them together.

The lot just beyond the dock on the east side of Cornhill fell to John Coggan, who opened there the first store in Boston. John advertised that he had for sale household goods, tobacco, clothing, and "crooked lane ware," whatever that may have been. After Governor Winthrop died, Coggan married the widow who outlived him by two years and died "not without suspicion of poison."

On the south corner of State Street lived Captain Robert Keayne, who was the founder and first captain of the Ancient and Honorable Artillery Company, a tailor, and a number of other things, including keeper of the pound. In the latter capacity he became embroiled in an argument whose repercussions caused a profound change in the government, a change which has continued to this day.

Mrs. Sherman was a sort of widow, her husband having returned to England. She kept a pig and a Boarder. There was a strong and persistent rumor that the lovely landlady granted many privileges to the Boarder which were neither legally nor morally defensible. The pig, distressed perhaps at being obliged to live in a house of sin, ran away. The Boarder, not distressed at all, remained.

At about this time a stray porker was found wandering about the streets and was duly delivered to the care of Pound Keeper Keayne. The Captain housed the pig with one which he owned and instructed the Town Crier to advertise the foundling. Now, having one more pig than he needed, Captain Keayne butchered one of them—his own, he claimed.

Shortly thereafter, Mrs. Sherman, accompanied by the faithful Boarder, visited the pound demanding "their" pig. They readily admitted that the remaining animal was not their missing porker and so accused the Captain of having butchered the wrong pig. This he denied and the matter was taken before the elders. The remaining pig was viewed, witnesses were interviewed, and the verdict was given that the Captain had undoubtedly killed his own pig, and that the remaining one was a stray. That it was not Mrs. Sherman's was unfortunate, but nobody's fault.

During the hearing, Captain Keayne had made some remarks about the alleged relationship between Mrs. Sherman and the Boarder which rankled in the bosoms of both. So, after due consideration, they entered a complaint before the Lower Court, not for slander, as one might suppose, but for the theft of the pig —yet once more.

Again the verdict was against the pigless matron; but this time the Court, a little weary of the whole affair, slapped on a fine. Mrs. Sherman was ordered to pay the Captain three pounds for his trouble in attending the Court and twenty pounds for the injury to his character.

This should have closed the matter, but it did not. The Boarder, anxious to impress his inamorata, finally found a witness who was willing to testify that he had committed perjury in his former testimony and was now, six years after the event, anxious to ease his conscience by telling the truth.

The General Court admitted the case for a hearing, but very shortly it became involved in a wrangle as to the respective powers of the deputies and the magistrates. The case of the pig and even the spicy details of the "Sherman-Boarder" affair were forgotten while the Court deliberated over this much more important issue. When the smoke of battle cleared, there emerged a Great and General Court split into two houses with almost equal powers. The bicameral system of legislature was born.

The Puritans of Boston were loyal subjects of the King of England. Even as late as the middle of the eighteenth century they were willing to bend the knee—albeit somewhat stiffly—to anyone with a royal title. Consequently there was Puritanical excitement and sober jubilation when, in 1637, the ship *Hector* arrived in Boston Harbor bringing a young man, a ward of Charles I, who rejoiced in the name and title of James, Lord Leigh, Earl of Marlborough.

We may be sure that the populance would find occasion to frequent the primitive cart road where His Grace might be encountered walking with his friend Sir Harry Vane, the Governor. To receive a "Good morning" from such dignitaries was something for a man to boast about over his mug of cider in the evening and to recount to his children as a great event. The townspeople did not get around to naming this bit of highway where His Lordship took his walks until 1708; but when they did it was, of course, Marlborough Street.

During his three months' visit in Boston the noble Earl lodged at Cole's Inn. Cole's was the first institution of its kind to open its hospitable doors in the town, and at the time of His Lordship's visit it was probably the only tavern in New England. There are more now.

Governor Winthrop extended a most gracious invitation to the Earl to lodge with him at his home, but received the somewhat ungenerous reply that Marlborough felt he could be fully as comfortable and private at the inn. It would seem that the accommodations at the inn were superior to the manners of its guest.

Samuel Cole, England's great gift to a thirsty town, opened his house of entertainment in 1634. He came from England in the first shipload of Puritans in 1630. His next-door neighbor to the south was Mrs. Anne Hutchinson and, to the north, the widow of the afore-mentioned Captain Keayne. Cole embraced the religious views of Mistress Hutchinson and was one of those disarmed for so doing. Presumably he also embraced the person of his other neighbor, for they were married shortly after the death of Captain Keayne.

Nothing is known now as to the size or appointments of Cole's tavern, but it must have been a considerable building. When Governor Vane entertained Miantonomo and other chiefs, the four sachems dined with the Governor; but the other chiefs, twenty in all, had their dinner at the inn. It was at this time and in this tavern that the treaty of peace between England and the Narragansets was signed.

Indians never used chairs, nor were they used to individual servings. In all probability, Landlord Cole sat them in a circle on the floor and placed an iron pot of food in the center. It was his thoughtful custom to give people what they wanted. He was not responsible for the fact that a constable always stood at the side of the drinkers in his establishment and arbitrarily cut off the supply just when the guests were beginning to enjoy themselves.

In 1669 a part of Governor Winthrop's land was chosen as the site for a new church, a small cedar building, where Benjamin Franklin was baptized at the early age of three hours. It was a bitterly cold day but, fortunately, it was only a short walk to the church from the little house on Milk Street where Ben was born.

The little chapel was replaced in 1729 by the noble structure now venerated under the name of the Old South Meeting House. The building is held in such national esteem that, when repairs were made in the interior, the wood which was removed was used to panel the walls of President Theodore Roosevelt's private elevator in the White House.

The Old South has echoed to the oratory of Sam Adams, Warren, Otis, and Hancock. It was here that General Warren, in 1775, delivered his famous address on the dangerous subject of the Boston Massacre. There was a considerable number of soldiers present and, it was learned later, they had arranged a plan to seize Adams, Hancock, and Warren on the charge of treason at this meeting. The plot was that an ensign would throw an egg at the speaker the moment he made any treasonable statement. This would be the signal for the seizure of the patriots.

Plenty of treasonable statements were made by the fearless Warren, but no egg was thrown. Perhaps Providence was on the side of the patriots, for on the way to the meeting the ensign had tripped and fallen, breaking not only the egg but his leg as well. The soldiers dared not move without the signal from their officer.

As the meeting progressed some of the soldiers shouted, "Fie! Fie!" This was the eighteenth-century equivalent of our word "baloney." Many of the spectators understood this to be a cry "Fire! Fire!" and a panic followed which emptied the hall much more rapidly than could have been done by force of arms.

During the siege of Boston the British soldiers, unable to lay hands on the patriots, took revenge on the building by using

Old South Meeting House

the pulpit and pews for firewood and the hall itself as a riding school. After the war the church was restored to its original uses. It is now a museum of Revolutionary memorabilia which is visited annually by thousands.

For more than two centuries, the Old South has watched over the city, and each second of those centuries has been ticked away by Gawen Brown's masterpiece, the old belfry clock.

That part of Washington Street which used to be called Marlborough is today some eight hundred feet of narrow, over-crowded, noisy city street where the swarming pedestrians over-flow from the inadequate sidewalk into the inadequate street. Here the horn of the taxi is loud in the ear. Yet above the roar of traffic, above the babble of the myriad shoppers, the mind at-tuned to such matters will hear the beating wings of passing centuries. For this is sacred ground. Here history was made at a pace more furious than the present-day traffic.

The section of the main street which lay between Summer and Essex Streets was named Newbury in 1708 and so remained until 1824, when at last it was given the name of Washington in honor of the general who was revered as being "first in peace, first in war and first in the hearts of his countrymen."

This section, formerly Newbury Street, now Washington, has been first in a lot of things, too. The first Roman Catholic weekly in Boston was published from the Pilot Building, 607 Washington Street. Established in 1838, it was for many years edited and in part owned by John Boyle O'Reilly. The first base-ball club, the Boston Red Stockings, had its home at 765 Wash-ington Street in 1880. In much earlier days the first stagecoach to Providence left from Lamb's Tavern, which was on the land where the noted Adams House was later located.

The first commercial house in the United States to use electric lights was the Continental Clothing Company at the corner of Harvard Street. This was in 1878. David Wheeler, a blacksmith, had a shop in Newbury Street where he made Bos-ton's first fire engine. Its value was amply proved at a fire in 1765.

The world's first telephone "central" was established at 342

Washington Street in 1877 with Miss Emma Nutt as the pioneer female operator. Previous to her appointment the company had experimented with men as "operators" but decided it was a woman's field.

Boston's first regular newspaper was published from an office at the corner of Avon Street. There had been, in 1690, an attempt to publish a monthly newspaper, but it had censor trouble. The Governor's Council issued an edict forbidding any further publication of the paper; it contained "Reflections of a very high Nature and sundry doubtful and uncertain Reports." That was that, and a second issue did not appear.

In 1703 John Campbell, postmaster, decided to try his hand at editing a paper; and Bartholomew Greene, in his shop on what became Newbury Street, agreed to print and publish it. They avoided the danger of censorship by keeping the paper so dull and uninteresting that the most conscientious censor could not endure to read it all. Most of the news items were scissored from month-old English newspapers. The local news seemed to be limited to pleas for advertisements and for delinquent subscribers to pay up.

Altogether the *News Letter* was as poor an apology for a news sheet as one could imagine. But it was all that the people had, so they kept it alive for eleven years. In 1719 Boston was electrified by the publication of a second newspaper, *The Gazette*, a much more sprightly sheet. As a result, and for the first time, the *News Letter* contained an item which really captured the interest of its subscribers. "I pity the readers of the new paper," it said; "its sheets smell more strongly of beer than of midnight oil." With this fragrant endorsement from its rival, *The Gazette* prospered and the *News Letter* quietly died from anemia of the advertising department.

Isaac Vergoose, in 1659, bought a house which was just across the street from Jordan Marsh Company. Of course, the great department store was not there then, for this was some two hundred years before Eben Jordan sold his first yard of cherry-colored ribbon.

Vergoose was a family man—definitely. When he became a

widower at the age of fifty-five there were ten little Vergooses—or should one say Vergeese?—for whose upbringing he was responsible. Following the custom of the time, Isaac promptly remarried. His second wife, Elizabeth Foster of Charlestown, was twenty-seven when they were wed. They had ten children of their own to add to the ten which Isaac had given his bride as a wedding present. Twenty in all—a considerable gaggle!

After fifteen years of active married life with Elizabeth, Isaac passed away serenely conscious of having materially helped a growing nation to grow. His widow carried on and, in spite of her busy life, found time to write a despairing little jingle of frustration.

> There was an old woman who lived in a shoe
> She had so many children she didn't know what to do.

Certainly Madame Vergoose had her problems, but fortunately poverty was not one of them. The family was always referred to as "the wealthy Vergooses," so the young Verganders left the maternal nest well provided for and the Vergeese carried liberal marriage portions to their husbands.

The records of marriages in the City Registrar's office show that "1715, June 8 was married by Rev. Cotton Mather, Thomas Fleet to Elizabeth Goose." By this time the family name of Vergoose had been shortened by the deletion of the "Ver."

Tom Fleet was an impecunious printer who ran a rented press in a rented shop down on Pudding Lane, which is now Devonshire Street. He was able to buy both the shop and the press with the liberal dowry the loving Elizabeth brought him. In addition to the dowry, the printer's bride brought him a Mother-in-Law; for Mother Goose, now alone in the world, went to live with them.

Contrary to what might have been expected, Mrs. Goose was a most welcome addition to the new home. The Fleets in due time had fourteen children; and Mrs. Goose, a motherly old soul who loved little folk, found her greatest pleasure in gathering them about her knee while she entertained them by singing or reciting countless little nonsense rhymes. Many of these she made up at the moment and some were remembered from her own childhood in London.

Fleet, who recognized a profitable thing when he heard it, collected the verses and published them under the title of *Mother Goose's Melodies for Children*. Through two and a half centuries this classic has held its place as one of the "best sellers."

Among antiquarians this is controversial ground. Some stoutly maintain that there never was a Mother Goose. They will tell you that there is no real proof that Fleet ever published the Mother Goose book. Pay no attention to these cynics. There is no proof that he didn't.

Mother Goose died at the age of ninety-two. As required by law, Fleet filed a meticulous inventory of her estate including such insignificant items as "1 small looking glass" and "1 old arm chair." Six months later he presented an accounting of moneys due him from the estate for her care:

To Meat, Drink, Washing and Lodging for fourteen years 9 mo. and 20 days at 6 pounds, 13 shillings and 4 pence a year.

To 4 years ditto when lame.

To cash paid for medicine.

To funeral charges.

It is interesting to note that the sum of the costs equaled—to the exact penny—the value of the estate. Fleet was a businessman!

In the days when Boston Town was young, the only way in which one could reach the mainland without using a boat was by traversing that narrow strip of land called "the Neck." Anciently the Neck presented a scene of desolation. Dank and dangerous marshes bordered its ill-defined road, Orange Street, which at times would be a foot or more under water. The presence of the gallows in no way enlivened the macabre picture. Wharves were built along its easterly side and, as noted before, when ships were tied up at Josiah Knapp's wharf, where Knapp Street is now, they caused a traffic problem as their bowsprits extended across the highway and tangled with passing carts.

Orange Street was important enough to be paved with "pebble" in 1715, two brickyards were built near it in 1770, and fortifications were erected across the Neck some four years later. A mint also was established near the fort in 1786 where the mint master struck off seventy thousand dollars in Massachusetts coinage—copper cents and half-cents for the most part.

Auchmuty Lane (now Essex) was the dividing line between the old Orange and Newbury Streets. It marked the beginning of the unsavory lowlands of the Neck. Quite early in the history of the colony a tavern was built at this corner. It was an ideal spot for an inn. Here the traveler could fortify himself against the dreary, and sometimes dangerous, trip out of town across the Neck. If he was entering the town, the inn was the fitting place to celebrate the end of a disagreeable journey.

A comfortable taproom with a blazing fire in the commodious fireplace offered a delightful spot for lounging in the winter time; but in the summer it was pleasanter to take a mug of cider or pot of beer at one of the little tables which stood under a huge spreading elm tree in the front yard.

Every public house becomes, sooner or later, a sort of club or gathering place for congenial people. The outdoor tippling place under the elm was the rallying place for a youthful gang of "South Enders" who delighted in occasional clashes with an equally mayhem-minded gang known as the "North Enders." Their mock warfare was often not so mock, and bloody noses and broken heads were a frequent result.

Fully ten years before the actual outbreak of the Revolution there were some patriotic colonists who realized that war with England was inevitable. They were not averse to fomenting the unrest that was every day more apparent. Chief among these far-seeing lovers of liberty was Samuel Adams. Sam looked with a speculative eye at the simulated warfare between the "North Enders" and the "South Enders." It seemed a waste of good material, for he realized the potentialities of the two "armies." A lot of skillful persuasion was necessary, but Sam knew how to influence men and accomplish his desires. Under his guidance the rival factions forgot their sectional differences and united as "the Sons of Liberty" against the common enemy, England. They became a factor of major importance in the years before the final outbreak.

"The World Should Never Forget the Spot Where Once Stood Liberty Tree . . ."

The shady front yard of the tavern where the "South Enders" had met became the headquarters of the united group. The mighty elm, christened "Liberty Tree," became their rallying point and symbol of the dreamed-of freedom. The open space under its branches was known as "Liberty Hall." A flagpole was erected which extended through and above the highest branches of the tree, and a flag hoisted there was the signal for action.

Much of the pre-Revolutionary activity in Boston was centered about this old elm. Upon its trunk were posted inflammatory cartoons and verses. Its branches bore the strange fruit of Tories hanged in effigy, and in times of victory—such as the repeal of the Stamp Act—the tree was gay with innumerable lanterns. Under its shade Secretary Oliver was forced to resign his post as Collector of Customs, which he did in as craven and mendacious a little speech as ever traitor uttered.

Strange, is it not, that these "Sons of Liberty," who were willing to fight and to die that liberty might be achieved, saw nothing incongruous in an advertisement that appeared in the Boston *Gazette* at about this time: "To be sold at public auction: Household furniture, sundry pieces of plate and a likely Negro lad. The sale to be at the house in Auchmuty's Lane not far from Liberty Tree." Even to the patriots of 1775, liberty was something exclusively for white men.

"Liberty Tree," symbol of liberty and focal point of Boston's early struggles against tyranny, was inevitably an object of hatred to the British soldiers. It was with great delight and joy that they cut it down during their occupation of the town. The size of the tree is indicated by the fact that it yielded fourteen cords of firewood. To the colonists it seemed nothing less than the divine hand of the avenging Providence when one of the axmen was killed by a falling branch.

When La Fayette made a post-Revolutionary address in Boston he said: "The world will never forget the spot where once stood the 'Liberty Tree,' so famous in your annals." Prophets should use the word "never" with extreme caution. Almost two centuries have passed since the Marquis predicted that the world would never forget the "Liberty Tree." Does the world remember? How many otherwise good and proper Bostonians could tell where it stood or what it was?

On a Washington Street building near the corner of Essex one may find a freestone bas-relief depicting the symmetrical branches of the "Liberty Tree." This carving is directly over the spot where the famous elm grew.

FROM FROGS TO FURS

It has long been an accepted custom in Boston to name streets after the most important or the most vocal of its residents. The colonists made no exception to this rule when they gave the name of Frogg Lane to the public way which ran "From Orange [Washington] Street through the marsh to the sea." The "marsh" is now the Public Garden and the "sea" came up to the corner of Boylston and Charles Streets.

John Josselyn, an English writer and traveler, visited Boston and wrote an on-the-spot account of the Boylston Street frogs: "some, when they sit upon their breech, are a foot high, and some as long as a child one year old."

The filling in of the Back Bay was a fatal blow to the family life of these fabulous frogs. Frogg Lane emerged from its primordial slime to become one of the show streets of the city. Elegant furs, exquisite gowns, and costly jewels gleam and glitter within the shops. Elegant furs, exquisite gowns, and costly jewels also gleam and glitter outside the shops, for Boston's most beautiful, chic, and attractively dressed women now promenade Frogg Lane.

Historic buildings, unusual types of architecture, and unexpected vistas line the highway. There is the decorative Masonic Temple, the Towne House Apartments on the site of the home of President John Quincy Adams, the historical Common, and the delightful Garden. One passes the Little Building (a misnomer if there ever was one), the Arlington Street Church, whose steeple was the first in Boston to be constructed of stone, and at last arrives at Copley's triangular Square with its delightful grouping of library, hotel, and more churches. And very fittingly located near the end of this street is the home of the Massachusetts Historical Society, oldest of all the historical societies in the country.

If one walks down Boylston Street with his eyes focused on the upper stories of the buildings he may have some unfortunate encounters with other pedestrians, but he will be rewarded with seeing odd, unexpected, and frequently charming bits of architecture: a colonnade of Corinthian columns from a third story to the roof of a building; tiles and mosaics after the Moorish manner; fanlights, grillwork, pillared balconies; frequent and intriguing glimpses of the blue roof of the old John Hancock Building and always the gleaming façade of the new; and the massive dignity of the New England Life.

Beyond Copley Square the pedestrian finds the Prudential Center and across the street an old building of red sandstone exhibiting more engaged columns and varied ornamentation than one could believe possible in so small a structure. Once a combined fire and police station, the building is now shared by the firemen and the Institute of Contemporary Art while the police occupy its small brick extension. Next come the beautiful

Arlington Street Church

shrine of Saint Clement, attractive apartment houses, and eventually the carefully landscaped Fens, where a bust of John Boyle O'Reilly gazes approvingly down the length of the street.

In 1812, Frogg Lane changed its name along with its character and became Boylston Street, honoring Dr. Zabdiel Boylston. From its beginning, Boston had suffered from periodic epidemics of smallpox, some of which were so severe that almost half of the population would be stricken at the same time. Few escaped and those who recovered were not considered socially acceptable until they had undergone certain semi-mystic rites as indicated in the following "passport," issued in 1776:

These certify that Ebenezer Stimpson has been so smoked and cleansed that in our opinion he may now be permitted to pass into the country without danger of communicating the Small Pox to anyone.

Signed:

Nathaniel Appleton

John Scollay

Selectmen of Boston.

The Rev. Cotton Mather was an omnivorous reader, and whatever he read immediately produced a profound fixation in his mind, for or against the subject. He was always positive and sometimes right. In the course of his miscellaneous reading, Mather ran across an interesting news item from Turkey. It was an account of the successful use of inoculation as a preventative for smallpox.

Fired with his usual zeal, the clergyman succeeded in interesting Dr. Zabdiel Boylston in this method of combating the dread disease. By way of testing the theory, Dr. Boylston inoculated his own son, Thomas, aged six, and two servants. They all responded well, and the doctor felt willing to try the experiment on the paying customers.

The opposition of the public to this type of treatment was terrific. Mobs, carrying ropes, hunted Dr. Boylston through the town with the full intention of hanging him if he could be found.

A crude bomb was also thrown into the bedroom of the Rev. Cotton Mather which, if the fuse had not been dislodged, would have killed him and wrecked his house. A paper tied to this infernal machine read, "Cotton Mather, you dog. Damn You, I will Enoculate you with this, with a Pox to you."

Dr. Boylston continued to inoculate all who would let him, and the results were so satisfactory that within a year the fickle public who had wanted to hang him were clamoring for his services. One of his most willing and importunate patients was a young man whose curiosity had led him to investigate a tomb in the Old Granary, the lock of which had fallen off. After spending some time in his gruesome investigations, the young man was horrified to read on one of the coffin plates, "Died of the Small Pox." Dr. Boylston had another convert.

When the advantages of inoculation had become fully evident, one of the oddest types of social gatherings ever to be known in Boston came into being. Ladies and gentlemen in the upper social brackets issued formal invitations to "small pox parties." A typical invitation would read:

> Miss Sally Pollard is invited to take the small pox at my home on the evening of June fifth together with a few friends.
> Tea and music will be enjoyed.

The terrible scourge was vanquished, and we named a street for the conqueror. We could do more.

ONE SIDE OF A STREET

Extending the entire length of Park Street on one side is Boston Common, while on the other side is much that has made Boston uncommon. History has been made and histories have been written on this short street.

Park Street is old, even as the city of Boston is old. They began life almost simultaneously. For the first fifty years the highway, then called Centry Lane, was a meandering path along

Park Street from the State House

which cows grazed. Over this trail the sentry traveled to his lonely but important duty atop Beacon Hill, where he kept watch for possible invaders, ever ready to light the tar-barrel beacon if it seemed necessary.

For the next hundred and fifty years or so the street was given over to public institutions of the necessary but unpleasant sort. These included the Almshouse, the House of Correction, the Insane Asylum, the Jail, and the Pound.

During the nineteenth century the lane was straightened, paved, and entirely rebuilt under the direction of Charles Bulfinch. Even its name was changed, from Centry to Park Street. After this face-lifting operation, the highway became residential in character and was graced by the homes of some of Boston's most distinguished personages, including three governors: Christopher Gore, James Sullivan, and Henry Gardner; three mayors: Josiah Quincy, Jr., Josiah Quincy II, and Harrison Gray Otis;

two Harvard Presidents: Josiah Quincy and Fisher Ames; a Secretary of the Navy: George Cabot; a Secretary of War: Samuel Dexter; and a host of other noteworthy persons.

During this period, when it was the home of so many notables, Park Street was the dividing line between the business and the residential parts of the town. This fact gave rise to the then popular axiom that "No gentleman takes a drink before three o'clock or east of Park Street."

During the late 1800s, residents of this favored thoroughfare gradually gave way before the inroads of business. The last family to leave removed to another part of the city in 1907. Today, the Houghton Mifflin Company, publishers, occupies the site of the home of historian John Lothrop Motley; the Union Club is in the home of Abbot Lawrence; the Paulist Center is on the site of Josiah Quincy's dwelling; and the famous Amory-Ticknor house has become both an antique store and the jewelry shop of Trefry and Partridge.

When Park Street was given over to public institutions, there was built at the corner of Tremont Street a huge barn, 2400 square feet in size. This was a sort of welfare project—the plan being to store corn and wheat in this structure and, in times of scarcity, to sell the grain to the poor at cost. The fact that such thoughtfulness was deeply appreciated by certain of the inhabitants is indicated by a report made to the selectmen that "the weevils have taken the wheat, and mice annoy the corn much, being very numerous." This seems as good a method as any for taking care of surplus products, but as a means of relieving the poor it was not overly successful.

After the failure of this "noble experiment" the building was sold to a manufacturer of canvas, who there fabricated the sails for the frigate *Constitution.*

In 1809 the building was torn down and the lumber used to construct a tavern in Dorchester, which was in dire need of another bistro. All that is left of the old granary is its name, which has been perpetuated by the nearby cemetery.

Shortly after the removal of the granary, the site was occupied by Peter Banner's masterpiece, the Park Street Church—

a building so attractive that Henry James spoke of it as "perfectly felicitous" and "the most interesting mass of brick and mortar in America."

There are some interesting "firsts" connected with the Park Street Church. It was here that "America" was first sung in public, on July 4, 1832. William Lloyd Garrison, on July 4, 1829, here gave his first antislavery address. It was without doubt the first church ever to rent part of its building as a tearoom—and to cancel the lease when the management permitted women to smoke. It surely was the first, and only, church to be invaded by a water-spout coming from the world's very first subway. When, on Sunday morning, November 24, 1895, a workman in the Tremont Street Subway struck his pick into a huge water main, a terrific geyser spurted upwards with such force that it broke the windows in the minister's study and half filled the room with the vilest of mud. The pastor, in his evening sermon, called the subway "an infernal hole" and "an unchristian outrage." Some of us moderns might go along with him on that. "And who," he thundered, "is the Boss in charge of the work?" After a dramatic pause he exclaimed, "It is the Devil!"

The site of this church has long been known to Bostonians as "Brimstone Corner." By tradition this is a tribute to the fiery sermons preached in the church; but actually, and prosaically, it received the name because brimstone, used in making gunpowder, was stored in the basement during the War of 1812.

In a building next to the church there was an auditorium where, in 1884–85, a small group met each Sunday in response to a notice which read: "The Church of Christ respectfully invites you to attend their Services at number two Park Street, Hawthorne Hall, every Sunday at 3 P.M.; and learn how to heal the sick with Christianity." The organizer and leader of this group was Mary Baker Eddy, and so this site might appropriately be called the birthplace of the Christian Science Church.

The Paulist Center and Chapel now occupy the building where for a while were the offices of the *Atlantic Monthly*. This was also the site, in the earliest days, of the old pound where stray animals were confined. The cows, regardless of ownership,

Park Street Church: Brimstone Corner

were permitted to graze at will on the Common; but the bulls, being town property, were given special attention. In 1703 a George Ripley was appointed to "take care of watering the bulls, and to put them by night in the Burrying Place." This not only took care of the bulls but protected the cemetery from trespassers, also saving the town the expense of cutting the grass and buying fertilizer.

Number 6 was the home of the noted physician, surgeon, and teacher Dr. Jonathan M. Warren. It was he who, with Dr. Jackson, was first to use ether as an anesthetic during an operation. At his home on Park Street the doctor had not only his office but also a small surgery with a demonstration room where he instructed a select group of medical students. The back windows of this house overlooked the Burying Ground. It must have been a great comfort to a surgeon of that day to look out of his window and be assured that if he had made any mistakes they were well and permanently hidden.

In 1720 the House of Correction stood on the lot now occupied by the Union Club. It—the reformatory, not the club— was built "for the accommodation of able bodied persons who were unwilling to work; the Almshouse never has been intended for the entertainment of such scandalous persons." The building contained two large rooms "one for men, t'other for women." The law provided that "a whipper should be in constant attendance."

During the residential period of Park Street, this site was occupied by a skillful and popular physician, Dr. John Jeffries. For relaxation, the doctor was interested in ballooning. On January 7, 1785, he, with a Frenchman named François Blanchard, made the first flight across the English Channel. The doctor was so anxious to make the trip that he not only paid all the expenses but also signed an agreement that if it were necessary to lighten the ship he would jump overboard. Dr. Jeffries was not obliged to make the supreme sacrifice, but it was close. Before they reached the shores of France everything in the balloon was thrown overboard, including most of the clothes of the intrepid aeronauts.

Amory Tichnor House

After the death of Dr. Jeffries in 1819, his house became the home of the great philanthropist Thomas Handasyd Perkins, who gave considerable sums to both the Massachusetts General Hospital and the Athenaeum. It was he who founded the Perkins Institute for the Blind.

The "Almshouse Lot" at the corner of Beacon Street was purchased in 1801 by the wealthy merchant Thomas Amory, who erected a mansion there in 1804. The wine and coal cellars built at that time still extend cavernously under Park Street. In 1806 this building was occupied by Mrs. Catherine Carter, who made it into a fashionable boarding house. It was here that General La Fayette made his headquarters during his triumphal visit in 1824. The doors were thrown open and the public invited to enter and meet the General. A tremendous throng responded to the invitation but, alas, did not have the pleasure of shaking his hand; for the moment the General entered the house he requested to be shown to the bathroom. There he remained so long that most of the guests left without seeing him.

Professor George Ticknor purchased the property in 1830. He possessed a magnificent library which was probably the finest private collection of books in the city at that time. Among the many friends who came to visit him—and his books—were the leading men of the town: Everett, Bowditch, Channing, Prescott, and Daniel Webster.

By the turn of the century the building had been taken over by mercantile interests. The interior has been altered past all recognition, but pictures of the original rooms may be seen at the Athenaeum.

TWO SIDES OF A STATUE

School Street was laid out only ten years after the Puritans arrived in Boston. There is no doubt that it was a much frequented lane for many years before that.

The first settlers of Boston were people of education and culture. Very strongly they desired that their children should have the advantages of a thorough education. However, the problems of establishing a home in the wilderness were too great to permit them to give much attention to this matter for the first few years. Yet in the town records for 1634, we find that "Philemon Pormont be intreated to become a schoolmaster for the teaching and nourtering of the children with us."

As Philemon was "intreated" so he did. In due time a schoolhouse was built just below the site of the present King's Chapel, on a lane or cowpath which meandered up that way. This was the first public school in America. A superior school it was. A superior school it still is. Now located in the Fenway but still under its original name, the Boston Latin School continues its high tradition of scholastic excellence. This institution has probably graduated more men of note than any other public high school.

Great men of the past received their early training in this famous school just as great men and women of the future are receiving training there now. Benjamin Franklin, John Hancock,

Robert Treat Paine, Cotton Mather, Samuel Adams, and many other men of renown occupied its hard benches.

The pathway where the school was located was called, very properly, School House Lane. Later it became Latin School Street, which was soon shortened to School Street. So it has remained.

When the present King's Chapel was built, it was found necessary to take the grounds occupied by the school building, but the church built a new schoolhouse on the opposite side of the street.

As with all civic changes, this was most displeasing to some citizens, one of whom expressed his wrath in a clever little quatrain:

> A fig for your learning! I tell you the town,
> To make the church larger, must pull the school down
> "Unhappily spoken!" exclaims Master Birch;
> "Then learning, it seems, stops the growth of the church."

A seemingly needless passageway leads from School Street into the graveyard of King's Chapel. According to the early records, this passageway "must be wide enough for a man with a wheelbarrow and so kept open forever." Oddly enough, this alley passes right through the vestry of the church. It must have been designed for an exceptionally narrow man with a very thin wheelbarrow.

Next to King's Chapel is Boston's Old City Hall (or "City Haul," as one disgruntled taxpayer wrote it). Built during the Civil War, this building reflects the influence of the French ideas in architecture which prevailed at that time. The lot upon which it stands has had only two owners: Thomas Scottow, who was one of the first settlers, and the Town of Boston, to whom he sold it in 1645.

On the front lawn of Old City Hall stand the bronze statues of two men, both graduates of the Latin School. Many citizens of Boston feel that those who occupy our municipal headquarters do not always display the civic wisdom we have a right to expect, but no one has ever criticized their wisdom in the choice of the two men who are given the places of honor in front of Old City Hall.

"Boston's Most Distinguished Son":
Ben Franklin in front of Old City Hall

One of the statues is of Josiah Quincy, who is represented as he was when mayor of the city, an office he held for five terms. Few men have done as much for the advancement of a city as Mayor Quincy did for his.

The second statue is of Boston's most distinguished son—Benjamin Franklin. Tablets on the side of the pedestal show Franklin (1) working as a printer, (2) signing the Declaration of Independence, (3) signing the Peace Treaty with France, and (4) conducting electrical experiments.

The Rev. Edward Everett Hale, who lived almost directly across the street from the statue, wrote to a friend: "Richard Greenough [the sculptor who made the statue] once told me that in studying for the statue he found the left side of the great man's face philosophical and reflective and the right side, funny and smiling." You will find that Greenough so delineated it. Viewed from the east one sees Franklin the statesman; from the west, the author of *Poor Richard's Almanac*.

BULFINCH BUILT

Houses with bay windows are quite in the Boston tradition, and a personal "bay window" is fairly common among our older residents; but of Boston streets having a definite and symmetrical bulge in the middle there is only one. Franklin Street, between Hawley and Devonshire, curves outward on both sides so that the street at this point has a very noticeable increase in width. This is no middle-age spread, however, for we must go back over two hundred years to find the reason.

As early as 1750, a pathway known as Vincent's Lane ran from Marlborough (now Washington) Street and ended in a large bog or marsh near what is now the corner of Franklin and Arch Streets. The owner, Joseph Barrel, a wealthy merchant, filled in the marsh and made it a most attractive part of his garden, beautified with a fish pond and a fountain.

In 1793, three public-spirited and far-seeing men, Charles Bulfinch, William Scollay, and Charles Vaughan, bought the land and developed what became Franklin Street. Bulfinch designed a block of sixteen buildings all joined together in a crescent form. This was built on Franklin Street and became Boston's first apartment house. In the center was a large arch which permitted the passage of a street, right through the building. This street was, and still is, known as Arch Street.

Bulfinch displayed his great artistic ability in the design of the archway, where Venetian windows and classical columns pleasingly broke the uniformity of the houses.

Tontine Crescent Arch, Franklin Street

The two rooms above the arch were then occupied by the Massachusetts Historical Society and the Boston Library Society. The beauty of the archway has been preserved for us by the skill and wisdom of the architectural firm of Putnam and Cox, who, in designing the façade of the Kirstein Memorial Library on City Hall Avenue, closely followed the design of this archway, the arch itself becoming the huge central window.

Across the street from the apartment building the business structures were erected in an outward curve to balance that of the block of houses. The resulting oval space, about three hundred feet long, in the center of the street was laid out as an enclosed garden ornamented by a huge urn which Bulfinch had bought in Bath, England. This he placed in the center of the garden as a memorial to Benjamin Franklin, for whom the street had been named. The urn is now in the Mount Auburn Cemetery, appropriately marking the grave of Charles Bulfinch.

The approach to the crescent was graced by two other buildings, both examples of the genius of the same incomparable Bulfinch—Boston's first theater and the city's first Roman Catholic cathedral. Bishop Carroll of Baltimore consecrated the cathedral in 1803, and the town was fortunate indeed in securing the services of John Cheverus as its first pastor. One of our public schools now bears his honored name.

The church property, which in 1799 cost $2500, sold in 1860 for $115,000, a sum which helped considerably in the building of the great Cathedral of the Holy Cross on Washington Street. In the crypt of this magnificent building is the altar from the Franklin Street church.

Not far from the site of the first cathedral there is today a narrow building which houses several Catholic offices and organizations including the Oratory of Saint Thomas More. Here one finds an island of peace in the midst of the noise and bustle of the city. Soft illumination, a mural of the All-Knowing and All-Forgiving Christ, and the deep-toned voice of an unseen priest combine to give rest and comfort to the weary and afflicted.

All day long visitors come—men and women of all creeds or of no creed. They remain long enough to absorb something of courage and strength, and depart, with faith renewed, to their round of business or pleasure.

About the time that the cathedral was built there was a printer and engraver of music, Gottlieb Graupner, who had his home and shop at number 6 Franklin Street. Here he organized an orchestra, the first to be formed in this part of the country. It grew into the Philharmonic Society. A group of singers which he gathered together at about the same time justified his faith by becoming the famous Handel and Haydn Society.

In the First Federal Savings & Loan at number 50 is a "Federal Room" which is, in effect, a little museum of Frankliniana. Exhibited here are a number of rare portraits of this famous Bostonian, books and papers published by him, and a well-chosen library of books about him.

An old-timer cannot leave this neighborhood without a nostalgic tribute to the memory of the old Arch Inn. Here, sixty years ago, the gourmet could find an excellent eight-course dinner deliciously prepared and graciously served. Such a meal was, of course, not cheap. The dinner, with a bottle of excellent wine included, cost seventy-five cents!

FIRE!

The constellation of the Great Dipper is a "natural" for a tavern sign: distinctive, easily remembered, easy to paint, and suggestive of long and satisfying drinks. Thomas Bannister, landlord, was pleased when the idea occurred to him and he wasted no time until the sign of the Great Dipper appeared, in 1689, on the tavern which he had recently bought.

Bannister's inn was located at "Ye Mylne Street," which ran "from ye Broad street to ye Widow Tuthill's windmill." To modernize these names—the tavern was on Summer Street near Hawley, and the mill was on the seashore about where the ocean covered the site of South Station.

Carrying grist to and from the mill was a thirst-provoking business, and the tavern prospered. The carters had little knowledge of astronomy; but they could count up to seven, and the tavern became generally known as Seven Star Inn. It was not long before "Ye Mylne Street" became Seven Star Lane.

In 1730 the tavern was sold to the First Episcopal Church Society, which built there a wooden edifice, the first building of Trinity Church. Peter Faneuil was a member. George Washington worshipped in the church—it is even possible that "George Washington slept here"—although Dr. (later Bishop) Parker was not a soothing speaker. The wooden building was replaced in 1828 by a granite church of Gothic design graced with square towers.

To the early settlers, the land at the junction of Summer and Bedford Streets had seemed an ideal spot for a future church so they named it Church Green. In 1715, the New South Church was built there, an octagonal white granite building with Doric columns and a graceful steeple. The church was removed in 1868 to make room for a store. It is a curious fact that the square was known as Church Green before the church was built. It has also

Church Green

been Church Green ever since the removal of the sacred building, but the name was not used while the church stood there.

The first half of the nineteenth century was unquestionably a socially pleasant period in Boston's history, and Summer Street was one of the most attractive of all the residential thoroughfares. Stately horse-chestnut trees lined both sides, and their interlaced branches turned the street into a cool, delightful, green tunnel.

The rustic beauty of the street inspired Bulfinch to design a special type of mansion exactly suited to these wide, tree-shaded spaces. Here the houses were set well back from the street and were surrounded by magnificent gardens. The list of residents of Summer Street at this time was also a list of the most wealthy, most cultured, and most socially prominent people of the city.

By 1850 stores had begun to replace the mansions, and in a few years Summer Street became a region of magnificent shops.

Came November 9, 1872—7:24 in the evening. A tragic date for the city of Boston, the beginning of a disaster such as the city had never before experienced. A watchman, strolling his beat along Summer Street, glanced at the four-story warehouse at the corner of Kingston Street. Even as he looked, the roof exploded into flames and a fountain of blazing hoop skirts cascaded into the air. As he sounded the alarm from box 52 at the corner of Bedford Street, a dozen other roofs were burning from the flying sparks. Emergency calls went out to neighboring towns. In a surprisingly short time men and apparatus arrived from thirty-five communities, including such distant places as Providence, New Haven, and Biddeford, Maine.

Red tongues licked the buildings hungrily, smoke billowed to the sky; the heat was so fierce that even above the crackling of the flames the wild scamperings of thousands of rats seeking safety could be heard.

The fire soon laid waste to a triangular area bounded roughly by Washington Street, Atlantic Avenue, and Milk Street. Sixty-five acres in the heart of the city consumed! Fourteen lives lost! Seventy-five million dollars' worth of property destroyed!

An amazing fact is that of the 776 buildings reduced to rubble, all but 67 were "fireproof" structures built of stone or brick. Boston learned the hard way that a "fireproof" building filled with highly combustible material and topped by a mansard roof of wood and tar is not as fireproof as it appears.

Even before the ashes of the great fire had cooled, the task of clearing and rebuilding began. A new and much more functional and artistic business area rose over the ashes of the old. Mark Twain in his *Life on the Mississippi* really went overboard in describing the rebuilt area. He wrote: "The 'burnt district' of

Boston was commonplace before the fire, but now there is no commercial district in any city in the world that can surpass it —or perhaps rival it—in beauty, elegance and tastefulness."

BOSTON COMMON AND BOSTON PREFERRED

By the laws and customs of the seventeenth century, the Rev. William Blackstone was the owner of the peninsula which became Boston. The group with which he had come held a grant from the King. He had lived here for eight years; he had built a house and improved the land. It was his.

When he made the mistake of inviting the Puritans to join him, they "gave" him some fifty acres of his own land which he sold back to them within a year. The sale also included all of his rights in and to the entire peninsula. Thirty pounds was the price, which indicates that the Reverend was a smart operator in real estate—when one remembers what Manhattan Island sold for at about the same time.

Each of the colonists contributed six shillings or more, according to his means, to make up the purchase price; so Blackstone's garden became common property and was set aside by Governor Winthrop as a grazing place for the colony cows and as a training ground for the soldiers. It is still common property— the Common, the oldest public park in the country.

The fact that the Common belongs to the people rather than the city is important. None of the land can be sold or leased, no building can be built upon it, no roads may run through it, and none of it can be taken for widening or altering of streets without the consent of the citizens. Even the chief executive of the city cannot dispose of any part of it, although it is a matter of record that some have tried.

During the three and a half centuries since its creation the Common has been the stage where many local dramas have been played—some of great historic interest, many humorous, and others downright grim. During the 1600s, executions were public and were much appreciated by the populace, who flocked to the

Beacon Street Mall: Boston Common

Common in tremendous numbers to see some unfortunate Quaker, pirate, or witch "turned off," as the phrase went. People who are denied normal amusements will turn to abnormal pleasures. The Puritans, who were not permitted to indulge in sports, games, dancing, theatricals, or music, derived an emotional stimulation from watching a hanging—even that of poor Rachel Whall, who was executed for stealing a bonnet valued at seventy-five cents.

The stocks, as well as the gallows, had an honored place on the Common and that was fun too. This seat of humiliation confined the wrists and ankles of the culprit, which in itself was not too painful. The real horror of the device was that it left the victim exposed to a barrage of fruit, eggs, and mud from the sportive minded. If the poor wretch was really unpopular he might expect stones and clubs to be hurled at him as well. More than one man was maimed for life after "an hour in ye stocks."

In 1634 a carpenter by the name of Palmer was hired by the town to make the first stocks. He did a good, workmanlike job, submitting his bill for one pound, thirteen shillings. The town elders felt this to be excessive and haled Palmer before the court

121

on a charge of profiteering. He was found guilty, fined one pound, and sentenced to spend a half-hour in the stocks—the elders wanted to try out the new apparatus without delay.

A few months later a man convicted of bigamy was fined a hundred pounds and also sentenced to be "set in the stocks for one hour on Lecture Day for two weeks so that all maids and widows might see him and not become number three." Evidently he was a man whose fatal fascination was feared.

A prowling Puritan reported to the watch one evening that there was a drunken English sailor loose on the town. After diligent search the culprit was found—in bed at his lodgings, sound asleep. The constable woke him, forced him to dress, and set him in the stocks. A French sailor, who had been the man's drinking companion earlier in the evening, felt that this was monstrously unfair so he released the prisoner. Horrified at this flouting of authority, the constable put the Frenchman in the stocks, receiving a black eye in the process. An international incident appeared to be in the making so Governor Winthrop was summoned. The Governor promptly released the Frenchman and made him a public apology. He also publicly reprimanded the constable for arresting the English sailor without a warrant, for putting him in the stocks, then for letting him escape, and finally for molesting the Frenchman. In private the Governor complimented the officer on his zeal and ability.

One of the uses to which the Common was dedicated originally was as a parade ground and training field for soldiers. The Puritans did not intend it to be so used by their enemies, but it was. Before the Revolution and during the siege of Boston the British soldiers camped on the Common, and it was from here that they left for their foray into Lexington and Concord. Many were brought back from that expedition to be buried in a trench at the foot of the Common.

Celebrations here have been many and spectacular. Salutes, illuminations, and fireworks greeted the repeal of the Stamp Act. A huge bonfire marked the surrender of Cornwallis. Fireworks, both visual and oratorical, marked the Grand Temperance Convention of 1844, the completion of a public water system in

Central Burying Ground: Boston Common

1848, the Railway Jubilee of 1851, the celebration of a visit by the Prince of Wales in 1857, and a greeting to Colonel Lindbergh in 1927. For over three hundred years the colorful drumhead elections of the Ancient and Honorable Artillery Company of Massachusetts have furnished an annual spectacle on the Common, a dramatic survival of an ancient rite.

Like London's Hyde Park, the Common has always been a forum for eccentrics. The radical and the crackpot are permitted to rave unrebuked; perhaps letting off steam prevents them from having a real explosion. In 1851 a woman mounted one of the benches and unleashed a flood of oratory on the crowd which quickly gathered. She was wearing a queer sort of trousers instead of a skirt. Strange to say, she was crusading for this scandalous type of dress for women. Her name was Amelia Bloomer, and the garment, with some changes, still occasionally bears her name.

It is quite typical of Boston that a cemetery should be a part of the public playground. The Central Burying Ground was not, as is often stated, the first cemetery of the colony. It was the fourth. The oldest stone bears the date of 1749, which is old enough so that the trunk of a tree almost encloses one of the tablets. There are more gravestones here that show the Square and Compasses, a Masonic emblem, than there are in any other burial ground in the city. Julien, Boston's first restaurateur, whose delicious soup still finds a place on the menu of the better-class eating places, rests here, as does the famous portrait painter Gilbert Stuart, although the grave of the latter is unmarked. Wishing to honor this distinguished artist, the Paint and Clay Club in 1897 prepared a bronze palette as a memorial to be placed on his grave. Unable to locate his final resting place they hung their tribute on the fence.

Near the Tremont Street side of the Common is a memorial to the martyrs of the Boston Massacre. A bronze plaque vividly depicts the scene, the most prominent figure being that of Crispus Attucks, the Negro who was the first to fall a victim to the British muskets. A superstitious belief has grown up that it brings good luck to touch the extended hand of Attucks, which now has a high polish from the frequent contacts. Shake hands with the statue some time. Who knows what effect it may have! Unlike kissing the Blarney Stone you can salute this statue without danger of apoplexy.

Another memorial of considerable interest is to be found near Beacon Street. This is a simple granite tablet bearing the inscription "On this field the Oneida Football Club of Boston, the first organized football club in the United States, played against all comers from 1862 to 1865. The Oneida goal was never crossed." Strictly speaking, the Oneida Club was not a school team, although all but three of its members were students at Mr. Dixwell's private school in Boylston Place. One of the pupils of this school in 1860 was Gerrit S. Miller, who became the father (if one may use that term for a sixteen-year-old boy) of organized football. Until he created the Oneida Club, football was merely a vague sort of game to be played at recess, but under his direction it became a recognized interschool sport.

Football in the days of "Gat" Miller was quite unlike the present game. There were no goal posts and no "gridiron." The goal was a line across the entire field. The object of the game

*In Remembrance of
the Boston Massacre:
Boston Common*

was to get the ball across the opponent's goal line, and the players were not hampered by many rules. The ball could be thrown, carried, kicked, or just plain shoved through the opposition. The team to first make two goals was declared the winner. There were no rest periods. The game continued without any interruption until one side had scored the necessary two goals. One game, against the Latin School, lasted for two hours and forty-seven minutes of continuous play. No protection equipment was used and the "uniforms" of the Oneida Club were red handkerchiefs knotted at the corners and worn as caps.

At the top of the tablet is carved a representation of a football—a modern oval pigskin—but the players really used a spherical rubber ball. The one used against the combined Boston High and Boston Latin School in the great game of 1863 may be seen at the Society for the Preservation of New England Antiquities on Cambridge Street.

125

Many visitors who view the tablet ask, "Why was it called the Oneida Club?" The question has been asked more often than it has been answered. Miller named his club for a beautiful lake near his home in Peterboro, New York.

Directly across Charles Street is the Public Garden. A visitor might easily think that the Common and the Garden were all one recreational area with a public street running through it; but actually they are two separate and distinct parks—different in age, history, and even ownership.

The Public Garden was a salt-water marsh until 1794, when it was filled in by the city. It was used for ropewalks until 1859, when it was converted into a beautiful public park.

There is a loveliness and grace about the Garden, a formal and controlled winsomeness that is to be looked at and admired, but with circumspection. Decorous children make the swan boat tour of the little lake passing under what was once the smallest suspension bridge in the world and past a Japanese lighthouse that formerly decorated the Momoya Palace of the Emperor Hideyoshi.

Slightly self-conscious adults walk sedately along the trim paths, admire the gorgeous flowers, and read the labels which give the species and the family name of each of the many trees. In Boston, family is important, even in the vegetable kingdom. It is quite fitting then that the swan boat concession should be a family affair. For several generations these foot-propelled craft have been operated by the Paget family, all descended from the original "Admiral" Paget, who invented this interesting type of boat.

Along the Boylston Street side of the Garden are four statues. Can you name them? If so, you are to be commended, for most of the hundreds who pass them daily cannot do so. There is Kosciusko, a native of Poland who was made a colonel in the American Army by George Washington; Thomas Cass, an Irishman who organized and commanded an all-Irish regiment in the Civil War; Charles Sumner, abolitionist, who was elected to the United States Senate by the uncomfortable majority of one vote; and Wendell Phillips, the Champion of the Slave.

Public Garden

Edward Everett Hale, writer, scholar, and preacher; William Ellery Channing, pastor of the Federal Street Church; and George Robert White, Boston's great benefactor, are all honored by beautiful memorials in other parts of the Garden.

The imposing Ether Monument, near the Beacon and Arlington Street corner of the Garden, commemorates the birth of the use of ether in surgical operations, which meant the death of pain. At the time the monument was erected there was a bitter dispute between two doctors, Dr. Jackson and Dr. Morton, as to which really was the discoverer of the use of this anesthetic. With admirable tact the inscription on the memorial does not mention either name. As Oliver Wendell Holmes once said, it is a memorial to ether or either.

The difference between the Garden and the Common in the public mind is the difference between the reception hall and the rumpus room. Within reason, anything goes on the Common— it belongs to the People. One may wade in the Frog Pond, walk on the grass, sleep on the benches, climb over the bandstand, make speeches—do anything, in short, that he could lawfully do in his own yard. The Garden, on the other hand, is city property.

One may not walk on the grass or pick the flowers. All is carefully supervised.

THERE IS A DIFFERENCE

The Common belongs to the People;
The People—that means Me!
I can sleep on the lawn
From twilight 'till dawn.
I can watch a ball game, free.

The Common belongs to the People;
The People—that means You!
You can stand on a chair
And find fault with the Mayor,
For nobody cares what you do.

BUT

The Garden belongs to the City;
The City—that isn't Me!
I'm restricted by signs
And threatened with fines,
And even the Swan Boats aren't free.

The Garden belongs to the City;
The City—that isn't You!
You're forbidden to wade
In the lake that they made,
You'd be stopped if you took off one shoe.

VANES

In a chapter about the arteries of a great city it is surely no impropriety to devote one section to the vanes.

When Boston was a community of farmers and fishermen the weather was of utmost importance. Later, in the gay and venturesome clipper ship days the direction and force of the wind could, in a moment, make the difference between poverty and wealth. Great fortunes depended quite literally on a breath of wind. Consequently, weather vanes were found on almost every house and stable.

Nearly all of these old landmarks have disappeared—gone with the wind. But a select few, constant in their inconstancy, still mark the winds that blow over our ancient, narrow, and crooked streets.

In 1744 a church was built on Berry Street (now Chauncy). A weather vane, the gift of Governor Hancock, was installed on its lofty steeple. The pastor, Rev. John Moorhead, watched his vane with understandable pride and was disturbed to note that as the days passed it was moving not at all. A steeplejack made the difficult—and expensive—trip to the top of the spire. Descending, he reported that all was well. And he reminded the pastor—after he had collected his fee—that the wind had been due east for a fortnight. The church, the vane, and even the street have ceased to be, but Boston's east wind is as faithful now as it was then.

To become world famous would seem to be an impossible achievement for a mere weather vane, but the grasshopper atop Faneuil Hall has this distinction. Made by "that cunning artificer" Deacon Shem Drowne, in 1742, it became a noted landmark and guide for ships entering the harbor. It is said that foreign consuls used to ask the question "What is the Faneuil Hall weather vane?" as a test for those who claimed Boston as their home port.

The insect was as carefully made as though it were to have a close inspection. Its glittering glass eyes, originally door knobs, have gazed into the heart of many a storm. It has endured hurricane, fire, earthquake, and theft; and, with occasional repairs, it has marked the shifting winds for over two centuries.

Why a grasshopper? Many reasons have been given: that there was such an insect on the Faneuil coat of arms (which there wasn't); that the farmers who frequented the market liked grasshoppers (which they certainly did not); that chasing locusts was connected with a boyhood romance of the Deacon's (which seems unlikely); and that the design was suggested by a similar one which was on the Royal Exchange in London. You may take your choice, but the last seems the most reasonable.

Grasshopper Atop Faneuil Hall

Deacon Shem Drowne, who died in 1774 at the age of ninety, was by profession a wood carver and a superior one. He specialized in ship's figureheads although he was not above carving an ornamental top for a pump or a gatepost. The fabrication of metal weather vanes seems to have been a side line. But, as frequently happens, he is remembered for his hobby rather than for his chief work.

When Boston ceased to be a colony, becoming a royal province, and the governors were housed in what had been the mansion of the wealthy Peter Sargeant, the octagonal cupola of the house was ornamented by a unique vane, four and a half feet high, in the form of an Indian with a drawn bow with the arrow in place. It was an exact copy of the Indian that appeared on the old Colonial seal of Massachusetts. As the ancient records say, "Shem Drowne made itt," glass eyes and all. After many years of faithful service, the Indian has now gone to his happy hunting grounds—the Museum of the Massachusetts Historical Society.

There was a bitter quarrel among the members of the congregation of the North Church in North Square during the winter of 1719. A small majority voted to install the Rev. Peter Thatcher as assistant pastor. The minority group did not want him at any price. The majority prevailed and the Rev. Peter was installed on January 27, 1720, but only after a fight that left black eyes and bloody noses in its wake.

During the ceremony of installation, the malcontents gathered in the balcony of the church and indulged in noises and actions of unbelievable vulgarity. They were even guilty of anointing the congregation under the balcony with a liquid which the records of the event say "shall be nameless." One justly indignant young lady who was present wrote to a friend, "The filthy creatures entirely spoiled a new velvet hood which I had made for the occasion. I could never wear it again."

After the installation, the insurgents left the church in a body and organized themselves into a new congregation, building for their services a substantial brick church on Hanover Street. There was some talk of calling this "The Revenge Church of Christ" (they were really mad), but saner counsel prevailed and it was officially named "The Second Church in Boston."

Shem Drowne, naturally, was commissioned to make the weather vane for the new building. He made a vane five feet, four inches in height from old brass kettles contributed by members of the congregation. It weighed 172 pounds.

Remembering the Bible story that Peter would deny his Lord three times before the cock crowed, the congregation had their vane fashioned in the form of a crowing cock. They felt it was a subtle way of showing their disdain of Rev. Peter—Thatcher.

For 140 years the insolent bird silently crowed his defiance. Then the building was torn down and the diminished congregation joined other churches. The rooster, still in excellent condition, could not give up his ecclesiastical life, so he joined another church. Today he may be seen, bravely turning to face the tempest atop the spire of the First Church (Congregational) in Cambridge.

Constantly moving, yet never leaving its appointed place, looking everywhere but going nowhere—that is the normal life of a weather vane. Yet some years ago one Boston vane made a tour of the whole United States. When the steeple of the historic Christ Church was blown down by "Hurricane Carol" on August 31, 1954, little was left to be salvaged save the beautiful old weather vane, another Shem Drowne masterpiece made in 1740. The vane, a banner surmounted by a star, was escorted on a tour of the United States, a trip made to remind the people of the entire country that the spire where the Revere lanterns were hung must be restored and that here was an opportunity to help. The old vane was successful in its objective, and the spire has been replaced by an exact copy of the original.

vi. Birds of a Feather

FLOCKING TOGETHER

In Istanbul, Damascus, and such exotic cities, we find highways which are designated as "Street of the Rug Sellers," "Street of the Coppersmiths," and the like. While Boston has no such streets given over to a single trade, we do find that there is a strong tendency for "birds of a feather to flock together."

Lower Summer Street is considered the wool center of Boston and was possibly at one time the wool hub of the nation, for this city once conducted 70 percent of the country's importing business in that commodity. Chauncy Street has a high concentration of cotton goods dealers, and South and Lincoln Streets are primarily devoted to shoes and leather goods.

Kneeland Street is given over to the garment trades, and the windows are a rainbow of "Ladies' ready-to-wear." Many stores on this street display "findings"—buttons and bows. No wonder people collect buttons. These windows gleam with little gems of art: cunningly wrought metal buttons, glittering jeweled buttons, colorful cloth buttons—every conceivable shape, color, and texture being employed. All are masterpieces of the craft of the jeweler, the metalsmith, the wood carver, or the weaver.

Three streets—Melrose, Piedmont, and Church—constitute the motion-picture distribution center of the city. This industry processes all human emotions and puts them up in cans like so many vegetables. Here is romance in reels for rental. The counters and shelves are crowded with flat metal containers filled with tears, laughter, adventure, and drama.

Antique stores cluster on Charles Street. Every few steps discovers a different one. There are all kinds: little, big, clean, and dingy. Several specialize in antiques of a particular type, a given era, or a specific country.

"Antique Stores Cluster on Charles Street"

Newbury Street is noted for its elegant specialty shops. Art galleries, antique and gift shops, and clothing and shoe boutiques line this impressive highway. Store windows laden with goods from every country entice the browser.

There are streets dedicated to the important task of keeping the Bostonian well fed, also financial streets sacred to that mysterious brotherhood who have the miraculous art of making money by the mere handling of money. There are streets where families of the same ethnic background congregate and other streets devoted to goods and services of strictly feminine appeal.

RIVERS OF FOOD

Through the years, most of the importing, processing, and redistribution of meats, fish, and produce took place in a section of Boston known as the Market District—a triangle formed by Faneuil Hall, Copp's Hill, and Fort Hill Square.

North Street (one end of it at least) dealt in wholesale meats, as did Blackstone and Clinton Streets—the latter containing a block-long two-story market adorned with a gilded bull's head. Here one could see the bones of beef cattle sliding down a wooden chute into waiting trucks. The bones were denuded with such skill that there was not a meal for a cat in the entire truckload, although a number of misguided felines waited hopefully with impatient paw.

Chatham Street, the only street in Boston where the house numbers run up one side and down the other, was devoted to eggs—all sorts of eggs: strictly fresh eggs, fresh eggs, and eggs. One company dealt exclusively in dried eggs, another in frozen eggs, and a third in broken eggs. There was even a sign for "Small Company—Eggs," which was possibly where the little ones came from.

While the market area still flourishes and one can still see sides, chines, loins, and rumps of various beasts, the bulk of the wholesale trade has migrated to South Boston and Chelsea, and today the area is primarily devoted to the retail of food.

The ever helpful and usually precise City Directory defines Faneuil Hall Square as "north, south, east, and west of Faneuil Hall." It also defines it as one of the boundaries of Dock Square, leaving the explorer in considerable doubt as to where the one leaves off and the other begins. Not that it matters, for it is in effect all one square. How far from the historic building Faneuil Hall Square extends on the other three sides also seems a bit uncertain. This is not the fault of the directory. Here, as in some other parts of the city, its compilers have done a remarkably skillful job of defining the indefinable.

There is no vagueness, however, in the minds of the merchants and market men. They have pre-empted the streets near the Hall and Quincy Market and sell their wares from trucks, pushcarts, and wagons parked thereabouts. There is, indeed, a widely believed tradition that the marketeers, not the city, own these streets. This belief has a basis in fact. An ancient law permits the sale of farm produce "from wagons or other vehicles in the streets, not including the sidewalks, within the market limits." Permission, however, must be had from the person in front of

Faneuil Hall

whose premises the cart is located. The result of this permissive law is to furnish one of the most picturesque sights of Boston. On market days, the crowded square and Blackstone Street overflow with vehicles of all types standing wheel to wheel; a colorful variety of farm products from apples to zucchini are offered for sale; and the vendors plead, boast, demand, and supplicate in their varied voices.

Each merchant tries every known device to divert your attention away from his rival and to focus your interest on his superior produce. Bitter rivalry, jealousy, hatred, and revenge are rampant. Strident noises, raucous voices, shouts, and imprecations crisscross through the air until to the spectator riot, mayhem, and murder seem just around the corner. Suddenly one realizes that it is all in fun—a magnificent pageant— and he is caught up in the spirit of high carnival, becoming no longer a spectator but an actor in the tempestuous and kaleidoscopic drama.

KIDS AND VAMPS

Some sections of Boston smell pleasantly of dressed leather. They should, for Boston was one of the great shoe and leather centers of the country. Over a century ago an antiquarian wrote, "The name of Sister Street has now been changed to Leather Square so that it rejoices in the name as well as the smell of leather." Back in Colonial days Thomas Atkinson willed his land "to my sister," and the highway which ran through it was consequently called Sister Street. When, in 1867, a tannery was built there, the name was changed to Leather Square. Pearl Street, now devoted to other trades, was named Shoe and Leather Street in 1869.

To the innocent abroad in this leather district the signs on the buildings were startling, to say the least: "Dealer in Men's Soles," "Colored Kids," "The Perfect Heel," "Foot Pads," "We specialize in Vamps," "Stripping," "Dressing," and "Dyeing." One can sympathize with the English lady who saw "Baked Indian Pudding" on the menu at Durgin-Park and exclaimed in horror, "Can such things be in a Christian country?" One advertising placard read: "Have you tried the Sterling Heel?" Penciled underneath was the despairing answer, "Brother, I married him!"

The leather district of today comprises a group of streets lying just west of South Station. The lower end of Essex Street, South, East, and Lincoln Streets deal almost exclusively with leather and leather products.

The stroller in the leather district cannot fail to be interested by the architectural arrangement of South Street, and, if one feels that variety is the spice of life, 105–147 South Street, between Beach and East, merits more than a passing glance. Built of red brick, this block displays an amazing diversity of ornamentation. The buildings, in actual physical contact with each other, are profusely dotted with windows, boasting no less than fifteen different shapes and sizes. The façade combines patterned brick, stripes of dark stone, arches and columns, and, below, the handsome gold-lettered signs of the leather merchants.

"Variety is the Spice of Life":
105—147
South Street

MONEY STREETS

There are streets in this busy world whose very names have become synonymous with financial matters: Threadneedle Street in London, Wall Street in New York, and State Street in Boston.

In our own city three other streets: Kilby, Federal, and Devonshire, although not so well known internationally, share with State Street the honor of being nerve centers of that vast network of financial operations which spreads over the entire civilized world. The failure of a bank in India, a business consolidation in England, or the revaluation of the franc in France has its repercussions in these streets.

Long before the Puritans arrived in Boston, an Indian trail led from the center of the peninsula to the water. The settlers

Old State House from State Street

made it one of their principal thoroughfares, "The Great Street to the Sea." Later it became King Street, and, when British royalty became unpopular, it was rechristened State Street. As marshland and shallow water were filled in, the shore line retreated; and the street, still running "to the sea" became longer until today it is some six times its original length.

As the years passed, State Street became the financial and civic center of the city. Commercial banking in New England really began in State Street, and in 1837, twenty-two of the thirty-five banks in the city were located on this street. Likewise the first insurance office in America opened, in 1724, at the site of 22 State Street.

In the early 1850s the Stock Exchange stood at what is now number 40, and the United States Bank was at number 28, the present site of the New England Merchants National Bank. The Royal Customs House was located nearby. At the same site was the Merchants' Exchange, where shipowners and their captains transacted business in the clipper ship days.

Number 66 marks the site of the offices of Thatcher Magoun, whose fleet of eighty-four ships traded in all ports of the world. It was here also that Enoch Train, the great ship designer, had his private office.

State Street's position as a great financial stronghold may be due in part to the fact that it led directly to Long Wharf, once the center of world trade. It has also prospered by the fondness of wealthy Bostonians to set up trust funds and by what Ben Franklin described as "the State Street prudence of buying by the acre to sell by the foot."

Great financial deals are consummated in the austere offices of banks and trust companies; but many have their inception in chats over a friendly glass or across the hospitable luncheon table. Hence State Street has always been famous for its taverns. The Royal Exchange Tavern, from which the first stagecoaches left in 1772 for their six-day trip to New York, had a ground floor intentionally left open as a sort of arcade so merchants might meet, discuss financial affairs, and transact business there. This tavern was also the scene of the quarrel between Phillips and Woodbridge which led to a fatal duel on the Common. Nearby stood the Admiral Vernon, whose proprietor, for some inexplicable reason, always signed his name "John Evard, alias Webb." The Bunch of Grapes, at the corner of King Street and Mackeril Lane (State and Kilby Streets), was known as the best punch house in Boston. The Tory headquarters during the Revolution was the British Coffee House on the site now numbered 66. It was here that Otis was attacked and received the wound which later caused his insanity. Pirates and other characters of low esteem consorted at the Crown Coffee House on Long Wharf.

Nearby Corn Court, a "wheel barrow way of full five feet" in 1650, took its name from the corn market which was situated near the dock in a veritable warren of markets, warehouses, and shipping offices. All of these traditionally thirsty trades made Corn Court an ideal spot for a tavern.

The old Brasier Inn met this demand. In 1780 the Brasier Inn, wishing no doubt to share the popularity of the first governor of the state, changed its name to "Hancock Tavern." It proved to be a wise choice, for Governor Hancock himself became a friend and patron of the proprietor. A large sign was prepared, ornamented with a portrait of the Governor, painted, according to one contemporary writer, in a style very like that of the celebrated Copley. By another it was characterized as "a wretched daub."

At the death of Hancock, the sign was draped with black crepe for several weeks. Over a century later the historian Samuel Drake, refers to the Hancock as the oldest tavern in Boston and writes, "A delapidated sign, bearing the weather-stained features of Governor Hancock, retains a feeble hold on its fastenings." Less than a year later, the "feeble hold" gave way and the sign fell to the ground, causing the death of a passing pedestrian.

The Hancock became the favorite stopping place for foreign visitors, especially those from France. In 1794, Talleyrand spent the summer there; the same year the French priest John Cheverus made his home at this inn; and a year later a man who signed himself as M. d'Orléans was a guest. These three men were alike in that they were all French refugees, all men of great ability, and all destined to play a part in shaping the history of the time. In every other respect they were as different as it was possible for men to be.

Talleyrand, traitor to his church, was excommunicated by the Pope in 1791. He was friend and adviser to Napoleon; but when it became to his interest to do so, he betrayed his benefactor and was instrumental in restoring the Bourbons to the throne. Louis XVIII made him Prime Minister in 1815. Not a lovable character, he was an astute, unscrupulous, and highly successful politician, always on the winning side.

John Cheverus was one of the noblest men who ever adorned the Boston scene—a true Christian, a man of serene faith, and sincerely beloved by all who knew him. Protestants and Catholics united to do him honor and to build, on Franklin Street, a fitting cathedral for his use. All the city rejoiced when he was consecrated the first Roman Catholic Bishop of Boston in 1810; and men of good will, regardless of creed, were deeply pleased when he became cardinal in 1836.

M. d'Orléans was a quiet, unassuming young man who spent much of his time in the coffee room of the Hancock Tavern discussing French politics with a Parisian barber and a French dancing master who also lived at the inn. All three were frequent visitors at the office of the newspaper *The Centinel*, in nearby State Street. Here they found files of foreign newspapers which recounted the current events in their beloved homeland. When the papers announced the fall of Napoleon, M. d'Orléans quietly returned to Paris, where some fifteen years later he assumed his rightful place on the throne of France, as King Louis Philippe.

The old tavern on Corn Court did not lack other distinguished visitors. George Washington once dined there. Benjamin Franklin was a frequent guest, and many other men of note enjoyed its hospitality.

During the War of 1812, the house was frequented by officers of the Army and Navy. For many years afterward it was a favorite resort for businessmen, who would drop in for a "drop" at the inn, which was especially famous for its noonday punch, prepared by the hostess.

President's Office: State Street Bank and Trust

All the taverns did their hospitable best to alleviate the mental stresses inevitably associated with big business deals. The tradition has continued. The area is not without its taverns of repute even today.

One may paraphrase Kipling by saying, "The old is old and the new is new and never the twain shall meet," but meet they did in the old Second Bank–State Street Trust Company. Here banking in its most modern phases was carried on in the atmosphere of a countinghouse of the early eighteenth century. Ancient lanterns hung from the ceiling. Tables and chairs were copies of old tavern furniture, and radiator covers resembled the fronts of early oak chests. The lamps on the depositors' tables were the old whale-oil type—electrified, of course—the pewter inkwells were originals from old English countinghouses, and even the lamp shades were worthy of study with their paintings of clipper ships. The office of the president was furnished entirely with genuine antiques. The mammoth fireplace contained an extremely rare "Governor Dudley" fireback; the desk was an early American refectory table; the president's chair was from the taproom of the Wayside Inn. A wastebasket (always overflowing) was an ancient fire bucket. A churn provided an umbrella stand, and an old sea chest held the wood for a cheerful fire. That president's office may still be seen at the State Street Bank and Trust Company at 53 State.

Devonshire is a busy street, a street of historic background and of imposing buildings; but primarily it is a money street. Throw a stone at random within its confines and the chances are ten to one you will hit a bank or a trust company.

One of these financially minded buildings has, on its side, two carvings in stone, each showing a male and a female figure. In one, the couple are holding hands and gazing fondly at each other. This is labeled "Fidelity." In the other, they are not holding hands and are looking in opposite directions with expressions of abhorrence. This is labeled "Security." There must be an explanation, but it eludes this observer.

Like many another Boston street, Devonshire has changed its name with a careless frequency. In 1640 it was Wilson's Lane, since it ran through the garden of the Rev. John Wilson. This sensitive gentleman sold his land to John Daws, a joiner, stipulating that he (Wilson) should "not be annoyed with any stincks." Later the names Daws' Lane, Crooked Lane, Dindale Alley, Theatre Alley, and Odeon Avenue were all used for the whole or parts of this thoroughfare. Finally the entire street became Pudding Lane, possibly because of its many restaurants, but more likely in memory of the London street of that name.

It was on Pudding Lane that John Allen and his associate "James the Indian Printer" had a press and published *The Psalter in the Indian Language,* along with sermons and religious pamphlets.

Taverns were numerous in Pudding Lane. One of them, the Rose and Crown, sorely disturbed the Puritanical proprieties. In 1682 the landlord put up a new sign which showed a crown held aloft by two chubby nude boys. This so shocked one of the elders that he made a complaint to the court and straitway mine host was ordered to have the most immoral sign altered. Back to the carvers the sign was reluctantly sent; in due time, it was returned, the offending boys transformed into two entrancing little girls. Upon reviewing the new sign, the irate court—even more horrified than before—ordered that the charming girls be modestly concealed by garlands of respectable roses.

Another tavern incident which bordered on a heartbreaking tragedy occurred in the Boston Exchange Tavern, also on Pudding Lane. The tavern burned to the ground, the fire interrupting an exciting card game in which Henry Clay was one of the players. The esteemed statesman escaped safely, but one can imagine his dismay when he found himself still clutching four aces which had been dealt to him, now useless.

The great fire of 1760 entirely destroyed all of the forty-one buildings on Pudding Lane and ruined many of the businessmen. Christopher Devonshire, a merchant of Bristol, England, generously contributed two hundred pounds to aid these afflicted persons. The new street which replaced Pudding Lane was named Devonshire in his honor, and so it has remained.

The manipulation of money is paramount in Kilby Street also. This thoroughfare has become a haven for all branches of insurance, and the ramifications of the insurance business are many and varied. The first automobile insurance policy ever to be written in the United States was issued here for a Stanley Steamer. At that time there was no such word as "automobile" and no law governing its insurance; but the attorney general was in no way disconcerted. He ruled that "a motor running on its own wheels is a marine risk and can be so insured." From this auspicious beginning the business has grown until today the street is almost entirely occupied by underwriters.

Places of entertainment are no new thing on Kilby Street. Over two hundred years ago the famous Bunch of Grapes was located there at the corner of State Street. This hostelry was a favorite resort of Paul Revere and his cronies of the Whig Club. Governor Burnet was banqueted here upon his arrival from England in 1728, and George Washington was entertained at the same lavish table after the siege of Boston. Washington really slept here, too, and so did La Fayette, Hancock, Adams, and a host of others whose names are in the history books.

A famous place for organization meetings was the Bunch of

Grapes. The first Lodge of Masons in America gathered here in 1733; the Society of the Cincinnati in 1787; and a chance meeting of good fellows over a bowl of the famous punch resulted in the formation of the Massachusetts Humane Society, the third oldest life-saving organization in the world.

The repeal of the Stamp Act was celebrated at this inn by a party which, it is hinted, was a bit merry although the diary of one of the participants records very properly that "every man was safe at home by ten of the clock."

Perhaps the wildest party ever held at the Bunch of Grapes was immediately following the reading of the Declaration of Independence. The carvings of the Lion and the Unicorn from the State House, the tavern signs from the King's Arms and the Royal Coffee House, the street signs of King and Queen Streets, with every other symbol of sovereignty in the town, were jubilantly torn down, gathered in front of the tavern, and there burned in a huge and thirst-provoking bonfire.

The Bunch of Grapes ceased its long and honorable career in 1798, when it was removed to make room for the New England Bank.

Kilby Street derived its name in exactly the same way as did Devonshire. Completely destroyed by the same fire, it was rebuilt under financing by a Boston merchant, Christopher Kilby.

Federal, another of the great "money streets" of Boston, also had its baptism of fire. The tremendous conflagration of 1872 swept across this street, wiping out ninety-two firms and destroying every building.

It is evident that those who rebuilt this thoroughfare were determined that such a holocaust should never again occur. Every building is of stone—massive, ponderous blocks of granite. Thieves shall not break in nor fire consume.

Altogether, Federal Street is impressive for mere size, weight, and—for Boston—height. Obviously the architects intended to relieve the somber effect of all this solidity by the introduction of carvings and sculptures in the stone itself. The results are not entirely happy. The human faces are sorrowful and the animal figures are such as the drug addict sees in his delirium. Most of the sculptors of that era served an apprentice-

Another "Money" Street: Congress Street

ship as gravestone artists. Their early training in gloom may have influenced their later work.

The animals sculptured on several buildings are less dolorous but more grotesque than the human figures. There are two creatures over the door of number 24 that are actually grinning —in a ghastly sort of way, of course. They are difficult to classify: dragons, perhaps—or maybe dogs—possibly horses—or lions. Anyhow, they have wings and are equipped with the most amazing tails, each in a tight spiral, with improbable things growing from them—roses, cabbages, pears, grapes, and such.

One obvious break from the tradition of human and animal sculpture is 100 Federal, the 37-story headquarters of The First National Bank. Encased in polished granite, this monumental structure, architecturally distinguished by its 8-story "paunch," rises 591 feet—one of the tallest and most impressive buildings in Boston.

The State Street Bank building at number 71 is tremendously inspiring in its architecture. Built in 1930, it is of a soft, buff-colored brick with a broad band of bronze panels encircling the building. The subjects of the carvings are, appropriately, the Evolution of Agriculture, Manufacturing, Transportation, Communication, Education, and the Arts. In the foyer and corridors one is impressed by murals of etched brass showing early views of old Boston Town.

Anciently Federal Street was called Long Lane. At one corner was a barn where the Scotch-Irish Presbyterians held services in 1728. Later the barn was replaced by the first purely Gothic church in Boston. It was here that the delegates met to decide whether Massachusetts should accept the proposed Federal Constitution. By a majority of nineteen votes, the Constitution was adopted on February 6, 1788. To keep this event in memory, Long Lane was renamed Federal Street.

WOMEN'S STREETS

To say that Boston is a woman-dominated town would certainly provoke debate and would probably not be entirely accurate. The fact remains, however, that women's interests loom very large in this city. There is an unusually generous number of women's clubs, of specialty stores catering to ladies exclusively, and of restaurants where mere men are admitted reluctantly, if at all. Cocktail bars, barber shops, and bowling alleys are no longer the exclusive domain of the retiring male.

Read the advertisements in any newspaper. You will find an overwhelming percentage of them beamed at the woman buyer. Even the stores which feature men's clothing do not neglect the feminine angle. Boston is full of rugged males who insist upon using their own judgment in matters of clothing; but, as these stores well know, their matured judgment frequently is that they should consult a woman.

Open the telephone book at random. You will find as many Anns, Marys, and Elizabeths as there are Williams, Johns, and Henrys. It may not be a women's city, but no one can deny that they are in there pitching.

Some of the Boston highways might with justice be called women's streets. Temple Place, for example, is largely devoted to the beautification of womankind. Hair stylists by the dozen and beauty shops by the score improve the top section; a quantity of chiropodists and foot specialists reconstruct the other end; and any number of dressmakers and foundation experts take care of the territory in between.

Temple Place was not always like this. In the early 1800s it was purely residential. At that time the street ended in a flight of steps which descended to Washington Street. As a result the highway was called Turnagain Alley. Possibly it was the proximity of both Summer and Winter Streets, or there was, perhaps, some other reason, but the records state that "the Aldermen, on May 15, 1865, voted to change the name of Temple Place to Autumn Street." Exactly ten days later, the same board voted to change the name back to Temple Place. It was the shortest Autumn ever recorded.

West Street has been under the feminine influence since 1840. In that year Elizabeth Peabody opened her famous Foreign Bookstore, a gathering place for women of culture and literary taste. It was here that *The Dial* magazine was published.

"Beautiful but dumb" was an expression which had never been heard in 1840, but the idea would have had the hearty endorsement of the men of that era. They preferred that their women be uninstructed in all things except those connected with homemaking and entertaining. Thinking and talking on any but the most frivolous subjects was, like a few remaining present-day taverns, "for men only." The women, bless them, did their best to conform to the standards set for them. There were, however, some outstanding exceptions. A few women dared to think, to talk, and to write on subjects long considered the exclusive province of men.

Chief among the rebels was Margaret Fuller, who later became the Marchioness Ossoli. Margaret had an insatiable appetite for study. She became a recognized authority in the fields of art, music, literature, and philosophy. At her home in West Street, she conducted a series of "conversations"—really lectures—with a group of intelligent and thoughtful ladies. It was these "conversations" which influenced the women of Boston to break the fetters of convention and to dare to lead more intellectual, more mature, and more interesting lives. They have been more fun to be with ever since.

West Street is quite short but it finds room for jewelers, shoe and fur stores, lingerie and millinery shops, beauty salons, corsetières, and many other emporia of predominantly feminine appeal—as well as the venerable Brattle Book Shop, which caters to both sexes.

The tremendous increase in the number of beauty parlors and "tonsorial artists" through the years would indicate that a preoccupation with hair styling is a new phenomenon. This is not the case, however. Witness an advertisement which appeared in the *Columbian Centinal* of October 17, 1807:

WILLIAM SMALLPIECE

At his DRESSING ACADEMY AND SCHOOL OF FASHION in Milk Street, opposite the south door of the Old South, Reminds the Sons and Daughters of Fashion and Beauty, that tho' they may possess every latent excellence; yet they require the improving hand of Art. And it is a lamentable fact that

> Full many a mind is rear'd with toil and care
> To waste its worth by Slov'nliness in Hair
> What though the Eye voluptuously roll,
> The Form possess each hevenly grace;
> Say, can they Any Heart control,
> Draw Friendship near—bid Love take place
> 'Till SMALLPIECE touch them: he whose trade is
> To make Gods of Men and Goddesses of Ladies.

CRUISING THE BACK BAY

It has been said that more students are at work within twenty-five miles of our State House than in any other area of the same size in the world. Most of these are in Back Bay. In the same confusingly named section of the city we find much that justifies Boston's reputation as one of the great cultural centers of the world. The serious student requires the facilities and tools for his work: libraries, museums, studios, and concert halls. Of these the Back Bay provides the very best.

Copley Square in the Back Bay is a rare jewel on the variegated tapestry which is Boston. Architecturally one of the most interesting as well as one of the most attractive squares in America, Copley blends seven utterly different types of architecture into a composite whole which is delightful and pleasing. Why this should be so is a problem for architects and artists, but it is the fact.

The Florentine Renaissance façade of the Boston Public Library forms one side of the triangular "square." The entrance is flanked by Bela Pratt's charmingly executed statues representing Science and Art. Science seems to be symbolizing Boston hospitality by offering a large bronze grapefruit to the public. On the façade are carved the names of men famous in literature, art, music, and science. While the library was being built it was dis-

Boston Public Library and the New Old South Church

covered that these names were arranged in such a way that the
initial letters spelled "McKim, Mead and White," the architects.
A new deal was ordered and the names were rearranged.

The library, opened to the public in 1895, was one of the first great book repositories in the world and, when built, the most artistic, functional, and costly building of its type in existence. Not only a collection of ancient and modern books, a literary workshop, and a mine of information, the library is a treasure house of rare volumes and special collections: the *Bay Psalm Book*, John Eliot's Indian Bible, the Bowditch collection of rare mathematical works, the Barton Library of Shakespeareana, and many other priceless volumes.

The interior of the library is illuminated like a medieval missal. The great marble stairway flanked with the stone lions by Saint-Gaudens is enriched by Puvis de Chavannes's murals of "Good and Bad Tidings" winging about telegraph wires. Abbey's "Quest of the Holy Grail" and Sargent's "Triumph of Religion" adorn other walls, while bronze and marble statues add to the beauty and interest of the building.

Unfortunately, the library lacks one magnificent work of art which it might have had. McKim, the architect, purchased a bronze statue—MacMonnies' "Bacchante"—and presented it to the city suggesting that it be placed in the center of the interior courtyard. Immediately, all of Boston broke out in a rash of Puritanism. The statue was a nude! On one arm she carried a baby—also nude! She wore no wedding ring! Worst of all she was tempting the infant with a bunch of grapes, which could only symbolize intoxication! The shocked trustees declined to accept the statue, but she was not homeless long. New York City was happy to give her an honored place in the Metropolitan Museum. A replica of the beautiful figure has graced our art museum for many years without noticeable effect on the morals of our youth.

Those who seek to undermine the virtue of a city never give up. The excitement caused by the "Bacchante" had scarcely subsided when a gift was received from the mayor of Athens. It was a bust of Bacchus!

Across Boylston Street from the library is the Italian Gothic New Old South Church—and there is a name to astonish the visitor. This church is a direct descendant of the historic Old

New Old South Church

South, which is in the northerly part of the city. Here is antiquity, indeed, and the gravestones of two early members, John Alden (1701) and Joshua Scottow (1697), which are affixed to the outer wall of the church help to emphasize its age.

This cruciform church is ornamented by a great and beautiful tower built of varicolored stones. It is pierced at the top by four large windows whose richly carved mullions give a lace-like effect. It is particularly attractive at sunset when the delicate tracery of the tower is seen against a backdrop of flaming color.

Although it is not true, as claimed, that the whole of Copley Square rises and falls with the tide, the underground water sometimes does have its effect. Some years ago it was noted that the church tower was beginning to lean—Pisa like. With every passing day it seemed to slant a little more. Tension mounted and soon passers-by began to speculate—even to place bets—as to when it would fall, and upon whom. By 1931 it was a full three feet out of line and action became necessary. Stone by stone the tower was taken down, each piece carefully numbered and stored. In 1940 it was rebuilt over a steel framework and now points directly heavenward, as a church tower should.

The massive New England Mutual Life Insurance building with its setback construction, while not actually in Copley Square, definitely forms a part of its total picture. When excavating for the foundation of this structure, the workmen uncovered the posts and wattle of a huge fish weir which scientists date from about 1400 B.C. Evidently the Indians had been long in this region, although their culture had not advanced appreciably.

Persons crossing Copley Square occasionally glance up at the tower clock on the New England Mutual to see the time and then look across at the colored lights on the tower of the old John Hancock Insurance building to note the weather: "Clear blue, clear view; flashing blue, clouds due; steady red, rain ahead; flashing red, snow instead."

Continuing clockwise around the square we find Trinity Church, which was built on this site after the great fire of 1872 destroyed its predecessor on Summer Street. This church is one of the choicest examples of ecclesiastical architecture in the country. Its marvelously rich carvings make this building unique, while the stained-glass windows are jewels of glowing artistry. They should be, for the genius of Sir Edward Burne-Jones, William Morris, and John LaFarge designed them.

Built into the wall of the appealing cloister is a window of delicately carved stone which came from Saint Botolph's Church in Lincolnshire, England, where John Cotton was Vicar before persecution in the name of Religion drove him to seek sanctuary in this newer Boston.

On the Boylston Street side of the church is the statue of Phillips Brooks, for many years its Rector. The irreverent claim that the inscription on the base of the statue is a perfect example of Boston smugness. It lists the four most memorable virtues that can be ascribed to this justly revered Bostonian.

Portico of Trinity Church

Preacher of the Word of God
Lover of all mankind
Born in Boston
Died in Boston.

While not directly in the square, it would be impossible to ignore the new 790-foot John Hancock Tower in any discussion of Copley. This 60-story rhomboid mirror, placed at an angle to dramatically reflect its 19th-century neighbors, is the tallest building in Boston. Much debate has transpired over the

Hancock Tower's physical beauty, as well as its effect on Copley Square and Boston's skyline, but no one can say it isn't striking.

Standing on the site of the old Art Museum is the Copley Plaza Hotel, beloved by all world travelers, whose severely Classical lines form an admirable foil for the ecclesiastical ornamentation of Trinity.

Not all of the beautiful and interesting churches of Back Bay are in Copley Square. A short way down Huntington Avenue is the center of a worldwide religion—the Mother Church of Christian Science, built of white limestone with a dome twice the size of that on the State House. This immense hemisphere rises to an inside height of 108 feet and is entirely without supporting pillars. The doors and also the pews—which comfortably seat four thousand persons—are of richly carved mahogany from Santo Domingo which contrasts pleasantly with the pure white interior.

There was at one time a spate of books with such titles as *Inside Asia*, *Inside U.S.A.*, and the like. If one cares to be inside the world, he may satisfy the desire by a visit to the Mapparium in the Christian Science Publishing House next door to the church. Here, standing on a crystal bridge inside a huge glass globe, one may view the continents and oceans of the world above, beneath, and about him. A number of little clocks show the correct time in every country of the world.

It is in this building that *The Christian Science Monitor* is printed and published—a newspaper of vast circulation and unimpeachable accuracy. "The Monitor says" is the synonym for "It is the fact." It never exposes its readers to the sordid details of death, crime, or scandal. It faithfully guards its readers' delicate perceptions. When other news sheets unblushingly published an advertisement picturing a nude baby, the *Monitor* refused to print it until its art department had clothed the infant in chaste diapers.

To find the most dignified and cultured of Boston's sons ornamenting a church tower is startling, but there they are on the tower of the First Baptist Church at the corner of Berkeley and Commonwealth. Bartholdi, the French sculptor of the Statue of Liberty, designed this tower and ornamented it with panels representing the four sacraments of the Christian Church; baptism, communion, marriage, and death. For his models he chose well-known personages: Longfellow, Emerson, Hawthorne, Sumner, and other great and famous figures.

The First and Second Church, at the corner of Berkeley and Marlborough, is sixth in direct line from the first mud-walled gathering place of the Puritans and can list among its former members such notables as Governor Winthrop, John Cotton, John Quincy Adams, Emerson, Hale, Prescott, and many more whose names are associated with great events in Boston. After the fifth building of the First Church was destroyed by fire in 1968, the present church was rebuilt around the surviving tower and today stands as a dramatic example of the successful mating of old and new architecture.

The churches mentioned are prominent because of their historical background. There are many others equally active in carrying on the great Christian work which is a Boston tradition.

As with churches, so it is with schools. Almost every conceivable kind of school is to be found in the Back Bay. The superb grouping of massive marble buildings about an impressive courtyard is the Harvard Medical School, the first medical school in the country and now, unquestionably, one of the finest.

The New England Conservatory of Music, oldest institution of its kind in the United States, lists many famous names among its graduates.

Here also are schools of art, science, education, languages, theater arts, and practically everything else. You can learn anything in the Back Bay—and the word "anything" is used advisedly.

Over the main portal of the Museum of Fine Arts on Huntington Avenue is an unfinished sculpture vaguely suggesting the head of a sphinx. It is symbolic of the truism that the creation and collecting of art are never finished. This thought has been the motivating force back of the manifold activities of the museum—never static, always growing, and always improving. Such a policy has resulted in the museum's having the finest collection of Japanese art outside of Tokyo. Only in Cairo is

Museum of Fine Arts

there a more complete exhibition of Egyptian art of the Old Kingdom, and the collection of Indian painting is unequaled anywhere in the world. Beauty and historic interest unite in the priceless examples of the work of Paul Revere and other Colonial silversmiths, of which there is an authentic collection.

But why make comparisons and listings? The Boston Museum of Fine Arts is a treasure house of the beautiful, of the sublime craftsmanship of many artists working in many media and with varied tools. A visit to the Museum is a visit to the world of dreams—dreams made manifest by the brush, the chisel, the graver, and the tapestry needle in the hands of those to whom God has given the transcendent ability to interpret and perpetuate His works. And it is ours, freely and completely ours, to enjoy as we may desire. It is open to the public for a small admission fee, but it is chiefly supported by gifts from individuals who love beauty and who generously believe in sharing it.

There is a palace in the Fens which is ours to enjoy, also— the Isabella Stewart Gardner Museum. Mrs. Gardner, our benefactress, was a Bostonian by marriage, not by birth, and though

J. S. Sargent, Isabella Stewart Gardner

she definitely was a member of Boston's "Four Hundred" by virtue of her marriage to John Lowell Gardner, by no conceivable standard could she be called a "Proper Bostonian."

"Mrs. Jack" as she was called, although never to her face, delighted in outraging the mores of Boston society. When others drank sherry, she drank beer and said that she liked it. She was known to have "walked" a lion through the Boston zoo, and to have hired and helped drive a locomotive at eighty miles per hour in order to beat her friends to a picnic site.

Once during Lent she indulged in an act of pious atonement for her misdeeds of the year. Arriving at Beacon Hill in her chauffeur-driven limousine, she took bucket and mop and scrubbed the steps of the Church of the Advent. Much advance publicity was given to this act of sanctimonious abnegation. The consensus was that, as full atonement for her sins against the traditions of Boston society, she should have scrubbed the entire façade.

The Gardners were avid art collectors. Between the years 1874 and 1898, they made frequent trips to Europe and Asia, increasingly motivated by "the hunt" for precious objects. In 1896, their collection was so extensive that Mrs. Gardner, called "Busy Ella" by her husband, turned her attention toward the creation of a palace suitable to house these fabulous artifacts. Purchasing columns, cornices, capitals, fountains, balconies, and sundry other architectural fragments from various Italian villas and shipping them, piece by piece, to Boston was the first step. Creating a Venetian palace in the Back Back Fens was the second.

After her husband's death in 1898, Mrs. Gardner devoted the rest of her life to the completion of the museum and the arrangement of her treasures. Being a millionaire in her own right as well as having inherited three million from her husband, she was well implemented for the task. Finally, when all was in place, she made her will, leaving her museum for "the education and the enjoyment of the public forever," with the proviso that none of its precious contents should be relocated and that nothing should be added or loaned.

The inner courtyard is, at all times, delightful with the color and fragrance of an ever-changing display of fresh flowers, while

The Dutch Room, southeast corner:
Isabella Stewart Gardner Museum

frequent concerts of chamber music form a background to the beauty that is all about.

The sculpture, furniture, stained glass, and tapestries are magnificent, but the display of old masters is superb. These include "The Concert" by Vermeer, "The Presentation of the Child Jesus in the Temple" by Giotto, Rubens' "Earl of Arundel," and the canvas which some have called the finest painting in America —the "Rape of Europa" by Titian.

The Isabella Stewart Gardner Museum is unique. There is nothing else like it in the world. It is a glowing example of what a woman of impeccable taste, sufficient funds, and tremendous energy can accomplish.

Many legends are still told about Mrs. Gardner's eccentricities. It has been said that she became exceedingly frugal in her later years, her passion for accumulating the beautiful having such priority that she was known to ration her servants' food when a particular objet d'art tempted her. Whatever her eccentricities, she was a woman of vision, and Boston is eternally grateful to her.

ITALIA NOVA

Folks of the same ethnic background tend to gather together, and the North End is now entirely occupied by people of Italian extraction. It was not always so. For the first two centuries of Boston's existence this was quite the fashionable end of the town, graced by the mansions of Lieutenant Governor Hutchinson, Sir Henry Frankland, and Governor Phips. Less wealthy but equally important residents were people of the type of the Mathers, the Reveres, and Mint Master Hull.

Came the Revolution, bringing with it many social and financial changes. The North End lost its supremacy and was soon abandoned by the rich and fashionable, who, by degrees, removed to the south and west parts of the town.

The failure of the potato crop in 1842 was an unmistakable warning to the Irish farmer that he must leave his overpopulated, undernourished land or face starvation. He left. By the crowded steamshipload he left. America, the land of promise, was his goal. He did not choose Boston, but since that was where the Cunard steamer left him, there he stayed.

Boston's North End received him, and in the already deserted mansions he made his home, usually on the basis of one family per room, and that family sometimes finding space for a boarder or two. Unskilled labor was needed in Boston then, and the men found pick and shovel work aplenty. The women and girls "hired out" as domestics, and, in a modest way, the families prospered.

The children attended local schools and learned more than the purely academic subjects. They explored American ways and became keenly interested in business and politics—especially politics.

As their condition improved, financially and socially, they moved out of the North End to Charlestown and from there to the many pleasant towns of Greater Boston's outer rim.

As the Irish left, families of other ethnic backgrounds arrived so that by the end of the Civil War there was a small but growing Italian colony centered about North Bennet Street, and a considerable number of Jews from eastern Europe in the section west of Salem and north of Prince Street.

There was surprisingly little conflict between the three groups, chiefly because their desires and interests were widely divergent. The main interest of the Jews was in buying and selling real estate; the Irish were chiefly concerned in politics; and the Italians had, as always, a longing to deal in the products of the good earth, meat and produce.

As time went on more and more of the Irish and Jewish people moved away and the Italians took their places until today the North End is once more homogeneous.

Placards in the window of a travel agency on Hanover Street urge excursions to Italy. Why? The North End *is* Italy. The liquor stores feature wine instead of whiskey, and much prominence is given to *strega* and *anisetta*. The hardware stores display wine presses, *salza* makers, and strange rolling pins for the manufacture of macaroni and ravioli. Live snails and squid crawl sluggishly over grocery windows, and every fourth store seems to be a bakery featuring cakes of rainbow colors with delightful shapes. There are very special types of macaroon-like cookies which are always served at weddings and christenings. Since weddings are frequent and christenings follow soon and often thereafter, the demand for these confections is brisk.

At Christmas and Easter time the sculptor in sugar produces his finest work. Little lambs, spring flowers, and religious scenes appear. Art is art, religion is a matter of daily life, and these kindly people see nothing incongruous in a figure of the Christ in a manger surrounded by adoring Wise Men—all done in pink sugar. The figures are tenderly preserved and admired until dust and much handling have rendered them unrecognizable, when they are broken up to sweeten the morning coffee.

Hanover Street

Eels on Christmas Eve are as much an Italian tradition as is turkey on Thanksgiving for the New Englander. A few days before Christmas, metal-lined pushcarts appear on the streets. These are full of sea water—and eels. A crowd gathers around one of the carts to help an old, wrinkled Italian woman select her banquet. With the approval of the bystanders she indicates a noble specimen, full five feet from stem to stern. The vendor grasps him expertly and places him on the scales. Immediately he slithers off and back into the tank before his weight can be established. A huge paper bag appears from under the cart and the eel is dropped in, tail first; but before the mouth of the bag can be tied, the eel splashes back into his native element.

Excitement grows! The crowd takes sides! Some shout advice to the old lady, some to the vendor, and a considerable number call upon the saints to aid the eel.

Now the operator changes his technique and drops the eel into the bag head first. An exploring tail oozes out. The vendor seizes it, giving it a vicious bite. The tail withdraws into the safety of the paper sack. Quickly the neck of the container is securely tied and the bundle triumphantly placed on the scales. By this time the paper is so water soaked that the lithe captive has no difficulty in pushing his way right through the wall of his prison and back to freedom. The salesman admits defeat, loops a strong cord around the eel, guesses at the weight, and hands the other end of the rope to the elderly purchaser, who departs with a long black tail wagging in the dust behind her.

Peace again descends on Salem Street.

There is an affinity between the Italian temperament and all growing things. To own a bit of the fruitful earth, to plant a garden, to watch the annual miracle of germination, growth, and fruition is, to him, one of the great satisfactions of life.

It is the tragedy of the North End that, in a region populated by a people who love all growing things, there is not in the entire area a spot which is not occupied by buildings, streets, or sidewalks. There is no room for gardens.

However, ingenuity, patience, and hard work have conquered these seemingly insurmountable obstacles. There *are* gardens in the North End—fine gardens, often containing rare and unusual fruits and flowers. In the homey little restaurants, in the snug, club-like bars, and over the coffee cups in pleasant pastry shops one may hear the gardeners comparing notes, giving advice, and, it must be admitted, boasting not a little.

If your interest is genuine and you have the gift for making friends you may be invited to see one of these gardens. The visit will entail a considerable climb up dark and noisome stairways, for buildings in the North End are tall and the gardens are on the roof tops.

With infinite pains the owner has brought carefully selected earth from the suburbs. This is carried up three or four flights of stairs by the basket or bagful. Mixed with carefully measured fertilizer the soil is placed in wooden boxes or tubs and the garden is ready for planting.

It is not the ordinary fruits and flowers that are grown in these roof gardens. Often the nostalgic longing for the well-remembered foliage of a garden in the homeland where childhood dreams were made will result in the cultivation of some exotic plants seldom seen in this climate. Little fig trees, orange trees, and even a lemon tree with an annual crop of five or six lemons may be found. Of course such semitropical plants must be taken into the house and cared for during the long winter. Generally they are moved in, box and all, early in September and spend a warm, comfortable winter in kitchen or bedroom. They receive as much attention and care as any other member of the family.

There is a solid satisfaction in sitting, with a few friends, at a table in your own garden of a summer evening. Here the wine has a better flavor, the stars seem more friendly, the conversation is more sparkling, and the problems of the day seem very remote. "The roof," as one old patriarch put it, "is that much nearer Heaven."

More than twenty thousand tourists annually visit the historic places in the North End and they *all* get lost. The streets and alleys which lead to the Old North Church and to Paul Revere's house are a tangled puzzle that few can solve. Italian children, fortunately, are plentiful and most willing to act as guides. For a small tip they will give you personal escort, recite "The Midnight Ride" if you wish, and flash you a million-dollar smile in the bargain.

The mere names of some of the North End streets carry an aura of romance. Wouldn't you like to live at the junction of Prince, Sun Court, Garden, and Moon Streets? Paul Revere did. So did the Mathers—Increase, Samuel, and Cotton. So did Governor Hutchinson and Sir Harry Frankland. The long, narrow triangle formed by the junction of these streets is the old and historic North Square.

The Revere house, still standing in North Square, was a century old when Paul bought it in 1770. It is now the oldest dwelling house still standing in Boston. The great fireplace, bits of the original wallpaper, furnishings of the period, and a collec-

Paul Revere House: North Square

tion of tools which Revere actually used in his manifold occupations make this one of the most interesting historical museums of the city.

North Square is a lively locality today and it must have been a sprightly spot in the 1770s. It had within its narrow confines a public market, guard house, town pump, and meeting house—all centers of excitement and gossip. The Revere family doubtless added their quota to the general animation, for Paul had sixteen children, eight by his first wife and eight by his second. These were all born at two-year intervals, and always on the even-numbered years.

The Revere house was built in 1676 and we are really traveling back in time when we speak of the house which stood on this site before that. The first house to be located here was the home of Captain Kemble, who was condemned to suffer for two hours in the stocks for "Lewd and Vicious" conduct. He had been seen kissing his wife on the Sabbath day.

The Kemble house was later occupied by the great and famous minister Increase Mather and by his no less revered son Cotton, whose church, the original Old North, was nearby. It was written of Increase Mather that "he was a blessing to his people who lived together in love and peace." After he became incapacitated, the church continued to pay his salary. Also, as a touching mark of their appreciation, they paid his funeral expenses—a dollar and a half for a coffin and twenty dollars for wine for the mourners.

Cotton Mather was a precocious youth, entering Harvard at twelve and being graduated four years later. In 1686 he married Abigail Phillips and recorded the event by a single line in his diary. Two Sundays later he preached in Boston choosing as his topic "Divine Delights."

The mansion of Governor Hutchinson in North Square was the house that was sacked and all but destroyed by an infuriated mob at the time of the Stamp Act riots.

Near the Hutchinson mansion was the luxurious home of Sir Harry Frankland. It was to this palatial residence that Sir Harry brought the beautiful Agnes Surriage, whose face and figure had delighted him when he first saw her as a chore-girl scrubbing the floor of a Marblehead tavern. Boston society was a little cool toward Sir Harry's explanation that he took her to his house because "he wanted to oversee her education." Fifteen years later, he was rounding out Agnes' education by foreign travel. In Lisbon he was in a building that collapsed during an earthquake. The fair Agnes rescued him at considerable risk to her own life. Shortly thereafter they were married and Agnes became Lady Frankland at long last; but it took a cataclysm to bring it about.

On Salem Street, just off North Square, is a beautiful, old, and historic church. If you wish people to know what building you are talking about, you will call it "the Old North," but its real name is Christ Church and has been since April 15, 1723, when the Rev. Samuel Myles of King's Chapel laid the cornerstone with the words "May the gates of Hell never prevail against it." Up to the present writing they haven't.

Christ Church, the oldest edifice of its kind in the city, stands on ground where no other building has ever stood, unless there happened to be a wigwam of some tribal chieftain on the spot. Since 1723 weekly religious services have been held here without interruption, save for a brief period during the Revolution. From its steeple flashed the lanterns "two if by sea" which started Paul Revere on his ride.

From this same steeple, a safe distance from actual combat, General Gage watched the attack on Bunker Hill which cost him his command. Old North is not only a church but a landmark and a shrine as well.

Christ Church is an almost exact copy of an edifice in the suburbs of London which was designed by Christopher Wren. The two-and-a-half-foot-thick walls are of brick, over 500,000 of them, all hand made in nearby Medford. In Medford, also, may have been manufactured the eighty-three gallons of rum included in the bill for raising the steeple, which towers 170 feet above the sidewalk. This steeple was blown down in the storm of 1804 and its successor fell before another hurricane in August 1954. Both of the replacements were accurate copies of the original.

In 1912 the interior of the church was restored to its original beauty: high box pews, each with its little door inscribed with the name of the first owner; the two graceful chandeliers over the central aisle; the Richard-Avery clock, installed in 1726, in front of the old organ; the staves in the pews of the church wardens; and the four wooden cherubim on the organ case which were the gift of the privateer (or possibly pirate) Captain Gru-

Paul Revere and His Mall

Interior: Old North Church

chy. They were taken from a captured ship which had been bound for Canada.

Remarkable historic treasures are preserved in the old church: the first portrait bust of George Washington; the "Vinegar Bible" printed in 1717; the silver communion service presented by George II; and, most beloved of all, the chime of eight bells, the first in America, cast in England in 1744. These continue to delight the hearers every Sunday morning. One of the early ringers of this chime was Paul Revere, who combined, as all bell ringers must, a musical ear and a muscular arm.

Under the church, in the old tradition, are tombs containing the bodies of the faithful, including, unfortunately, that of Major Pitcairn, whose mortal remains were supposed to have been sent to England for honorable burial in Westminster Abbey. It has been quite definitely established that a careless and indifferent sexton sent the body of a Lieutenant Shea instead of that of the Major. The sexton was presented with a gold watch for his care and trouble. Whether Major Pitcairn's mortal remains be in Westminster Abbey or in Christ Church, he rests in peace surrounded by beauty, reverence, and historical tradition.

KWANGTUNG IN BOSTON

A little section of Kwangtung Province has crossed the sea and been dropped in the center of Boston's business district. Small in area, being bounded by Shawmut Avenue, Oak Street, Harrison Avenue, Essex Street, the Southeast Expressway, and the Mass Turnpike, it is, nonetheless, the fourth largest Chinatown in the United States, exceeded only by those in New York, San Francisco, and Los Angeles.

Chinatown is increasingly showing the signs of a self-sufficient neighborhood with its many groceries, book and record shops, and beauty parlors. But, to many visitors, the large number of restaurants in the area is its most notable feature. It is a good place to dine if you like Chinese food, as who does not? The food is excellent, the décor is interesting, the service is friendly, and the prices are moderate. While most restaurants in Chinatown specialize in Cantonese cooking, the appropriately named Shanghai Restaurant is expressly noted for its regional style. "Fast-food" restaurants and luncheonettes have cropped up in recent years. Fortunately they appear to have been able to rise above or bypass the computerized qualities and atmosphere of their Western-style counterparts.

There are also a number of clubs and associations in the district. The Chinese are great "joiners," often by necessity; and, several years ago, every family group had its "Fong" or association for mutual help. The "Fong," literally translated as "room," was rented by each group as a means of providing shelter and a meeting place for those male immigrants who, forced to leave their families behind, arrived alone in the United States some fifty years ago. While the concept of "Fong" has died out, there are still a number of organizations that fill many of these same needs and more.

Assorted Delicacies: A Chinese Grocery

Chinese Merchants Association Building

On the corner of Hudson and Kneeland Streets is the headquarters of the Chinese Merchants Association. Built in 1952, this structure is an interesting combination of Eastern and Western architecture. The façade is ornamented with four large plaques in which the East and the West, the ancient and the modern, have joined. Cast in one of the most distinctively American metals—stainless steel—are represented, in low relief, figures from one of the oldest and most characteristically Oriental of religions: the Pa Hsien, or Eight Immortals, of the Taoist cult.

Oxford Street, in spite of its Puritan origin and its English name, is entirely Chinese. There are interesting spots to be visited in this short, narrow highway. The Chung Wah Gong Shaw—the Chinese Consolidated Benevolent Association of New England—is located at 14 Oxford. Comprised of representatives from business, civic, and social organizations, and family-name associations, this umbrella organization, with its 50-member council, has traditionally served as Chinatown's main spokesman both inside and outside the community. Its far-reaching interests and activities range from negotiating civil and business disputes, forming ad hoc committees for problems of urban renewal, sponsoring housing (such as Tai-Tung Village), and sponsoring the New Year and August Moon Festivals to supervising the community bulletin board and sponsoring an intercity volleyball tournament every three years.

At number 16 Oxford, in the basement, is the Shanghai Printing Company. This firm is equipped to print booklets, menus, laundry checks, and other job printing in either Chinese or English. The English type case carries the twenty-six letters of our alphabet. However, the Chinese is different. Every word is a different symbol, and the walls are lined with cases holding over ten thousand characters, no two alike. The amazingly learned proprietor, Mr. Henry Wong, gallops up and down in front of these cases. He selects a character here and another there, to compose those Chinese phrases which are as perfect as his faultless English. A Chinese compositor must possess high intelligence, a prodigious memory, and powerful legs. Mr. Wong has all of these.

Next door at 18 Oxford is the On Leong Theater. Once a focal point for Chinatown's theater and entertainment, it is now converted into classrooms. The children of Chinatown, of course, attend the regular Boston public schools, but in the late afternoon they are to be seen at this Chinese school, where there are five teachers, a principal, and some hundred and fifty boys and girls ranging in age from six to sixteen.

Here the children are taught a mixture of both the classical and contemporary usage of the spoken and written language of the homeland, which some of them have never seen. In an attempt to revitalize their culture, Chinese dances and songs are taught as well as the Analects of the great sage Confucius. It would be no bad thing if all children—and adults—memorized and pondered some of these sayings. To quote a few:

Henry Wong

"The superior man cherishes books, the common man cherishes his pig."

"Let those who produce the revenue be many and those who consume the revenue be few and let the consumers practice economy."

"In a neighbor's melon field do not stoop to tie your shoe lace."

Down the street from the school is the Yee Hong Guey restaurant. Here one finds no Oriental décor, no dragons, lanterns, or colorful hangings; but he will find Chinese food at its succulent best. The chef of the Yee Hong Guey is an artist supreme, and the memory of his Lobster Cantonese, Butterfly Shrimp, and Chicken Foo Yong will remain with one until he descends into the hungry grave.

A very large proportion—75 percent—of Chinatown's residents don't read or speak English, and the community has no Chinese-language newspaper. Instead, opposite the Yee Hong Guey restaurant is The Bulletin Board. Here are posted announcements of meetings, notices of births, marriages, and deaths, as well as news items and advertisements. Seventy years ago this was the only source of world news for many of the local residents. Today many subscribe to the New York and San Francisco Chinese-language dailies.

Though Chinatown lacks a newspaper, there is no lack of entertainment. The China Cinema at 84 Beach Street is noted for its Chinese movies, most of them imported from Hong Kong and Taiwan. The greater part of these deal with the legendary gods and heroes of the olden times, though there is a rise in martial arts subjects, such as Kung Fu and Tai Kwan Do, and the Western type of melodrama and sentimental love story is creeping in.

A Chinese opera is something to see—and hear. Usually presented in the Hancock Hall or the Bradford Hotel, the performance lasts for hours; years ago, it used to last for days. The audience drifts in and out, walks about, munching melon seeds, and never, never applauds. One claps his hands to frighten away evil spirits, and it is impolite to imply that there are such beings about.

There is little or no scenery, but the costumes are startling in their gorgeous beauty. The orchestra members—in American clothes—sit on the stage and scrape, thump, and blow the instruments of their native land. To some Occidental ears they produce the wildest cacophony. Perhaps some Oriental ears also need respite, for it is no uncommon sight to see a player in the midst of this never-ending barrage of sound casually reach beneath his chair for a shiny Thermos bottle in full view of the audience. Nonchalantly he lifts this to his lips for a long satisfying drink of hot tea. This ceremony performed, he rejoins the orchestra and again vigorously applies himself to fervent squeaks and scrapes.

The property man, in shirt sleeves, sits on a chair also in full view of the audience. He hands the actors such properties as they may need and often rearranges the furniture. He spreads out a skirt here or a petticoat there so that it may be admired. He may even forcibly turn an actor around to face the spectators; or, if the actor is a bit slow about kneeling, as the story might

12 Tyler Street

require, he may suddenly give him a smart push in the right direction.

One can find neither monument nor tablet at number 12 Tyler Street, but such a memorial would not be out of place. At about the time that the Puritans were getting settled in Boston, the Manchurians attacked and conquered China. They overthrew the great Ming Dynasty, which had endured for centuries, and placed a Manchu on the throne. Some of the conquered Chinese united into a secret society, "The Brotherhood of the Golden Lily," whose objective was to recapture the government of the Chinese.

A great leader of revolt, Dr. Sun- Yat-sen, came to the United States, in 1905, in an effort to enlist the moral and financial support of his compatriots in this country. An attempt to overthrow a dynasty which had reigned for over 250 years was no light task, and Dr. Sun was not given too much encouragement. Arriving in Boston he found but seven men—five laundrymen and two restaurateurs—who were willing to work with him. These, men of education and ability, were political refugees from China. They met in a basement room at 12 Tyler Street, into which humble headquarters poured a great stream of money, freely given by the Chinese of America to finance the undertaking. It was here that much of the strategy of the Chinese Revolution was plotted until its ultimate success resulted in the creation of the Chinese Republic on the "double ten"—the tenth day of the tenth month of 1911.

VII. Streets of Sin

VICIOUS HIGHWAYS

Seventy years ago there were certain streets in Boston, as in every other city, which were never mentioned in polite society. Merely to speak the name of one of these streets from the stage of a burlesque theater would cause gales of ribald laughter. That is all in the past. Such segregated sinks of sin no longer exist. It is not that the city's morals are purer or that the police and social agencies have achieved any great triumph against the forces of evil. Rather it is a change in customs and manners. The "call girl" and the amateur have supplanted the old-time professional prostitute, and what was once focused is now diffused.

The worst of all vicious highways of the past was Anne Street, which was laid out along the original water front from Dock Square to North Square. For some twenty years during the middle of the nineteenth century this street was the home of thieves, murderers, prostitutes, and gamblers. Its proximity to the wharves made it a playground for men from the ships; and in those days sailors played rough.

A ship's crew would be discharged at the wharf and a group of young men, virile, vigorous, and lusty, would be suddenly decanted on the town. Behind them were weeks, even months, of lonely life at sea under the most rigorous discipline. Each man would have his pay for the voyage in his pocket and his pent-up desires and longings fermenting within him.

Anne Street would be ready and waiting. Anne Street, lined on both sides with brothels, "jilt shops" into which sailors were enticed and robbed, saloons, rat pits, dance halls, theaters of lewd entertainment, gambling joints, and boardinghouses of the lowest type. How closely packed were these dens of iniquity is indicated by the fact that a single police raid on the night of

April 23, 1851, resulted in the arrest of 165 persons guilty of every sort of crime. Another raid a few weeks later netted 150 prostitutes. Even as late as 1870, it was not safe for a police officer to go alone through this street. The police always went in pairs and were careful to walk in the middle of the street.

A hopeless task, one might think, to try to combat the forces of evil rampant on the waterfront in those days, but one man attempted it and with considerable success. The Rev. E. T. Taylor established a Bethel and a "Mariners' House" in North Square. A former sailor, a vigorous orator, and a sincere Christian was Father Taylor. When he preached to the sailors he used a wealth of illustrations drawn from the sea itself and from the life of the sea. He talked in a language the sailors understood and his services were always well attended.

The "Mariners' House," a four-story building of over forty rooms, was designed with a complete understanding of the needs of the people it served. A storage room for the seamen's luggage, a laundry, bathing rooms, and a library were provided as well as the usual sleeping and dining rooms.

The needs of the growing city did for Anne Street what neither the police nor Father Taylor had been able to do. The swarming undesirables were driven out and respectable warehouses and much needed shops took the place of the disreputable and dangerous dens. Even the name of the thoroughfare was changed. It is now North Street.

The region has lost something of color but it has gained in dignity.

THE BLACK SEA

During a great part of the nineteenth century, Richmond Street, with its immediate environs, was known as the Black Sea. The street was lined with low-class boardinghouses, gambling dens, dance halls, bistros, and brothels. Every ground floor and many of the cellars were combined dance halls and saloons, while the upper rooms were used for even less savory purposes.

It was considered high adventure at that time for a group of young men from "uptown" to spend an evening "slumming" in the Black Sea area, dancing with the painted sirens, treating the crowd at the bars, and generally having an uproarious time. When such a group invaded a barroom, the floor would be cleared for them; partners would be chosen, the band would blare out its most provocative music, the girls would smile alluringly, and the dancing would be wild and unrestrained. But only for a brief period. After a very few minutes of dancing, the proprietor would shout, "Promenade all—and you know where." This was the signal for the boys to spend some money at the bar. Expert "bouncers" would ease them out into the street as soon as their money was exhausted; it never took long.

If the boys remained together in a band of ten or a dozen, they would come to little harm—physically, that is—but woe betide the man who permitted himself to become separated from his companions. The Black Sea would engulf him and the next morning would find him cast up on the shore, alive if he was lucky, but stripped of his cash, his jewelry, and most of his clothes.

One type of entertainment popular in the Black Sea is now, happily, no longer to be seen. It may be there is a more civilized and humane attitude toward what constitutes sport or it may be there is a growing scarcity in the supply of the necessary rodents, but the rat pit is as extinct as the dodo. Around 1850 the "sport" of ratting was popular, though illegal. The "pit" was an octagonal pen about four feet high built of tight boards. Twenty large, live rats would be lifted by tongs out of a barrel and placed in this ring. A dog, usually some famous "ratter" well known to the spectators, would be dropped into the ring and the bloody and disgusting contest would begin. The dog always won—or almost always. The interest, and the betting, centered on the length of time it took him to kill the twenty rats. Anything under a minute was considered excellent and the record was, reputedly, fifteen seconds.

The limited police force of the time did what they could— it wasn't much—to enforce law and order in the Black Sea, and occasionally the public would assist, as they did on the evening of

July 22, 1825. At that time there was a notorious establishment near Blackstone Street which was called the "Beehive," partly from the shape of the building itself, partly because of its buzzing activity and the incessant passing in and out through its narrow door. A group of young men decided that this disgrace to the city should be removed, so they elected themselves to do the job. Perhaps they were motivated by ideas of stern morality and high civic duty; or it is possible that the baiting of a group of abandoned and helpless women offered more excitement, even, than the sport of the rat pit. In any case they started out intent on destruction.

By the time these champions of reform reached their destination, their number had been increased to about two hundred. Disguised with whatever they could find of bizarre clothing, with faces blackened, armed with pitchforks, iron bands, and axes, they made a motley and fearsome spectacle. A "band" with fish horns, tin pans, and conch shells accompanied them.

The crusaders descended on the "Beehive" and the frightened, hysterical inmates fled, screaming, in all directions. The axmen lost no time in getting to work, and, although the building was left standing, every bit of furniture, as well as most of the walls and windows, was demolished. Although it was midsummer, a violent blizzard seemed to be raging about the house. The "reformers" ripped open a multitude of feather beds and emptied their contents out of the windows. The wind swirled them high and low. For weeks thereafter, these feathers blew about the Boston streets, making miniature snowstorms here and there, finally piling in gray, sordid drifts against the buildings.

A good time was had by all—except the girls. Formerly merely hopeless and friendless, now they were homeless as well. Morality and righteousness were triumphant.

CROSSROADS OF HELL

In its innocent youth Scollay Square was a cow pasture and so it remained until 1684, when a schoolhouse was built "over against Sam Sewall's house." In 1790 this school was discontinued and William Scollay bought the building. He also purchased a number of other buildings nearby, living in one and renting the rest. These became known as the Scollay Buildings and were occupied by tradesmen of various sorts and the largest tea store in the city, a store whose advertisement read, "Our tea is almost intoxicating." A beverage "almost intoxicating" would have been coldly received in the Scollay Square of a later date. However, tea continued to be featured there, and the steaming tea kettle in front of the Oriental Tea Company delighted children for nearly a century.

In 1847 when the kettle was new, the company offered a prize of a chest of forty pounds of tea to the customer who could make the nearest guess as to the capacity—one guess with each purchase. When the contest closed, a crowd of some 15,000 people gathered to view the measuring. A platform had been built around the kettle, where a Boston court judge and the City Sealer of Weights and Measures presided over the ceremony. The lid was removed and a small boy poked his head out of the kettle. He was lifted out and was followed by another—and another until eight boys and a man wearing a tall silk hat had emerged.

Steaming Kettle

A local newspaper wrote that its editor had guessed that the kettle held three hundred gals. and was astonished to find it held only eight *boys*.

The 13,000 guesses handed in ranged from one gallon to 3,500 gallons. According to a newspaper account, published at the time, the correct amount of 227 gallons, two quarts, one pint, and three gills was guessed by eight persons, who shared the prize. This, Boston's second tea party, caused almost as much excitement as did the first.

The Scollay Buildings were torn down in 1816 to make room for a new street, Cornhill. Shortly thereafter, great hotels were built in the square—the American House in 1835, closely followed by the Quincy House, the Crawford, and the Revere. These were admittedly the finest hotels in the United States at the time. Their guests included such notables as the Prince of Wales, the Grand Duke Alexis, President Pierce, and our own Daniel Webster. The Crawford House had the first passenger elevator in the country, and the Quincy House certainly had the slowest.

Gradually, almost imperceptibly, the character of the square changed: the visitors of note went to newer hotels and people of notoriety took their places. The theaters became second rate, or worse. Things deteriorated until in 1903 even the bronze statue of Governor Winthrop, which had graced the square for a hundred years, couldn't take it any longer and removed to the First Church in serene Back Bay.

Scollay Square was well on its way to becoming a disreputable slum when it experienced an unexpected renaissance. Two world wars in rapid succession caused the Navy Yard at Charlestown to be thronged with battleships being repaired and refitted. Boston was inundated with scores of bluejackets intent on having a final fling before going overseas.

During the war years the much maligned square lived by, and for, the boys of the Navy. Its restaurants, stores, bars, and other services were keyed to the tastes of the Navy personnel. Lunchrooms offered the toothsome hot dog, the nutritious hamburger, and the succulent submarine. Prices were low and the places were reasonably clean although unreasonably noisy.

Photo studios enabled Jack to secure a lasting memento of the current girl friend, or vice versa. Tattoo studios catered to that strange artistic longing which seems at times to attack all men associated with salt water. The artists of the needle would execute any design from a simple cross to a "bird's-eye view of Sydney." They advised against girls' names. A tattoo is apt to outlive a light o'love, and it was highly embarrassing for a sailor to contemplate matrimony with Helen in his heart and Tessie on his torso. Explanation was required. It was far wiser to have a simple wreath and the word "Mother." That is a love which changeth not.

Brass knuckles are socially unacceptable, but a huge and heavy ring worn on the middle finger was quite as effective and a lot more legal. To give weight and authority, there was an ornamental lump of metal on the top of the ring. Favorite designs were the heads of girls and Indians. Many a man taking inventory after a street fight was astonished to find the profile of a woman or a warrior stamped in intaglio on his face or skull. Rings of this type were featured in Scollay Square, where all things could be had for a price.

A burlesque theater, a penny arcade, two or three dine-and-dance spots, a bowling alley, a shooting gallery, and several taverns with discreetly dim booths completed the picture of what Jack Ashore considered the requisites for a well-spent evening.

Scollay Square, like the ladies who frequented it, was best seen in the evening. By daylight both seemed a little tawdry and to have a lying-in-wait look, impatient for the night.

It was during the war years that a police court judge characterized Scollay Square as "the crossroads of Hell" and intimated that the city would be much improved if the entire area were dumped into the harbor. This seemed over severe. Scollay was garish, raucous, and uninhibited, but it was not sinister. Its atmosphere was of youth and it was vividly and throbbingly alive. Scollay had a reputation to maintain, and it did its best.

In March of 1963 the earnest desire of the upright judge was realized. The voice of municipal progress decreed that Scollay Square should be razed and that in its place would rise a Government Center of great beauty, dignity, and benefit to the city.

Scollay Square Before: 1961

Scollay Square After: 1971

Many a staid and proper citizen felt that the passing of this many-sided "square" was one of the best things that could have happened to the City of Boston.

But there was a minority report. Many former Navy men felt a nostalgic pang as they remembered the days of World War I and II when the gay, raucous, and uninhibited square offered a form of entertainment which could make them forget for a few brief hours the miseries of life in a total war.

Last to fall before the onslaught of the wreckers were two buildings at the corner of Franklin Avenue and Brattle Street. Both had been there since Revolutionary days—the Brattle Book Shop and the Brattle Tavern.

The tavern, occupying the easterly corner, was a small, low-ceilinged bistro of little beauty but of great appeal to a group of good fellows who met there to enjoy a brief interval between the rigors of the business day and the sometimes exacting duties of domestic life. Most of the clientele were lawyers or officials from the nearby courthouse, and the talk was frequently of legal matters, although politics, current events, and philosophy received their proper attention. There was always worthwhile conversation at the Brattle. At times it seemed more of a salon than a saloon.

The unpretentious barroom, founded in 1766, claimed to be, and probably was, the oldest continuously operated tavern in the nation. It was here that the Irish poet and patriot, John Boyle O'Reilly, made the negotiations leading to the purchase of the whaling ship which subsequently traveled halfway around the world to rescue six Irish patriots confined in an Australian prison colony.

On the westerly corner was one of those truly Bostonian institutions—an ancient bookstore. Old books, venerable prints, and forgotten literary treasurers of a bygone age were piled haphazardly on its sagging shelves. Here would gather the antiquarian, the student, and the casual reader. The genial proprietor, George Gloss, knew them all, knew their tastes and interests, and could unerringly find the exact book to meet their needs. He could instantly recognize the impecunious booklover who would come in for a quiet hour of reading and who never made a purchase. These "customers" were welcomed as cordially as the others and were never urged to buy.

The tavern died quietly, with a final round of drinks and a final reading of a bit of verse which a newspaper columnist had written on the back of a menu some years before.

> What is the lure of the Tavern?
> Why do we gather here?
> There must be a common interest
> That is more than the whiskey or beer.
>
> It isn't our job or our station.
> It isn't the year we were born,
> For some are facing the sunset
> And some are greeting the morn.
>
> Why do we keep returning
> Where the décor's chiefly dirt,
> Where the air is let out of the windbag
> And the stuffing removed from the shirt.
>
> It's because with our proper home life
> And the daily scratch for pelf,
> There's a torturing need for one short hour
> Where a man can be himself.
>
> So a toast to our motley cohorts
> All learned—all full of gin,
> Who strike the shackles from their wrists
> For an hour—at the Brattle Inn.

The 139-year-old Brattle Book Shop on the opposite corner made its exit in the truly grand manner. On the final day Mr. Gloss, instead of moving his stock to his much larger store still doing business nearby, invited the public to come in and help themselves without fee or cost. Never was invitation accepted with greater enthusiasm. An orderly but highly excited crowd of over five thousand persons stormed the narrow doors and, by closing time, the entire stock of some 50,000 volumes had dis-

George Gloss

appeared. Nothing was left but torn newspapers and a partial copy of *Moby Dick*. Fortunately for the booklovers of Boston, though Brattle Street has disappeared, Mr. Gloss is still in business at a new address, 5 West Street, and his treasure house still bears the honored name: "The Brattle Book Shop."

Scollay Square is gone, and from its ashes has risen Government Center—as exciting and as architecturally startling as any group of buildings in the country.

HIGH HANDED WICKEDNESS

"Mr. Shrimpton, Capt. Legett and others come in a Coach

from Roxbury about 9 aclock on Post, singing as they come. At Justice Morgan's they stop and drink healths, curse, swear, talk profanely and baudily to the great disturbance and grief of good people. Such high handed wickedness has hardly been heard of before in Boston!" So wrote Justice Sewall in his diary for September 3, 1686.

The virtuous judge would be even more disturbed could he visit the same locality now, for Justice Morgan's place was on Essex Street near the corner of Washington. This region has become a tiny tenderloin, rivaling even Scollay Square. Here Jack Ashore finds a warm and friendly welcome. Here the amber lights gleam luridly, jiggers are generous, the saxophone moans sobbingly, and predatory Peris prowl. Here the shore police always work in pairs, preserving a semblance of good order. "What shall we do with the drunken sailor?" runs the old sea chanty. These lads know the answer to that question, and things never get out of hand.

A raucous corner in 1686, an uproarious spot today, this locality was none too quiet in the vivid decade preceding the Revolution. In another chapter mention is made of the riotous gang of "South Enders" who periodically fought pitched battles with the gang of "North Enders" at that time. This corner was their rallying point, and it was here at the "Liberty Tree" that the combined forces of the two gangs staged some terrific orgies in the name of Liberty.

Essex Street also had its exciting moments in the animated days before the Civil War. Wendell Phillips, the fiery orator and dynamic abolitionist, lived here near the junction of Harrison Avenue. Nearby was the home of the Rev. Theodore Parker, another uncompromising antislavery advocate. Only a few steps down the street from these two was the Union Congregational Church, where the Rev. Nehemiah Adams preached just as fiercely that slavery was a divine institution ordained by God. There is no record of physical violence ever having been indulged in by these consecrated men with such divergent views, but the door of Wendell Phillips' house is now part of the historic collection at the Old State House.

Perhaps the Rev. Nehemiah tore it off!

VIII. Boston Binges

NOT SO PROPER BOSTONIANS

Traditionally, Boston has been a city of erudition and culture. The typical Bostonian is pictured as cold, remote, and unemotional. Never believe it! We have had our full share of bigots, crackpots, and fanatics. Mass hysteria has played its part in our history, and any screwball who is sufficiently vocal —and most screwballs are—can raise a considerable following. Sometimes the most staid and proper citizen will become involved in an orgy through no fault of his own. This is always unfortunate and frequently amusing.

Certainly there never lived a more proper Bostonian than Major Melville, friend and adviser of Samuel Adams and Paul Revere and a member of the "Long Room Club"—that board of strategy which engineered the events leading up to the Revolution. He was also a participant in the Tea Party and a brave and efficient officer during the war.

Major Melville was chief of the fire wardens for forty years and was long remembered as the last man in Boston to wear the cocked hat and knee "britches" of earlier days. The man and the costume were immortalized in Oliver Wendell Holmes' poem "The Last Leaf."

While Melville was a member of the "fire wards," the town purchased a new fire engine, a "pumper," operated by man power, six men on each side. The firemen celebrated the event in due and ancient form. Toasts were drunk to the new pump, to its builder, to Major Melville, to bigger and better fires, and to anything else that would furnish an excuse for another glass. When the festivities were at their height, some joker raised the cry of "Fire!" The doughty smoke eaters staggered out, harnessed themselves to their proud new engine, and dashed off in the direction of a brilliant glow in the sky. Down State Street they galloped, knocking an occasional brick from the buildings on either side; out onto Long Wharf where the illumination seemed brightest and where they decided_to make their stand to fight the all-consuming enemy. Dropping their suction hose into the harbor, they bent their backs to the pumping. An hour of hard work in the cold sobered them sufficiently to realize that they had directed their efforts at the glow caused by the full moon rising through the harbor mists. Sadly they returned to quarters, dragging their pump behind them.

Bostonians have always had the happy faculty of expressing their opinions, not by writing letters to the newspapers, but by overt and wanton acts. Always there is a picturesqueness and gaiety to these merry outrages, as well as a charming taste in masquerade. When, in 1733, the town built a market in Dock Square, the populace, who preferred to have their vegetables delivered by cart, did not hold meetings or boycott the new venture. No, they simply went forth one night and took the building apart. The lumber of which it was built furnished repairs for every barn and outhouse from Copp's Hill to Boston Neck. The mob that did this bit of demolition was "disguised as clergymen"!

In the gay days preceding the Revolution the task of goading the King's men to desperation was joyously taken over by mobs, more or less under the direction of Sam Adams. When the detested Stamp Act was passed, a building on Kilby Street, which was intended to be used as a stamp office, was razed. Of course the razers had to make a production of the event, and the building was carried piecemeal to the top of Fort Hill, where it became a funeral pyre for an effigy of Mr. Oliver, who was to have sold the stamps. Later the mob attacked Mr. Oliver's home, breaking windows, defacing walls, and tearing down fences. Intoxicated by success and the all-potent Medford rum, the patriotic vandals also attacked Governor Hutchinson's home in an orgy of destruction.

The day following these riots, a meeting of "the better class citizens" was held in Faneuil Hall. Here a unanimous vote was passed declaring an utter detestation of such violent actions and

The Boston Tea Party Revisited: 1973

calling upon the selectmen to suppress similar disorders in the future. In Tory circles it was firmly believed that the same people were present at both affairs.

Frenzy reached its peak when the tax-polluted tea was thrown into the harbor from the British ships at Griffin's Wharf. The "tea-slingers," with faces smeared with grease, soot, and lampblack, called themselves "mohawks" and brandished "tommyhawks" to prove it.

More recent attempts to control affairs by mob demonstrations have not been so successful. The mob which, in 1919, attempted to aid the Boston police strikers by staging crap games and worse on the Common succeeded only in getting some score of their hoodlum members killed outright and a hundred or so wounded by the National Guard. They also created a breeze which wafted the then governor, Calvin Coolidge, into the White House.

LIBERTY AND LICENSE

We might as well admit it. Staid old Boston was really jumping. Half the population was high as a kite and the rest, including the ladies, were enjoying the spectacle.

The date: January 24, 1793. The place: Liberty Square and points west as far as the Old State House. The occasion: A celebration in honor of the French Revolution.

An ox weighing over a thousand pounds was barbecued somewhere up Fort Hill way and then hoisted on a wagon and drawn through the principal streets by fifteen horses. Following this cart was another carrying eight hundred loaves of bread and still another with hogsheads of punch. Then followed the crowd, growing hungrier, thirstier, and more excited by the minute. At the "Liberty Stump" at Essex Street they paused to drink a toast to freedom; then past Governor Hancock's home (A toast to you, Governor!); down by Lieutenant Governor Adams' house (Your health, Sam!); and so to the Old State House and Liberty Square, where tables had been placed and where the gilded horns of the ox had been set up on a sixty-foot liberty pole.

January is a cold month for an outdoor banquet, but the punch was potent and there were no complaints. Every window, doorway, and even rooftop was crowded with ladies, watching with well-simulated horror the revels below. In a short time, the air was filled with chunks of meat, bones, and bread, each diner striving to score a direct hit on some fair observer. The ladies were shocked, frightened, and mortified—several fainted—but it is not recorded that any left.

While this orgy was progressing in the streets, the Governor, Lieutenant Governor, French Consul, and the elite of the town, some four hundred in all, were getting politely and privately plastered at a more refined banquet in Faneuil Hall.

Weeks later, when the true and bloody character of the French Revolution became manifest, the Bostonians ceased to favor it, and the ox horns on the liberty pole were draped with black. By this time, however, the name of "Liberty" had become firmly attached to the square where the liberty pole stood; and

Looking Upward: Liberty Square

Liberty Square it has remained until the present day, although few realize that it honors French rather than American liberty.

LA FAYETTE—HE WAS THERE

Strong men were bursting into tears, publicly and unashamed, women were fainting, children were shouting themselves to exhaustion, dogs were barking, cannon were booming, and bells were clanging. Boston was enjoying an emotional orgy not at all in keeping with her sedate reputation.

The visitor whose mere presence was sufficient to arouse the city to such a frenzy of sentimentality was a man nearing his seventieth year and a foreigner; but none can say that the tremendous ovation which was accorded him was not richly deserved. The man was the Marquis de La Fayette and the occasion was his visit to the city in 1824.

Never before had so many people been in Boston at one time. They came from all parts of New England and many from even more distant places. Thousands attended the reception at the State House, where La Fayette was formally presented to the citizens of the city.

It was on this occasion that the national standard—with twenty stars—was first flown from the State House. One of the contemporary accounts of the reception makes the rather startling statement that the Marquis was "greeted by a host of his former comrades in arms *including* a large number of ladies."

A tremendous crowd gathered outside the Amory House, which still stands at the corner of Park and Beacon Streets, hoping for a glimpse of the great man. Even his shadow seen on a window shade was greeted with prolonged cheers. And, when he was crossing the Common on his way to the reception, La Fayette passed between a double row of schoolchildren, who welcomed him with cheers and strewed his path with flowers.

The love and hero worship which the people of Boston lavished on La Fayette was not misplaced. This French statesman and officer withdrew from the military service of his native land in 1777 to come to this country, in a ship fitted out at his own expense, to offer his services as a volunteer in the Continental Army in any capacity and without pay. General Washington immediately commissioned the Marquis as a major general. Except for a furlough which he spent in France advancing the American cause, he served throughout the war, not only as a military officer, but as a friend and adviser of General Washington himself.

During his stay the Marquis paid a visit to his friend Governor Brooks, in Medford. As he entered the town, he passed under a floral arch which bore the inscription "Welcome to our hills and *Brooks*." This was considered a right merry jest in the days before the radio and television entertainers introduced a more sophisticated type of humor.

After the visit from the beloved hero, the legislature was flooded with requests for changes in street names. Everyone

The Recessed Doorways of Fayette Street: Bay Village

wanted to live on La Fayette Street. The legislators did their best to comply and, as before mentioned, Boston broke out in a rash of Fayette and La Fayette streets, places, malls, squares, and parks. We still have a few of these streets which were renamed at the time. One of them is Fayette Street in Bay Village. This highway now contains a row of almost identical houses, each with a deeply recessed doorway and vestibule. If, as tradition maintains, they were built by the French Huguenots, it is quite fitting that the street should bear the name of the great French soldier and statesman.

IN THE NAME OF RELIGION

In 1740, our city had a visitation from a great revivalist, the Rev. George Whitefield. Not that Boston really needed a new minister, but outside talent is always welcome. The Rev. George "drew" well—so well in fact that he was obliged to hold his meetings on the Common, where audiences variously estimated at from eight to twenty thousand gathered to hear him.

Whitefield's auditors differed sharply as to the value of his sermons, but none more so than did the Rev. Mr. Chauncy and Whitefield himself. When the revivalist played a return engagement in Boston, he was met at the wharf by Rev. Mr. Chauncy, who greeted him with the words, "Mr. Whitefield, I am sorry to see you return to Boston." "Yes," replied the Rev. George, "so is the Devil!"

The emotional excitement aroused by the forceful speaking of Whitefield was unbelievable. Even the record cards of several hospital patients of the time show, under the heading "Cause of Illness," the statement "Rendered insane by listening to Rev. Whitefield." There are always those whose reason is so precariously balanced that a little enthusiasm about anything will upset it. Whitefield's sermons, which have been preserved in book form, are logical, scholarly, and dignified.

Mr. Whitefield organized and endowed a number of charity schools in England. In this country, he was the benefactor of many educational and civic projects. He was instrumental in securing the patronage of Lord Dartmouth for Dartmouth College and he personally gave fifty thousand dollars to the same institution. The good that he did is incalculable, the harm comparatively negligible.

In 1843, half of Boston flipped its unstable lid in a mass madness caused by the dire predictions of a mathematical-minded minister, one William Miller. Feeling that his style was cramped by the small New Hampshire community where he lived, Mr. Miller came to Boston to find a larger and more sympathetic audience. He found them, he preached to them, and they all went quietly mad together.

The Rev. Mr. Miller drew most of his texts from the Book of Revelation; and, by research and abstruse calculations, he deduced that the end of the world was imminent—very imminent indeed. Having this fine flair for mathematics, he was able to take certain data from the Book of Revelation and, after considerable manipulation of figures, to come up with the exact date for the final destruction of the earth and "all they that dwelt therein." The date of the holocaust was to be April 23, 1843.

Miller preached at the Chardon Street Chapel while a disciple of his, Elder Knapp, established himself in a church across the way. Miller was calm, mathematical, and coldly convincing. Without any emotionalism he presented his "facts" and stated his conclusions. Elder Knapp, a magnetic, dynamic, and forceful orator, described in fervid detail the celestial joys awaiting those who would repent and follow Pastor Miller. He also drew a colorful and frightening picture of the agonies in store for those who would not. The two men made a great team, and thousands of converts joined their ranks.

A huge tabernacle was built and decorated with representations of the monsters described in Revelation, grotesque and terrible. The excitement was intense! The day—the hour—was approaching! The Millerites, as they called themselves, closed their shops, gave away their possessions, and gathered in the tabernacle, where, amid scenes of almost insane frenzy, they awaited the end.

April twenty-third, the fatal day, came—and went. Miller recast his figures and arrived at a new date, October 18, 1847; but the spell was broken and most of his followers deserted. All that was left to them was the struggle to pick up the pieces of their ruined businesses and scattered fortunes. Only a very few remained faithful.

In 1845 the wooden tabernacle was removed and replaced by a magnificent structure of Quincy granite. Its Gothic design with three huge ecclesiastical windows was by the justly famous architect Isaiah Rogers, who also designed the Astor House in New York and the Maxwell House in Nashville.

The Old Howard

Since this noble structure was on Howard Street it was named the Howard Athenaeum. It rapidly gained fame as the most noteworthy of Boston theaters. Diamonds sparkled and rare silks and satins glowed in its gilded balconies, where the elite of the city occupied its cushioned seats, never before found in a Boston theater.

The audiences applauded the efforts of such actors as Joseph Jefferson, Charlotte Cushman, and Edwin Forrest. The first time that grand opera was sung in Italian in the United States was at this theater. Few of the socialites who attended this musical treat understood Italian, but all listened attentively and appeared delighted. Boston was laying the foundation of its reputation for culture and erudition.

Around 1870, the Athenaeum, which was beginning to be called the Old Howard, met the changing taste of the time and introduced vaudeville. The top talent of the four-a-day entertainers enchanted new, and somewhat different, audiences. Still remembered are the raucous Maggie Cline, the broadly farcical Weber and Fields, and the Roxbury Strong Boy, John L. Sullivan, whose bulging muscles were tremendously effective when he took the lead in that mellowest of old-time melodramas, *Honest Hearts and Willing Hands.*

Vaudeville degenerated into what was politely called burlesque. From then on, scantily clad girls of the bump-and-grind circuit cavorted, to the enjoyment of those who found that type of entertainment stimulating.

The footlights of the Old Howard—first candles, then kerosene lamps, and later electric lights—illuminated the best that came to Boston: the best of the old-time legitimate actors, the best of vaudeville, and, yes, the best of the strip-tease and exotic dancers.

The lights are now extinguished, never to blaze again, the dance has ended, the play is played, the curtain has fallen. The Old Howard has been razed.

IX. Crime and Punishment

THREE-LETTER MEN

Probably Calvin Coolidge never said it, but the story is usually attributed to him. When he returned from church one Sunday his wife asked what the sermon had been about. With characteristic brevity the President said, "Sin." Pressed for further details as to what the minister had said about sin, Cal replied, "He was against it."

So are we all. Every decent person is against sin. The point where we differ is in our definition of what sin may be. The Puritan idea was, apparently, that anything that was any fun to do must be sinful. They forbade cockfighting, not because it gave pain to the fowl, but because it gave pleasure to the spectators. Dancing, card playing, singing, except for a few lugubrious hymns, "taking tobacco," and "making love without the consent of friends" were all considered crimes in the seventeenth century.

A list of the offenses for which men and women were punished during the first twenty years of the colony included the following crimes:

Eavesdropping
Meddling
Neglecting work
Scolding
Naughty speeches
Pulling hair
Pushing his wife
Riding behind two fellows (This was a girl named Nancy)
Selling dear
Sleeping in meeting
Repeating a scandalous lie

Selling strong water by small measure
Spying into the chamber of his master and mistress and
    reporting what he saw
Dissenting from the rest of the jury

On Sunday, of course, laws were especially strict. It was forbidden to ride, run, or even walk on the public streets, except "reverently to goe to meeting." One unfortunate was fined for riding to fetch a midwife, whose immediate services were greatly needed.

Punishments were varied and severe. Jail was easily attained. One poor fellow, Wilbur Johnson, was sent to jail for life for stealing squirrels on the Common. Hangings were frequent and often for comparatively minor offenses—robbery, counterfeiting, and impiety—as well as for the more serious crimes of murder, rape, bestiality, adultery, and the sin of being a Quaker or a witch.

The condemned was always forced to attend church before his execution and to listen to an hour-long sermon in which his sins and his probable punishment in the hereafter were vividly portrayed by an expert in that field.

Sometimes other mental tortures were added. In 1673 Benjamin Goad was found guilty of bestiality. Not only was he sentenced to be hanged, but it was decreed that his partner in the crime "shall, before your execution and in your sight, be knockt on ye head."

To make fun of the honorable Court was not considered funny by the honorable Court. We find that Captain Stone "is sentenced to pay one hundred pounds and prohibited coming within the patent without the Governor's leave, upon pain of death, for calling Mr. Ludlow [a justice] a 'just ass.' "

To protest the findings of the Court was equally dangerous. In 1675 Maurice Brett was tried for adultery. He was found "Not guilty, but guilty of very filthy carriage." For this he was "to stand on the Gallows with a Roape about his necke to stand half a hower and thense tied to the Carts taile and whipt severely with thirty-nine stripes and be banished." To Mr. Brett this seemed over severe and he made the mistake of saying so.

A postscript was immediately added to his sentence. "For his Contemptuous Carriage Confronting the sentence of this Court he shall stand in the pillory on ye morrow at one of ye clock his ears nayld to ye pillory and after an howrs standing there, they to be cut off and he to pay twenty shillings for his swearing or to be whipt with ten stripes." In the seventeenth century it was unwise to talk when you should be listening.

For minor offenses there were the stocks, the pillory, cropping of ears, slitting the nose, and branding on the cheek or the hand with a red-hot iron. The brand, a cleft stick on the tongue, and the ducking stool seem to have been reserved chiefly for female scolds, although these were also used to punish brewers of bad beer and bakers of bad bread.

Whipping at the post or at the cart's tail was much used and provided a "source of innocent merriment" for the populace. Men and women were stripped to the waist and publicly whipped for lying, swearing, perjury, drunkenness, selling rum to the Indians, sleeping in church, and for slander. One, Thomas Dexter, was given twenty lashes for "prophane saying, dam ye come."

A sailor, just home from a voyage, was publicly whipped for publicly kissing his wife on the Sabbath day. Apparently he learned his lesson too well for about a year later he was again before the court, this time for "neglecting his wife and living apart from her." You just couldn't win.

A milder form of branding was to force an offender to wear a large letter sewn in a prominent place on his clothing—A for adultery, B for blasphemy, R for rogue, D for drunkenness, and so on. It is not recorded that there were any three-letter men in the colony, but it seems probable that some gained that distinction.

Public penance was another popular form of punishment—popular, that is, with the spectators, not the culprit. The guilty person, dressed in white, was obliged to sit or stand on a stool in the "middle alley" of the meeting house with a placard hung about his (or more frequently her) neck stating the nature of the offense. In 1672 a young lady "having binn above fower years in England absent from her husband and bringing with her a child of About two years old" was adjudged to be guilty of something—indiscretion at least—and the court ruled that "shee stand on a stoole in ye meeting house with a paper on her breast with ye inscription, 'Thus I stand for my adulterous and whorish carriage.' "

QUAKERS AND RANTERS

It was bad enough to be a Puritan in Boston Town, but it was infinitely worse to be anything else. In spite of their pious talk of religious freedom, the first settlers were just as narrow and intolerant as were the Lord Bishops who had forced them to leave England.

The Quakers in particular were given a rough reception. The first to arrive, Mary Fisher and Ann Austin, were promptly jailed and their books were burned by the official hangman. They remained, moaning low in the jail house, until their ship, the *Swallow*, was ready for its flight back to Barbados whence they had come. They were then hustled on board and warned that the result of a return would be particularly dire.

Hardly had the *Swallow* left its nest when another vessel arrived with four men and four women of the same detested faith. They were accorded the same treatment.

Feeling that the community was too soft toward these accursed nonconformists, the General Court held a hasty meeting and passed some rather severe laws, providing for fines, imprisonment, whipping, and banishment for all "Quakers, ranters and other blasphemous heretics." To all this was added the death penalty for any who should return after banishment.

It is only fair to record that these laws were passed by the narrow majority of one vote; and that a deputy who was absent on account of illness said that, had he known what was afoot, he would have crawled to the meeting on his hands and knees in order to have prevented it.

The year after these laws were passed, three Quakers each had an ear cut off, several were banished, and, in 1660, four of the sect were publicly hanged on the Common.

In spite of this severity, the Quakers had the temerity to hold a meeting in Boston in 1664. The twelve men and three women who attended suffered the then popular punishment of being "whipped through three towns," which meant that the victims would receive a number of lashes on the bare back in Boston and would then be carted to two nearby towns, where the whipping would be repeated. This not only brought some amusement into the drab lives of the suburbanites but, by giving the wounds an opportunity to partially heal, greatly increased the suffering of the victims.

News of the persecutions of the Quakers finally reached the royal ears of the King himself. Charles II was really horrified at the tales which were told to him and he issued a stern mandate forbidding the colonists to hang, imprison, or torture anyone for the offense of being a Quaker. The royal mandate was immediately sent to Governor Endicott by a trusted messenger empowered with all the authority of a King's courier and agent.

The story of the delivery of the King's order would be known in modern terminology as "Operation Hat." The interview between the Governor and the courier belongs in comic opera. The King, with a touch of royal humor, perhaps, chose as his messenger Samuel Shattuck, a Quaker who had previously been banished with the promise of being hanged if he returned.

Shattuck arrived safely in Boston and demanded an audience with the chief executive. Governor Endicott, to show his contempt, put on his hat to receive the Quaker. Shattuck entered, also wearing his hat. He was ordered to uncover in the gubernatorial presence, which he did. The Quaker then produced the royal letter and, as the King's representative, put on his hat and handed the missive to the Governor, who was now obliged to remove his own hat in the presence of the royal seal. Having fulfilled his duty, Shattuck ceased to be the King's envoy, so he was again ordered to remove his hat, while Endicott, having read and laid aside the royal edict, pompously resumed his own.

Relieved from immediate fear of punishment, the Quakers began to feel their oats. Purchasing land on Brattle Street they erected the first brick church to be built in Boston, and here they met and worshiped for sixteen years. In 1710 they removed to a new location near Congress Street.

In the colorful days just before the Revolution the British barracks were located on Brattle Street on the site of this first Quaker church. Here the brawl started which culminated in the so-called massacre of the so-called martyrs on State Street.

It was at the British headquarters, located where the church had been, that General Gage sat out the siege of Boston. Food was scarce, but Gage and his officers had beef at least once. They dined on the twenty-year-old town bull, which had been stolen and sold to them by a dissolute camp follower. She was well and publicly whipped, but whether for the theft or because of the toughness of the meat the record saith not.

Many years after the Revolution, this same spot became famous for beef of a very different quality, for here was located the justly famous Quincy House. The succulent steaks and fabulous lobster salads of the Quincy House are only a memory, for the hotel has been razed and the site is now part of Government Center.

When the Quakers left Brattle Street they built a smaller

Mary Dyer, Quaker: "Witness for Religious Freedom, Hanged on Boston Common 1660"

church near Congress Street and established a cemetery there. The site was sold in 1827, the bodies in the graveyard being removed to Lynn. The paths through the cemetery became, and still are, Quaker Lane.

Take a walk down Congress Street toward Dock Square and you will see, on your left, a sign reading "Quaker Lane." Continuing along Congress Street you may be a bit confused to find that the very next street you pass is also Quaker Lane. Turning left onto State Street you encounter Quaker Lane yet once more. Turning left again you are on Devonshire, and the first highway that you pass is—you guessed it—Quaker Lane again.

How come?

Let's look in the directory. That factual and unimaginative volume locates Quaker Lane as "From 11 Congress to 50 Devonshire *and* from 31 State to 25 Congress." Investigating the street itself we find that it crosses itself at right angles, runs parallel to itself for a bit, then emerges into Congress Street— twice; and that the whole street, with all of its ramifications, is hardly more than three hundred yards long. Well, that's the way the paths were in the cemetery.

A modern psychologist could doubtless explain the fact that, under the severest persecution, the sect of Quakers throve and grew in numbers, but when the severity was relaxed, the members became less active so that by 1848 hardly a Quaker was left in Boston.

It would, in fact, take a psychiatrist to explain the actions of these people. They came to Boston for no apparent reason save to be nuisances and firebrands. Their conduct was unseemly and indecent past all belief. Women entirely nude and with their faces blackened invaded the churches, claiming that this behavior had some deep symbolic meaning. Two of the women broke bottles over the head of the Rev. Mr. Norton while he was conducting a service. This, they explained, was a sign of the emptiness of his doctrines.

For the most part, these early Quakers were people of low breeding and little education. One of the magistrates in rebuking them said, "If, as you claim, you speak with the voice of God, you ought, at least, to use good grammar, for even Balaam's ass did that."

Although, in Boston, the Quakers suffered imprisonment, whipping, ear cropping, and hanging, they didn't have to. Every sentence pronounced against them carried with it the offer of immunity if they would only go away and stay away. In nearby Rhode Island they would have been, if not welcome, at least tolerated and sheltered. But they would not go.

Most difficult of all to understand is the fact that from this beginning has grown the Society of Friends—the Quakers—for the past two centuries a fellowship of men and women eminent for the qualities of culture, high character, sincerity, and moderation.

AROINT THEE, WITCH

Altogether too much importance has been given to the witchcraft delusion in New England. Reading the accounts in some books of history one might be led to believe that the good people of Salem and Boston invented witches. Nothing could be further from the truth.

During the sixteenth and seventeenth centuries, all of Europe had a firm and frightening belief in the vicious power of the Devil acting through his chosen agents—witches. During these two centuries, 100,000 "witches" were put to death in Germany, 75,000 in France, 30,000 in Great Britain, and a proportional number in other European countries.

In America the epidemic of superstition and panic lasted for forty years only, and the total number of alleged witches put to death in the whole of New England was thirty-two, of whom only four were in Boston. In 1648 Boston hanged one witch—its first—while in England nearly three hundred were executed the same year.

The Puritans believed in witches, of course. Why should they not? The Bible, their guide in all things, repeatedly warned them of the dangers of witchcraft and laid down the stern mandate, "Thou shalt not suffer a witch to live." They brought with them books of English law which outlined the legal methods of discovering and punishing witches and they had studied the methods of Matthew Hopkins, the professional Witch Finder General of England.

The Hopkins method of discovering a witch was by "searching" and "watching." It had the approval of the courts, and the findings were accepted as evidence. It was an outrageous and indecent procedure.

The "Hopkins Method" was based on the belief that every witch had a familiar spirit, or personal imp, who was obliged to obey the commands of the sorcerer and who acted as a sort of liaison officer between the witch and the Commander in Chief— the Devil. It was a necessary function of the witch, whether male or female, to furnish nourishment for the imp from his or her own body. "Also," Hopkins claimed, "the Devil leaveth other marks upon their body, sometimes like a blue or red spot, like a flea-biting, and they be often in their secretest parts, and therefore require diligent and careful search." Examining the accused for these witch signs was the legally approved "searching."

The "watching" meant keeping the suspect under careful observation every moment for twenty-four hours. During that time the imp must visit his patron for sustenance and would be seen by the watchers. Since the imp might assume the form of a child, a mouse, a cat, or even an insect, a visitation was fairly probable.

Margaret Jones was a neighborly soul and something of an amateur physician. She explored the woods and fields for medicinal herbs and roots with which she treated ailing friends. Unfortunately, her ministrations were remarkably successful and Margaret acquired a considerable reputation, not as a doctor, but as a witch. When a neighbor's cow died, Margaret was accused of putting a spell on the unfortunate animal. "Searched," "watched," sentenced, and hanged, she became Boston's first victim. This was in 1648.

Those of us who are jealous of Boston's reputation feel that it is unfair to list Mary Parsons as one of the four persons executed in the town for witchcraft. Although tried and convicted in Boston, her home was in Springfield and it seems probable that her execution took place there. There is no proof either way. In any case, it was never established that Mary was a witch. She was arraigned on two charges: first, of having bewitched the two daughters of a Springfield minister and, second, of having murdered her own child. She pleaded innocent to the first and guilty to the second. She was executed for murder, not for witchcraft.

Ann Hibbins, the third victim of the delusion, was hanged in 1656. Her story is told in a previous chapter. She was suddenly reduced from a wealthy and socially prominent wife to a poverty-stricken and neglected widow; her naturally turbulent and quarrelsome nature became worse, and the neighbors relieved themselves of a nuisance by way of the gallows.

John Goodwin, a brickmason, lived on the south side of Blott's Lane (Winter Street) near the Common. John was a virtuous and highly respected man, but he had four terrible little monsters for children. The eldest, a girl of thirteen, accused a laundress of stealing the family linen. The Widow Glover, mother of the laundress, gave the child a tongue-lashing for defaming the character of her daughter. Being Irish and gifted in conversation, she did a thorough job of vituperation which left Miss Goodwin crushed, humiliated, and thirsting for revenge.

The four children got together and "put on an act" which for histrionic ability and sheer vindictiveness was unparalleled. They claimed to have been bewitched by Mrs. Glover. They had fits. They raved and screamed, and with contorted limbs they would fall, writhing and shrieking, to the floor. The mere sight or any mention of Mrs. Glover would throw them into convulsions.

It is conceivable that the children were sincere. A thirteen-year-old girl who has been brought up in an atmosphere of repression and who has been denied most normal amusement may have strange, although very real, delusions. The actions of the Goodwin children show many of the classic symptoms of genuine hysteria.

In any case the girls' dramatics were good enough to convince the judges; and Mrs. Glover was hanged on Boston Common at high noon on November 16, 1688.

Cotton Mather became extremely interested in the Glover case; but his sincere, although misguided, efforts to suppress witchcraft merely added fuel to an already hot fire. The entire community was on the prowl, and witches were being pursued everywhere. No one was safe. There were no more executions, but many were jailed and otherwise tortured.

For several years witch hunting was a major sport. An effective form of retaliation against an enemy or a rival was an accusation of witchcraft. The surest way to secure yourself from being indicted for this crime was to accuse someone else, so this was frequently done. It was especially dangerous to show any sympathy for one who was on trial.

John Alden, Jr., was one of the results of a previous Alden's willingness to "speak for yourself, John." Junior was a man sixty years old, with an unblemished reputation; a deacon in the church, a ship captain, and active in civic affairs. One would think that such a man would be safe from scandal and calumny, but in 1692 when one of the poor, deluded creatures who posed as victims of witchcraft pointed—merely pointed—at John Alden, he was promptly seized by the marshal of Salem. His sword was taken from him and he was thrown into jail to await the usual mockery of a trial.

But John had a friend, a tried and trusted old companion and shipmate, a Mr. Gedney, who, he felt sure, would speak in his behalf and save him from being convicted. This character witness was immediately called. Gedney testified that he had known Alden for twenty years and had always believed him to be an honest man, *but now he had cause to alter his opinion.* Such is the force of superstition.

Alden offered bail, but the authorities refused to accept it. He was carried to jail in Boston, where he remained for fifteen long weeks. Finally, when opportunity offered, he escaped. The details of this jail break are not known, but it is believed that he fled to Duxbury, where relatives secreted and cared for him.

By April, 1693, the people of Boston were recovering from their witchcraft madness, considerably aided by the irascible Governor Phips, who took a firm stand against the foolishness when his own wife was accused. John Alden felt it was safe to return to Boston and stand trial. This he did and, as no one appeared against him, he was discharged.

DEAR DIARY

Judge Samuel Sewall, Chief Justice of the Boston colony, presided over most of the witchcraft trials both in Salem and in Boston, becoming noted for the severity of his attitude toward the unfortunate defendants—nineteen of whom he condemned to death. The fact that some of these were later reprieved was no fault of Sam's and he violently protested. Later, the Judge stood up before the congregation of the Old South Church, confessed the error of his judgments, and asked forgiveness of God and the people.

That took courage!

Although he was a man of considerable importance in his time, Judge Sewall's great legacy to us of the twentieth century is his diary, which he kept in great detail for many years. He has little to say on days when great events were going on. He was too busy. But at other times he tells of inconsequential events in great detail, giving us a vivid picture of life in the colony from 1674 to 1729.

The Judge had a delightful style and could turn a neat phrase. His notations "A pretty deal of Thunder this day" and "Neighbor Fifield brought me the news, who had it from the Cryer of Fish" are fresh and charming. "Judge Bulkly buried because could not be kept" is a masterpiece of convincing brevity.

On February 16, 1677, the Judge prepared for fatherhood. He reports that he "Brewed my wife's groaning Beer." Two months later he notes the birth of a son and writes, "I named him John and Mr. Thatcher baptized him into the name of the Father, Son and H. Ghost."

Like all diarists, Sewall has considerable to say about the weather although the item "Much New England Weather" seems to sum it all up. We have all seen just such a day. One January day it was "so cold that the Sacramental Bread is frozen pretty hard and rattles sadly when broken into the plates." Again, "At six a'clock my ink freezes so that I can hardly write by a good fire in my Wive's Chamber."

But at last spring came and he records, "I saw six Swallows together flying and chirping very rapturously." Spring also had its effect on the sober Judge for he "Visited Madame Horseman, formerly Dulcibella Dunch" and "I spent a pretty deal of time in the burying place to see the Graver of Tombstones; Push caterpillars off the Apletrees, goe to meeting of Mistress Averyes." But the day was not all play and dalliance, for "I cut down the Elm that annoy'd the Coach House."

Nathaniel Emmons, Samuel Sewall

Samuel took a grim pleasure in death and funerals and he records the details in sprightly fashion. Regarding the funeral of Governor Dudley he writes, "Were very many People spectators out of windows, on Fences and Trees, like pigeons." On the death of John Ive, "Had gloves sent me but the knowledge of his wicked life made me sick of going—and so I staid at home, and by that means lost a ring." "Mr. Turner dies suddenly at Scituat. He has the Character of a Drunkard and Striker of his Wife."

Of tragedy in his own family circle the Judge speaks just as briefly, "My Grandson John Sewall dies aged 16 mo. and 10 days. Matthew brings him in his coffin to my home and is set in best Room; a goodly corpse."

Sermons were duly recorded in condensed form: "Mr. Willard speaks to the 7th commandment, condems naked Breasts and seems to be against the marriage of first cousins." And on another Sunday, "Mr. Joseph Eliot preached the lecture, parallels the diseases of New England with Corinth; among others mentioning itching ears, harkening after false Teachers and consequently sucking in false Principles, and dispising, sitting loose from the true Teachers."

Sewall did not neglect his duty as justice, and we find this report of his activity: "With seven constables dissipated the players at Nine Pins at Mount Whoredom." But justice is tempered with a sweet reasonableness, for "Mr. Larkin sought after Mr. Mather this week to Arrest him, Mr. Mather on Tuesday was taking Physic and so was free, and since hath purposely avoided him."

Sewall married Hanna, the only daughter of Captain Hull, the wealthy mintmaster. Her dowry was said to be her weight in pine tree shillings—and she was a buxom lass. The Judge, his wife, and the shillings lived happily together for forty years, having a nicely balanced family of seven sons and seven daughters.

Mrs. Sewall died in October, 1717, and the Judge, then sixty-six, began—almost immediately—to look about him. He records visiting Widow Ruggles, Widow Emery, Widow Gill, and Widow Winthrop. To the last he sent several gifts, including a book with the provocative title "Smoking Flax Inflamed." Evidently the Judge was beginning to smolder also.

The Widow Winthrop was definitely leading the field until, on March 22, the Judge attended the funeral of his friend Mr. Denison of Roxbury. He went home from the services with the newly made widow and a few days later visited her again, bearing gifts—"Dr. Mather's Sermons, neatly bound" and "a pound of raisins with proportionate Almonds."

Other gifts and other visits followed until, in November, Sewall made a formal proposal of marriage. Mrs. Denison seemed willing until the ardent suitor insisted that she sign a financial agreement, very much in his favor. This she refused to do. At this point Samuel confided to his diary, "My bowells yearn toward Mrs. Denison but I think God directs me to disist." Evidently the Judge's head ruled his—bowells.

Apparently Widow Tilley was the next on the list. Here persistence paid off and Sewall's suit was successful. They were married on October 25, just two years and five days after the death of his first wife. The new bride was taken seriously ill on the very day of the wedding and, after a sad honeymoon, died on May 20.

Again Mr. Sewall consulted his rapidly diminishing list of eligible widows and selected Mrs. Winthrop for another try—he was on the second time around. The widow was coy, but determined. She would accept, provided he would agree to keep a coach and to wear a wig. Both requests were indignantly refused and so ended the fourth wooing.

Time was running out for the Justice so, with no delaying preliminaries, he wrote a formal offer of marriage to a Mrs. Gibbs, a new entry in the field. Mrs. Gibbs accepted but, since she had no dowry, the canny judge made her children sign an agreement that, in case of her death, they would pay him one hundred pounds. They signed but did not have to pay, for, after eight years of happiness with the former Mrs. Gibbs, the good Samuel Sewall departed for a land where we are assured there is neither marriage nor giving in marriage.

x. Unsung Battles

THE ONE-MAN ARMY

The unwary pedestrian who is lured into using Hamilton Place as a possible short cut from Tremont to Washington Street is likely to find himself wandering into a department store or theater without any very clear idea of how he got there, for the street ends unexpectedly in the entrances to Gilchrist's and the Orpheum.

Hamilton Place was the site of Boston's first large manufacturing project and it was also the locale of a battle in which a British regiment was put to rout by an army of one lone man.

A long time ago, about 1718, a group of emigrants arrived from Londonderry bringing with them the tools and skills necessary for the manufacture of linen. Very welcome they were. The Boston women had gotten along with coarse homespun, but they had never liked it. The thought of linen was to them as is catnip to a kitten. They all wanted to learn the new craft. The men were in favor of the idea, especially as the women would do all the work, so the legislature voted to establish a spinning school. An excise tax was laid on carriages and other luxuries to finance the plan, and the Manufactory House, 140 feet long, was built. A female figure, distaff in hand, ornamented the façade.

Spinning became the rage. The Manufactory House was crowded to the doors, and those who could not be accommodated there took their wheels to the Common and spun, like spiders, in the open air.

Like all fads the "spinning craze" wore itself out in two or three years, and the Manufactory House was rented by the Province to private families.

This brings us to the amazing story of Boston's one-man army. In 1769, when the British troops held possession of the town, a Mr. Elisha Brown was living at the Manufactory House.

Colonel Dalrymple was expected to arrive at any moment with his regiment, the Fourteenth Royal Regulars, and it was Governor Bernard's duty to find a barracks where they could be quartered. The huge Manufactory House seemed to be ideal for the purpose, so the governor sent a formal and official notice to Mr. Brown that he was to vacate the premises forthwith.

Elisha, feeling that his home was his castle, refused to leave. The enraged governor wrote an order of eviction which was served by Sheriff Greenleaf. Brown tore it up. The sheriff and his deputies forced an entrance into the cellar. Brown locked them in. A file of soldiers from the Common rescued them but could not force an entrance into the house.

Meanwhile Colonel Dalrymple and his regiment arrived, encamped on the Common, and kept the Manufactory House surrounded by soldiers day and night. For seventeen days Mr. Brown endured the state of siege and kept possession of his house. He barred the windows and doors and was living comfortably on the family supplies. In those days one did not run to the store every day or so. Each family kept enough staples on hand to last for weeks, so Elisha had no food problem. Finally, completely out-maneuvered, Colonel Dalrymple withdrew and quartered his soldiers in Faneuil Hall.

Elisha Brown died in August, 1785, at the age of sixty-five years and was buried in the Old Granary Burying Ground where on his gravestone we may still read of his valiant deeds.

ELISHA BROWN
of BOSTON
who in Octr 1769, during 17 days
Inspired with
a generous Zeal for the LAWS
bravely and successfully
opposed a whole British Regt
in their violent attempt
to FORCE him from his
legal Habitation
Happy Citizen when call'd singley
to be a Barrier to the Liberties
of a Continent

THE BATTLE OF BROAD STREET

Both sides enjoyed the fight—the great Broad Street Riot of June 11, 1837. Broken heads were common, bloody noses were a dime a dozen, and anyone who left the fray with all his teeth was scorned as a sissy. It was necessary to call out the militia before the fighting ceased.

Throughout the entire affair not a shot was fired, not a knife drawn. It was a "gentlemen's fight" all the way. Fists, sticks, stones, and boots were the only weapons used.

To understand the underlying causes of this fracas one needs to know a little of the history of the place where it occurred—Broad Street. This highway was built in 1708 by that great public benefactor Uriah Cotting, who also built Cornhill and in whose active mind originated the far-reaching Back Bay development plan. At first, Broad Street was given over entirely to commercial interests; but a few years later, when India Street was opened, the business concerns moved there and Broad Street became residential. It was occupied by recent arrivals from England, good, substantial citizens of the upper middle class.

After the War of 1812 a great number of Irish people arrived in Boston. They had found life in the old country unendurable and they dreamed of acquiring riches and happiness on this side of the ocean. These newer comers took over Broad Street, and the former residents moved elsewhere.

It was inevitable that there should be stresses, strains, and jealousies between the first settlers—the English—and the second settlers—the Irish. Matters came suddenly to a head when a company of volunteer firemen on their way to a fire encountered an Irish funeral cortege on its way to the cemetery.

It has been a long-established custom that the grief of a funeral procession is to be respected, and its progress is not to be interrupted. Even today, the automobiles of a funeral may, and do, ignore traffic lights. On the other hand, everything stops to let the firefighters through on their errand of mercy where every second is of importance.

Both the firefighters (English) and the mourners (Irish) felt, with some justice, that they had the right of way. Each group had other grievances which they were in no way averse to settling by the most direct and time honored of all methods. There was not room enough for the two groups to pass each other— Broad Street wasn't *that* broad. One side or the other had to give way. And neither would. Apparently the irresistible force had, at last, met the immovable body. Each man felt that he would rather die than retreat. Some nearly did.

The impasse had dramatic possibilities; and, as the statesmen say, the situation deteriorated rapidly. The firemen plowed into the funeral procession, and the mourners attempted to push through the smoke eaters. The hearse was hauled into a place of safety in a side street. The occupant was the only one who did not take an active part in the subsequent events.

After a few minutes of pushing and shoving, fists began to be used and soon a need for more effective weapons was felt. The shillelagh, traditional aid to the Irish, was wanting; but an efficient substitute was quickly supplied from railings and balustrades of neighboring houses. The block and cement construction of the pavement offered nothing helpful, but the contestants knew the surrounding terrain. A courtyard and an alley in the vicinity furnished an easily removable type of cobblestones. They were round, smooth, and about the size of an orange. They were effective. The firemen found them first, but the opposition soon had a supply of their own. The battle continued with plenty of gore and glory for both sides.

The militia was summoned; by the time it arrived, both armies were willing enough to declare a truce. Those who could still walk escorted the dear departed to his last resting place while the others were carried home to nurse their wounds.

The fire had long since burned itself out, or had been extinguished by someone else. No one now remembers where or what it was. The firemen neither knew nor cared. They said that they had not had so much fun since the Hanover Street Church burned eight years before. On that occasion they had found a great quantity of liquor in the basement of the church. No one came forward to claim it and no one ever knew where it came from—but the firemen knew where it went.

The question of who started the Broad Street affray, who was at fault, and who won has never been satisfactorily settled; but one result of the fracas was the disbanding of the volunteer and semi-official firefighters and the organization of a full-time, paid fire department under the direction of Chief Barnicoat.

BELEAGUERED BRICKS

A street of dignified tranquillity exemplifying the gracious charm of a bygone age. A retired highway of soothing antiquity where the brick houses with their deeply recessed doors, inside shutters, and oriel windows reflect the restrained architectural genius of Asher Benjamin and his contemporaries. This is West Cedar Street. One recalls that here was introduced the felicitous custom of placing a lighted candle in the window to guide the Christ Child on Christmas Eve; and here, also, originated the carol singing which has become a Beacon Hill tradition.

All that West Cedar Street ever asked for itself was to be let alone. It enjoyed its calm exclusiveness, as who would not? But the heavy hand of municipal "progress" was against it. In 1947 the City Fathers decided that this quiet backwater was to be "modernized" and "improved."

It was a sneak attack. The residents awoke one morning to find that workmen armed with picks and shovels had descended upon their street and had begun to dig up its sacrosanct brick sidewalks.

All of Beacon Hill has an overwhelming admiration for brick, a love that passeth all understanding. Bricks are the accepted thing. They belong! In Boston, wood as a building material is illegal and on "The Hill" stone and cement are considered, if not actually immoral, at least highly regrettable.

And the Public Works Department was actually openly and brazenly removing the hallowed bricks with the avowed intention of replacing them with sidewalks of cement.

"Beleaguered Bricks": West Cedar Street

Not West Cedar Street alone, but all of Beacon Hill, arose in protest crying, "Workman, spare that walk! Touch not a single brick!"

The Street Commissioner replied that brick sidewalks were a menace to life and limb—people might trip and fall. Serious injury could result. What was even more unfortunate, they might sue the city. "Whenever a person breaks a leg," he asserted, "his friends drag him to the nearest brick sidewalk and then sue the city."

Considerable heat was generated on both sides, but the laborers were ordered to proceed with the work of destruction. The women of West Cedar Street and some of their neighbors, however, turned out to protect their bricks, which they most effectively did. They sat on them!

The workmen continued languidly to remove the bricks, one at a time, in the unguarded spaces, producing an effect somewhat resembling a small lake crowded with little islands. The imaginative and irreverent pretended to be able to trace, in these islands, the outlines of the matrons who had occupied these spots, but their claim was without foundation. The ladies sat in chairs.

The tide of battle ebbed and flowed for several days, but the Beacon Hillites eventually won—they frequently do. The bricks remained and the happy calm of West Cedar Street was restored.

May it endure forever!

TONG WAR

Those who cherish the false illusion that Chinatown is a place of mystery and danger should visit a little alley, Oxford Place, which crookedly connects Oxford Street with Harrison Avenue. It perfectly fits the popular idea of what a Chinatown street should be: dark, narrow, and apparently sinister, a street of odd angles and reticent doorways. From it runs a nameless passageway about fifty yards long and so narrow that a man of any portliness would have difficulty negotiating it. It leads to a small, dingy, dark, and forbidding door.

To the imaginative, this appears to be the entrance to all the weird, unfamiliar mystery of the East. In sober, prosaic actuality it is the rear entrance to a tenement housing several Chinese families whose domestic life might well serve as a model for others in the city. Nevertheless, the whole impression made by this little alley is one of evil. The very stillness which blankets the street seems not the silence of honest repose but the supernatural calm of the hypnotic. The alley seems to dream of things of the past, evil things, things to be told in whispers.

In truth, this little highway has seen dark deeds and strange intrigues, during the deplorable days when war between the rival tongs was rampant—some fifty years ago.

To comprehend the tong it is necessary to understand the

Chinese conception of "family," which is quite different from ours. To many overseas Chinese "my family" means, not his immediate blood relations, but all who share his same surname. Perhaps "clan" would be a better word to use. The tie is often very strong, and some members of a clan feel bound to help their "cousins" in every way possible. Had we the same system, one can imagine the tremendous power which would be wielded by the Smiths, the Browns, the Sullivans, and others whose names occupy so many pages in the directories.

For years the members of the large clans controlled the business, the politics, and the finances of the Chinatowns in America. Those of smaller clans hardly had a chance to do more than earn a precarious living in some menial and unpleasant job. The answer to this intolerable situation was found, in 1870, by one Mock Wah, who lived in San Francisco. Mock Wah organized some thirty small "families" into a fraternity which he called the Kwong Dock Tong. In effect it was a new and large clan. The members were sworn to aid and protect one another, by peaceful means if possible, by violence if necessary.

A second organization, the Hip Sing Tong, came into being soon afterward. In a short time the idea spread, with a dozen or more tongs being created. In Boston there were only two, the On Leong and the Hip Sing. The On Leong was by far the more powerful.

In 1924 there was a bitter antagonism between the On Leong and the Hip Sing Tongs throughout the country. A sanguinary fight occurred in a theater in New York's Chinatown in which four Hip Sing men were killed and a number wounded. Sing Dock with Yee Toy, the leaders of the Hip Sing in that affair, found it advisable to leave New York. They came to Boston intent on revenge. They brought the tong's Boo How Doy (private army) with them.

At that time most of the amusement places of the On Leong were in Oxford Place, and Sing Dock determined that this should be the scene of the battle. Sing took plenty of time, drilled his men for weeks, studied the habits of his intended victims, and made a careful survey of the ground.

Oxford Place has only two outlets, one on Oxford Street and one on Harrison Avenue. When the prearranged time arrived, one group of Hip Sing gunmen under Sing Dock entered from Harrison Avenue and another group under Yee Toy approached from Oxford Street, thus bottling up the On Leongs.

When the police arrived, they found four dead and a score of wounded Chinese—with no one else in sight. Following the usual police technique they picked up and questioned all unknown Orientals. Strangely enough, they actually captured Sing Dock, who had fled to Somerville. A patrolman saw him on the street and decided to take him to the station for questioning. While they waited for the patrol wagon, a young man dashed out of a nearby store with a woman in hot pursuit shouting, "Stop thief!" Prompted by an age-old instinct, the patrolman took off after the moving target, and Sing Dock, badly wanted for murder by the police of two states, quietly walked away, a little puzzled but grateful to the two-bit thief who had saved him. He escaped to New York but was killed a year later in another tong outbreak. Yee Toy managed to get to Rhode Island and ultimately to China—where there are no tongs.

Before condemning the tong members as "heathen" or "alien murderers," give a thought to some of the bloody incidents which occurred when our labor unions and protective organizations were in the making. The tong "wars" were mild by comparison.

xi. Beasts of Boston

DON'T BLAME THE COWS

If one gave heed to the many commentators on the subject of Boston streets he would be forced to believe that the Colonial cows had no other duties than to wander about the Boston area laying out streets. Every time a stranger finds himself on one of our numerous crooked or curvaceous highways, he heaves an ecstatic sigh and murmurs, "Ah, an ancient cowpath." It is seldom the fact.

Actually the streets that are definitely known to have been cowpaths are reasonably straight and direct. Among these are Winter, West, Park, School, Bromfield, Walnut, and Spruce Streets. Even High Street, which used to be Cow Lane, is quite direct except where it made a complete circle around Fort Hill Square, now obliterated by the Fitzgerald Expressway.

All of the streets of Back Bay, as well as those stemming from Harrison Avenue and Albany Street, were laid out at the time those areas were filled in and raised from the sea. There was no bovine assistance.

The disastrous fire of 1872 completely wiped out a large section of Boston's business district. Every building was destroyed and few streets could even be located. The entire section was rebuilt. Men and horses labored gallantly—but no cows.

If we are not to lay the blame on the hoofs of meandering cattle, where, then, is the reason for the countless bends and curves of our tortuous highways? What accounts for their running, quite literally, in all directions?

Boston was not laid out like a suburban development, first the streets and then the houses. The earliest settlers built their homes, their churches, and their taverns where they wished in the open fields. As they visited back and forth, attended church or patronized the taverns, they made paths which later became roadways and still later crystallized into streets. Thus where we find a number of different streets converging on one spot, we may reasonably deduce that at that place was once a church, or more probably a tavern—the Puritans being not only godly but also thirsty.

Six streets meet at Dewey Square, where the Bull Tavern once stood. It was at a session at the Bull that a group of men decided to build a church at Church Green, which is, itself, a junction of four streets. Six streets lead into Dock Square, where the principal market and also the Town House were located. Scollay Square, where there had always been a tavern or two, was the focal point of seven streets.

The popularity of churches and taverns explains the fact that hardly any of Boston's streets are parallel, but what about the numerous curves and angles? Cows? Again, probably not.

As the early inhabitants made their paths from place to place they would go around any natural obstructions—a hill, a marsh, a pond, or even a big tree or rock. The obstructions have long since been removed; but some streets still avoid them.

We must also remember that not a house could be built, not a steeple raised, or a schoolhouse constructed without the accompaniment of gallons and hogsheads of rum. It is possible that the early path makers were even more devious than the cows.

In the early days, several of the important streets ran along the shore and naturally followed the indentations and projections of the coast line. Owing to the tremendous amount of land which Boston has reclaimed from the sea, many of these streets are now as much as half a mile inland. But they still follow the long-vanished shore line.

As early surveyors, cows were not too active; nonetheless, they keep popping up in the oddest ways in the story of Boston's development. The Puritans found no cows here when they arrived. The Indians were not interested in domestic animals. As one of the early historians expressed it: "Tame cattle they have none, excepting lice." The colonists, knowing this, brought a number of cows with them; and when they bought Blackstone's land for a cow pasture, the dispossessed hermit purchased cows from them with the money he received. These he took as companions on his search for a sanctuary in the hinterlands. When he returned, many years later, he triumphantly entered the town riding that great bull which he had broken to harness.

The Common was used as a training ground for the militia as well as a cow pasture, and sometimes the two functions became a little mixed. In 1661 General Atherton, on his way home after reviewing his troops, ran his horse into a cow and was killed. The record of the fatality says, "The cow also suffered." It was conceded that the General died in the service of his country. When the British were encamped on the Common, a frightened cow ran into a stand of bayonets with such force that several of the sword-like weapons penetrated her thick hide. Terrified, she hurried as fast as she could for home, an animated pincushion, thus making her personal contribution to the slender military equipment of the patriots.

Cows have even influenced Boston architecture. As noted in a previous chapter, there are houses whose height is limited and other houses which must be set well back from the street so that cows on the Common might be kept in view. The cows have left, but many of the laws governing the size and position of the houses are still on the books.

THE SACRED COD

It would be ridiculous to say that without the codfish there would be no Boston. We may, however, with perfect truth assert that without this succulent and prolific fish Boston would be a different place from what it is, both in its past history and in its present condition.

The Puritans could not have survived without the cod. It furnished them with food when they had little else. Salted or dried it became their first export and, for many years, their only source of outside revenue. Shiploads of salt fish were traded up and down the coast for tobacco, grain, clothing, and other necessities as well as for a few luxuries.

It was the cod that started the shipyards, which first built small craft for the fishermen, then larger ships for the delivery of the cargo along the coast, and finally much larger vessels for the trade with the West Indies and England.

In time there developed the highly profitable "three-cornered trade." A Boston ship would carry salt fish to the West Indies, where the cargo would be sold and the vessel loaded with sugar, molasses, tobacco, or other island products. These would be carried to England, France, Spain, or any other country where such products would command a high price. In the European port the shipmaster would once again sell his cargo and reload with goods that were in high demand at home.

Later, when Boston had developed its great distilleries, this schedule was reversed. Rum would be carried to Africa and there exchanged for ivory, gold dust, mahogany, and slaves. The next stop would be the West Indies, where the slaves would be exchanged for molasses, the basic ingredient of rum, and then the ships would return to Boston. Great fortunes were made in this manner; and, with true Boston thrift, some of them remain as trust funds today.

By the middle of the eighteenth century many a Bostonian was growing rich. His wealth was reflected in the gorgeousness of his attire, the splendor of his house, and the magnificence of his table. It was all because of trade, and the trade had a firm and solid base in the lowly cod. The British recognized this, and in envy and derision coined the phrase "codfish aristocracy."

John Rowe, Grand Master of Saint John's Lodge of Masons and member of the House of Representatives, gave thought to the debt of gratitude that the town owed to the noble fish. Ever a man of action, he did something about it. On March 17, 1748, Rowe made a motion before the legislators that "leave might be given to hang up a representation of a Cod Fish in the room where the House sits, as a memorial of the importance of the Cod Fishery to the welfare of the nation." His suggestion met with

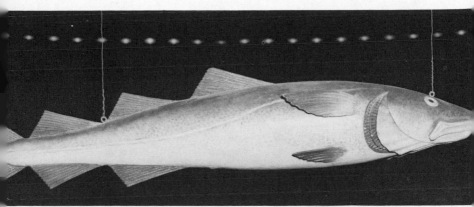

Sacred Cod: State House

hearty approval, and a large wooden cod was made and installed. The fish was carved from a single block of wood by John Welch, an active patriot and captain in the Ancient and Honorable Artillery Company. In 1895 the carved figure, or its successor, was taken down, reverently wrapped in an American flag, and transferred to the new State House. Here it has patiently and successfully withstood the waves of oratory and storms of debate to which it has been exposed.

John Rowe, who may be called "the father of the Codfish" (perhaps his name should be spelled "Roe"), deserves more than a passing mention. Although he was part owner of one of the ships which brought the unwelcome cargo of tea to Boston in 1773, he was sufficiently patriotic to sacrifice private gain for public good. At the mass meeting in the Old South Church which protested the landing of the British-taxed tea, it was Rowe who propounded the question, "Who knows how tea will mingle with salt water?" The colonists applauded the suggestion wildly —it was definitely their cup of tea.

Mr. Rowe lived on Pond Street in a house that later became the home of Judge Prescott, father of the noted historian William H. Prescott. Near the house was a small pond which gave the street its name and which was the only watering place for the cattle and horses of the neighborhood. John was rightly looked upon as a citizen worthy of honor; so in 1803, the private way, Pond Street, was given to the town as a public highway with the proviso that it should be called Rowe Street forever. In this case "forever" was not quite twenty years for, in 1821, the name of the street was changed to Bedford at the suggestion of Jeremiah Fitch, who had a summer home in Bedford, Massachusetts.

John owned a wharf down on the water front which, like the street, was named for him. It is still Rowe's Wharf and will probably continue to be so called for a much longer "forever" than was granted to the street.

CATS OF THE CITY

The city cat is an alert and agile animal. He has to be. Traffic being what it is, he must be deadly quick or he is quickly dead. Even the fat, lazy, and smiling beasts of the butcher shops can move with amazing speed when occasion demands. These favored felines of the Market District, while not in the highest social brackets, are unquestionably the gourmets of the cat tribe. Highly discriminating in matters dietetic, the cat of the market will sit for hours in a warm corner of a store, purring disarmingly. Spread out before him are the gastronomic treasures of the earth, but he seems not to see them. Apparently he sleeps; but beneath the drooping lids is an alert and active eye, casing the joint for that perfect tidbit, that ultimate delicacy which will furnish the supreme ecstasy known only to the connoisseur. Kitty arises languidly, stretches and yawns with elaborate leisure, and walks aimlessly toward the door. As he passes the selected morsel, there is a lightning flash of predatory paw, a sudden burst of speed, and cat and cutlet have disappeared together.

In Boston's South End, particularly in the Skid Row section, may be found an entirely different breed of cat. Technically

"The Socially Elite of Boston Catdom"

these creatures would be listed as "domestic short hairs," but it is a misnomer. Short haired they are, but domestic they most emphatically are not. Perhaps the nearest thing to a wild animal to be found in the city, the Skid Row cat, may be seen only at dusk or in the very early morning—a shadow among shadows, a derelict among derelicts. He slinks furtively along, close to the sides of buildings, never in the open. His life is precarious and he dies a sudden and mysterious death. One never sees an old cat in Skid Row.

In nearby Chinatown are the contented cats, happy, well fed, and much petted. Always appreciative of grace and beauty, the Chinese loves his pet, especially if it is a "money cat," one whose fur is a tapestry of five blending colors. Such a cat brings good luck and riches to its fortunate owner.

The socially elite of Boston catdom are the Beacon Hill cats. Faultlessly groomed, impeccably mannered, and exuding an aura of culture, they doze fatly on front steps or in drawingroom windows. Occasionally they pay formal visits to the neighbors or take sedate walks along the street, tiptoeing mincingly from brick to brick of the ancient sidewalks. These are the frontdoor or refined cats.

Here, also, are the back-door or alley cats. They, like the animals of Skid Row, are seen only at night as they roam the dark and twisting alleys that abound in this region. They dine disgustingly on scraps retrieved from garbage pails; they unite in hideous choruses; and the yowls and shrieks which accompany their frequent battles and their unspeakable amours make the night a torture for the musically sensitive.

The contrast between the front-door patricians and the back-door hoodlums is extreme, but the startling paradox is that —they are the same cats.

The codfish watches over the legislators in the State House, but it is not as widely known that a cat once presided over the meetings of the directors of the United States Bank. This bank, erected in 1824 by Solomon Willard, was of Classical design with massive granite columns. As so often happens to works of art in every city, the pediment of the bank soon became a favorite roosting place for pigeons. The president of the bank, Gardiner Greene, was quoted as saying that he sometimes liked to show his marksmanship by shooting pigeons but he did not intend to permit the sport to be reversed. Being a man of ideas, he had a huge cat carved out of wood and placed on the pediment. For a few days the pigeons were frightened away, but they soon returned and perched even on the wooden figure itself. The cat was removed and placed in the directors' room, where for many years it presided over the activities of the board.

ALAS, POOR DOBBIN

Visit any of the big town garages and you will find a flock of English sparrows in residence. These ubiquitous and adaptable birds make a comfortable living by picking insects from radiators of cars recently in from the suburbs. The insects are not only garden fresh but appetizingly grilled as well. The sparrow has achieved a triumph of adjustment to the changing conditions in a changing world!

The advent of the automobile and the virtual disappearance of the horse from the Boston scene have brought about profound changes other than in the gustatory habits of the sparrow.

During the nineteenth century the horse was the dominant figure in the Boston picture. Edward Savage, police chief in 1870, reported that 3608 teams and 1478 horsecars passed the corner of Boylston and Tremont Streets in a single day. Every family with any claim to wealth or social position maintained its own stable with attendant driver and groom.

Today, not many traces of the horse era remain in Boston, but there are a few. Hitching posts accent some Beacon Hill doorways, and on the brick walls of a few ancient buildings in the North End and on "The Hill" one may still discern almost obliterated signs reading "Boarding and Baiting Stable." This double-barreled hospitality was a feature of all taverns a hundred years ago.

Most of the "solid" families of Beacon Hill maintained their own stables, many with pleasant living quarters for the coachman in a second story. So numerous were the stables on the lower part of Chestnut Street that this section of the thoroughfare was, in the 1800s known as Horse-chestnut Street. Here we find most interesting tributes to the ingenuity and artistry of the remodeler—stable doors changed into imposing entrances, hay doors transformed into studio windows, and the iron brackets originally supporting the hay hoists now displaying swinging signs showing the house number.

The coachmen whose horses occupied these stables lived in comfortable homes on nearby Acorn Street. Their Old World charm, as well as their relative privacy, makes these houses most desirable residences. Similarly delightful houses which were built for the highly privileged class of coachmen are to be found in Rollins Place, Cedar Lane Way, Pinckney Street, and a few other of the hidden highways of "The Hill." Here bull's-eye glass, diamond-paned windows, hand-wrought iron railings, knockers, and door handles are used with good effect.

A Beacon Hill Dobbin

Converted Stables: Beaver Place

Most imposing of all the memorials to the departed Dobbin is the huge granite drinking fountain in Post Office Square. This was built by the contributions of Boston school children as a memorial to Dr. George T. Angell, founder of the Massachusetts branch of the Society for the Prevention of Cruelty to Animals. The city has an unfortunate habit of parking its huge snow removal equipment around this memorial during the winter. These vehicles look very like a group of brontosauri clustered around some primordial spring.

While on the subject of horses—and fountains—it may not be amiss to quote an item from the *Boston News Letter* of 1773: "there is newly erected in the Town of Boston by John and Thomas Hill at their distillery a Fire engine drawn by a horse which delivers a large quantity of water twelve feet above the ground."

In the days agone it was the gracious annual custom to erect, near the Angell Memorial, a Christmas tree for the horses. From its branches any visiting beast would receive a measure of corn and oats, an apple or a carrot, a lump of sugar, and other equine delicacies. He might also have a drink of water from the fountain if he so desired. Even the driver would be regaled with a cup of coffee and a box lunch.

Could we not revive and bring up to date this kindly custom and offer some Christmas cheer for the horse's successor—a jigger of high octane, maybe, or a little extra air for the tires?

xii. Here Lies

THE POPULAR BODY

The tiny ship which brought the first Puritans to Boston was named the *Arbella* in honor of the Lady Arbella, daughter of the Earl of Lincoln, who, accompanied by her husband, Isaac Johnson, was herself a passenger on this historic trip. Many later historians assert that Isaac Johnson died while the Puritans were still in Charlestown, but Lieutenant Governor Hutchinson in his *History of the Colony of Massachusetts*, printed in 1764, tells the story differently.

Mr. Johnson, says Governor Hutchinson, was an important person in his own right, as well as being the husband of a "Lady," and so was given first choice, after the Governor, of what land he would like to have in the new settlement. Isaac chose wisely, selecting that section which is now bordered by School, Tremont, Court, and Washington Streets. He did not live long enough to get any great enjoyment from his property, for he was one of the first of the company to pass away. With his last breath he whispered a request to be buried in the upper part of his garden. This would be near the present corner of School and Tremont Streets. It was so ordered.

Alive or dead, Isaac was a popular man; and others, as they saw the Grim Reaper approaching, asked to be buried "alongside Brother Johnson." It was done.

In one of the old records we find the ominous note, "Brother Johnson's garden is getting to be a poor place for vegetables." So the garden was abandoned and that corner of his land was set aside as a burying ground—which it already was. For the first thirty years of the colony this was the only repository for the dead in Boston.

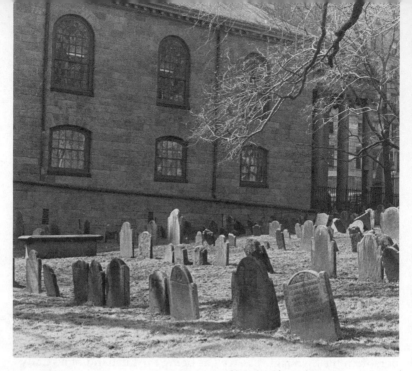

King's Chapel Burying Ground

Today this graveyard is the oldest man-made thing in the city. Here, amid the busy traffic, and directly over the thundering subway, sleep Boston's earliest residents, including Governor Winthrop, Lady Andros, and Governor Shirley. The earthly remains of the beloved minister John Cotton also lie here.

In 1686 Governor Andros, smarting under the refusal of the colonists to give or sell him land where he could build a chapel in which to hold the Church of England services, arbitrarily appropriated a corner of the burying ground and there built a small wooden chapel. This highhanded action in seizing the land against the will of the people was characterized by the antiquarian Bowditch as "a bare faced squat," which is quite a phrase when you analyze it. Some years later, in 1710, the chapel was considerably enlarged.

The present King's Chapel, designed by Peter Harrison, is well over two hundred years old. The cornerstone was laid in

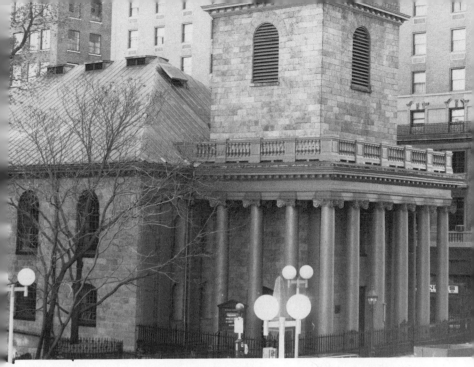

King's Chapel

1749 with Governor Shirley at the trowel. Services were not interrupted by the building operations, for the stone chapel was constructed so as to completely enclose the wooden structure, which, when the new building was completed, was torn down and thrown out of the windows.

King's Chapel was the first of many buildings to use Braintree (which is now Quincy) granite. Having little knowledge of quarrying, the builders used boulders from the top of the ground, and there was so much fear that there was not enough granite in Quincy to finish the job that a special clause was inserted in the building contract to cover this contingency. Fortunately the supply proved adequate, and enough stone remained in Quincy to build many more large and imposing buildings throughout the country.

It is interesting to note the contrast between the rough effect of the large hand-hammered blocks in the Chapel and the sleek surface of the stones of the Parker House, just across the way. Both are from the same vicinity. It is improved methods of stone dressing that make the difference.

There is another point of similarity between the Chapel grounds and the neighboring hotel. Both are filled with Boston statesmen and politicians, but those in the Parker House are very much alive while those next to the Chapel are very very dead.

King's Chapel was first in other things besides its use of Quincy granite. It was the first Episcopal church in New England, and after the Revolution it became the first Unitarian church in America.

In Colonial days King's Chapel became a sort of royal pet. Queen Anne gave it a set of red cushions and vestments, James II presented the pulpit, and George III gave the silver communion plate. The beautiful interior in Georgian design still features the pew used by the royal governors, and many emblems of royalty are displayed.

During the Revolution all royal symbols were, of course, anathema in Boston, and the colorless name of "Stone Chapel" was substituted for King's Chapel in much the same spirit that "Liberty measles" replaced "German measles" during a later conflict. In both instances, when the madness was over, the original names were restored.

Near the entrance to the Chapel is a monument, the most imposing one in the burying ground, with a lengthy inscription in French. This cenotaph honors the memory of Chevalier Saint Sauveur, an officer in Admiral d'Estaing's squadron, who was killed attempting to quell a street brawl while he was a visitor in Boston in 1778. Fearing international complications and as a gesture of good will, the House of Representatives voted to erect this memorial, with a parade and all fitting ceremonials. Having passed the vote, they apparently felt that their consciences were at rest and nothing further was done at that time. Saint Sauveur was buried, by candlelight, in the "Stranger's Tomb" under King's Chapel. In 1917, 139 years later, the provisions of the motion were carried out. The monument was carved and put in place with the parade and all other ceremonies exactly as they had been outlined in the original vote. The parade was led by Governor McCall, Lieutenant Governor Coolidge—later President of the United States—Mayor Curley, and J. C. J. Flamand, the French Consul in Boston.

OLD GRANARY

Boston has a high regard for cemeteries. For a store or an office building to overlook an ancient burying ground is a distinct asset. The occupants of the building are proud of it. They mention it in their advertisements.

Few, if any, cities outside of Boston can boast of five graveyards located in the very busiest centers of commerce. No other city would boast about it if it did have them.

The visitor to Boston is always taken to see some of these last resting places of our illustrious dead. He pretends to see some connection between this preoccupation with cemeteries and the wild and unrestrained traffic in our streets. Usually the first to be shown to the visitor is the Old Granary of Tremont Street.

The word "charming" hardly seems fitting when applied to a graveyard, but there is a gentle charm to the Old Granary. Pigeons and squirrels enjoy its peaceful atmosphere, birds nest in its trees, and employees from nearby offices sometimes find it restful to eat their lunches sitting on the horizontal slabs that were placed to protect the graves from the depredations of wild animals.

It has frequently been said, and it is probably true, that there are more people buried in the Old Granary who are known to more people than in any other cemetery in America. The long list includes three signers of the Declaration of Independence— John Hancock, Samuel Adams, and Robert Treat Paine; eight governors; many members of the Boston Tea Party; the victims of the Boston Massacre; John Phillips, the first mayor; and, some believe, Mother Goose, herself.

Andrew Faneuil, the old Huguenot, was one of the wealth-

The Old Granary

iest merchants of his time. In his will he cast off his nephew Benjamin with a bequest of "five shillings and no more," apparently for no better reason than that he did not approve of the fact that Benjamin had married without his full knowledge and consent. He bequeathed his entire estate to his other nephew, Peter, a confirmed bachelor. Some of this fortune Peter gave to the town to finance the building of the market and meeting hall still bearing his name and some he invested in rare wines and "five casks of brandy, disguised as rum" for his own use.

Peter did not live very long to enjoy his fortune, the epicurean banquets and rare vintages which he was wont to serve in his palatial home being, perhaps, a contributing cause of his early demise. By an ironic twist of fate the entire estate then went to Benjamin—in addition to the five shillings which he had already received.

On the tomb in the Old Granary where Peter, Andrew, and Benjamin repose—we hope amicably—together was, originally, the family crest. Later some forgotten stonecutter inscribed the name as it was probably then pronounced: "P. Funel." The true Bostonian still uses this pronunciation. At a still later date the

246

name "Peter Faneuil" was carved on the tomb in large and imposing letters. Today the crest has entirely disappeared, the "P. Funel" can be faintly seen, but the "Peter Faneuil" is in a good state of preservation.

Originally the Granary graves were arranged in sociable little groups, but some methodically minded sexton of earlier days took up all the stones and rearranged them in orderly rows. He thought they looked better that way and it made the mowing much easier. As a result no one can say where any particular person may be buried, and we are obliged to reverence our honored dead in mass rather than in detail.

The largest and most attractive of the memorials is the cenotaph which Benjamin Franklin erected in memory of his parents. It may be seen from Tremont Street, framed by the massive and somberly beautiful entrance gate. Both the monument and the entrance are the work of the architect Solomon Willard. Willard, originally a wood carver, became so enamored of granite as a building material that he bought a quarry in Quincy and constructed America's first railway—the Granite Railroad—to carry his stone from the quarry to tidewater.

Some of the monoliths in the Granary's retaining wall along Tremont Street are fully thirty feet long. They could just as well have been cut into shorter sections, but Willard enjoyed meeting and overcoming the transportation problems incident to the moving of huge masses of rock.

The symbolism of the winged globe and the inverted torches of the main gate is easily understood, but many have been puzzled by the "flying dumbbells" carved on the corner posts. That is exactly what they look like—a pair of dumbbells with wings. Actually they represent the old type of hourglass with wings attached, smoothly illustrating the classic phrase *"Tempus fugit,"* which may be somewhat freely translated as, "It's later than you think."

Why a burying ground should be called a granary has been explained in a previous chapter. It seems perfectly logical to a Bostonian.

CORPSE HILL

"Corpse Hill," some of the ancient records call it. This is not surprising since it is estimated that over ten thousand people have been buried in this North End cemetery. The correct name, however, is Copp's Hill, honoring the memory of the original owner of the land, William Copp, whose mortal remains lie here in an unmarked grave.

Little is known of William Copp. He was one of the very first of the Boston settlers. He is listed as a cordwainer or shoe-maker by trade, a respected member of the community, and an elder in Cotton Mather's church. This about completes his known biography. That he was a lovingly impartial father is indicated by an item in his will: "I give to my daughter Ruth my great kettle and little pot and I give to my daughter Lydia my little kettle and great pot." What could be fairer?

In the early days of the colony the North End was the home of the more prominent and wealthy citizens. The roster of those who found their last resting place in Copp's Hill Burying Ground would form a comprehensive "Who's Who" or, more literally, "Who's Through" of Boston's elite during its first century. The Mathers — Increase, Cotton, and Samuel, sleep here. Edmund Hartt, builder of the frigate *Constitution*; Deacon Shem Drowne, the fabricator of weather vanes; Captain Robert Newman, who hung the lanterns that started Paul Revere on his epic ride; the father and grandfather of Governor Hutchinson; and a host of other famous persons have found here a lasting peace.

The epitaph reader and the amateur antiquarian will find a stroll through the old Burying Ground richly rewarding. The stones are chiefly of slate and feature the urns, weeping willows, hourglasses, and death's-heads all so dear to the hearts of the macabre artists of the early days. It is noticeable that the death's-heads of the nineteenth century grin in a clearly jocular manner, while those of the eighteenth century are definitely sneering.

A few of the more pretentious stones display well-executed coats of arms. Near the main gate is one of the finest of these. It is the tomb of William Clark, whose epitaph describes him as

Copp's Hill Burying Ground

"an eminent merchant, an honorable counselor and a despiser of sorry persons and little actions."

Many years ago the sexton of a nearby church removed the body from this tomb and substituted his own name for that of Mr. Clark on the stone. In due time he was himself buried in the tomb—thus stealing the grave, the coat of arms, and the epitaph of the "despiser of sorry persons and little actions." The body of the estimable Mr. Clark no longer lies beneath the stone, but assuredly the stone *lies* above the remains of the despicable sexton.

A much more kindly and honest sexton of a later day had this tender tribute on the stone which marks the grave of his wife: "Betsy, wife of David Darling, died Mar. 23, 1805. She was the mother of 17 children and around her lies 12 of them and 2 were lost at sea. Brother sextons: Please leave a clear berth for me near this stone." Despite this moving plea the loving husband is buried in an unmarked grave in a distant part of the enclosure.

Vandalism has left its mark even in this sacred spot. Over a hundred years ago someone with a perverted sense of humor—and a cold chisel—changed the date on one of the stones so that it appears that Grace Berry was buried in 1625, five years before Boston was settled. Some of the stones show the marks of bullets from the muskets of the British, who used them as targets during the siege of Boston.

Through the years, many of the gravestones were stolen by neighboring residents and used for chimney covers, flagstones, drain covers, and even brick oven floors. When some of the patrons of a bakery became jittery over the death's-heads and funeral urns which appeared on the bottom of their loaves of bread, the theft was discovered, and over forty of the missing stones were found and restored to the graveyard.

There is a grim humor to be found among the ancient stones —and some color. John Green, Mehitable Scarlett, Hannah White, and Sarah Brown may be located. Captain William Trout and Sarah Bass have long been food for worms; Samuel Mower and Theadora Hay have fallen before the Grim Reaper; Betty Toot and Thomas Scoot are near neighbors, as are John Water, William Beer, and John Milk.

Nearby are the remains of Prince Chew, and Colo Jarvis. The fondness of our ancestors for these odd given names is evidenced by memorials to Onesimus Brown, Love Rawlins, Silence Barnard, Temperance Coleman, and Prissiella Woodward.

xiii. Saints and Sinners

THE INDUSTRIOUS APPRENTICE

No streets, no schools, no great insurance companies have been named in honor of Thomas Hancock. He merely earned the money which his nephew John spent with such a lavish hand. Nevertheless, he was a man worthy of honor and remembrance. It is highly probable that without the wealth and social position bequeathed to him by his uncle, John Hancock would have lived and died in complete obscurity.

Thomas came of a deeply religious family. His grandfather was a minister, his father was a minister, and his older brother was a minister. Evidently his father felt that enough was enough, for he apprenticed Thomas to his friend Daniel Henchman from whom he was to learn the art and mystery of bookbinding and bookselling.

Thomas proved to be an industrious apprentice. He worked hard and acquired the skills of his trade rapidly and well. As was customary at the time, he lived with his employer's family where he soon became much liked by all. At twenty-one years of age he had "served his time" and, to celebrate the event, took a brief trip to Plymouth, England, the home of his ancestors. Upon his return he opened a bookshop on Anne (now North) Street near the corner of Blackstone. A swinging sign painted with a picture of a Bible and three crowns decorated the front of the shop.

To marry the boss's daughter was quite in the Colonial tradition, so on November 5, 1730, Thomas was married to Lydia, the daughter of his former employer. It was a fortunate event for the young merchant. The bride's unusually large dowry furnished Hancock with a nest-egg which he developed into one of the largest fortunes in New England.

John Singleton Copley, Thomas Hancock
(1702/3—1764)

By his marriage with Lydia, Thomas acquired not only a considerable amount of money but also a considerable amount of girl. Miss Henchman was a buxom lass, nor did she diminish in size as the years went by. When her husband ordered a chariot from London he specified that it be unusually high and large. "Because," he wrote, "you know Mrs. Hancock is none of the shortest and smallest of folks, though I'd prefer as light a one as possible to her size." He also asked that the step "must be uncommonly low for Mrs. Hancock is a little weak in the knees."

As a businessman, Hancock was remarkably successful. When other dealers paid for their imports of books, paper, and supplies with cash, he paid with exports of dried fish, furs, whale oil, tar, and turpentine. Both parties profited by the deal.

In 1728 Hancock joined with Benjamin Faneuil, Henry Phillips, and his future father-in-law, David Henchman, in the venture of establishing, in Milton Lower Falls, America's first paper mill. This new business together with his bookselling and other interests brought much wealth to the versatile merchant. He was said to be the richest man in Massachusetts and the second wealthiest in the American colonies.

On the sunny slope of Beacon Hill the prosperous bookman built for himself and his Lydia a handsome mansion well fitted to his wealth and position. In later years this was to become famous as the "John Hancock mansion," but it was Thomas who built it.

On the first day of August 1764, Thomas Hancock was just entering the Council Chamber of the State House when he was stricken with an attack of apoplexy. His friends tenderly carried him to his home, where he lived for only a few hours. A contemporary newspaper noted his passing with the words, "He came to Boston as an apprentice to Mr. Henchman, Stationer— but having a Genius for more extensive Commerce, turned his views that Way and by the Smile of heaven acquired a plentiful fortune."

When his will was read it was found that the worthy merchant had provided gifts for a number of public organizations. The list forms an interesting key to the character and interests of the donor. Included are $5000 to found a professorship of Oriental languages at Harvard College; $5000 to the Society for Propagating the Gospel among the Indians; $3000 to the Town of Boston toward an insane asylum; and $1000 to the Society for the Carrying on of the Manufacture of Linen.

The union of Thomas and Lydia had not been blessed by any children, so he left the bulk of his estate to his favorite nephew, John, who was then twenty-seven years old. It had taken Thomas a lifetime to accumulate the fortune which was so great that it took John nearly a lifetime to spend it all—but he succeeded in doing so.

A WILY INDIAN

In ye days when ye Indian lived in ye land there was one, John Wampus, whose name appears frequently in the early town records. As a rule the Puritans had little truck with the red men, but they seem to have made an exception in the case of John. He was permitted to buy and sell a considerable amount of real estate in Boston and also in Connecticut.

As a young man Wampus attended the so-called Indian College. The "College" was a small brick building located on the Harvard campus. It had been founded by the Society for the Propagation of the Gospel in New England. Here Wampus acquired a fair knowledge of spoken English although he never learned to read or write well. On legal documents he always "made his mark" instead of signing his name.

At first the settlers had a high opinion of Wampus. He ate his corn instead of drinking it, led a quiet life, and seemed fair and honest in his business dealings. Later, however, he changed. He was frequently drunk, always tricky, and proved to be a fast man with a string of wampum. He claimed to be a chief of the Nipmucks and, as such, the owner of large tracts of land in both Massachusetts and Connecticut.

At a court held in Natick in September 1681, several of the older Indians testified that they had known John Wampus from a child and that he was no more a chief than they were. In spite of this testimony, John sold to Joshua Hewes and other Bostonians a tract of land eight miles square which is now the township of Sutton. The General Court confirmed the sale and, by that action, confirmed John's ownership and right to sell.

Becoming a sailor by profession, he made many voyages to England and became well known there although he always considered Boston his home port. Owning a tract of land on Tremont Street, just where St. Paul's Cathedral now stands, there Wampus built himself an attractive home and attempted to live among his white neighbors on terms of equality. The old records show many business transactions among them.

The records of the Court, however, show "information against John Wampus, Indian, that since he came out of England,

St. Paul's Cathedral

about four months past, he takes no employment, but travels up and down in a vagrant, idle way, among English and Indians, vaporing of the great quantity of land he has; offering to sell that which is other man's possession and improvement, both English and Indians. The said Wampus is a very disorderly person."

After recounting a few examples of these shady dealings, the record continues, "about the beginning of September he came to Natick where he bought a barrel of cider, and got about fifteen or sixteen women and men, and drank it all out presently, whereby himself and all the rest were made drunk.

"He hath escaped from prison, and is runne away upon Oct. 1, 1677."

John did often escape to London where he alternately enjoyed himself with his white companions and languished in jail for various misdemeanors. During his absences his squaw, Preske, had always kept the home fires burning in the house on Tremont Street.

Preske was the daughter of an Indian chief of the Aspetuk tribe and claimed to be the owner of considerable land in her own right. However, the squaw—known to the whites as Ann —died in 1676. Her husband had been absent at the time on one of his numerous trips to England. He was also on one of his numerous trips to jail, having been imprisoned in London on account of a small debt.

The Indian must have had some powerful friends in London, for a letter dated August 22, 1676, was written in his behalf by no less a person than King George himself. Addressed to "Our trusty and well-beloved Sir John Leverett, Knt; Governour of Massachusetts Bay in New England," the letter said that John Wampus owned lands in the colony, which he had held for many years, having taken the oath of allegiance as a British subject. The missive directed that Wampus be restored to his lands, or have liberty to sell them for his present relief.

The records of the Probate Court (vol. 12, p. 10) show that Preske had willed the Tremont Street property to Joshua Hughes, but the King's letter apparently restored it to John, so he sold it to the same Joshua Hughes (spelled Hewes this time) for the sum of twenty pounds.

It is evident that John was a thorn in the flesh of the good Puritans, but his chief crime seems to have been that he "took" them when they were trying to "take" him.

THE GALLEY SLAVES

For many years Boston has been recognized as one of the great printing and publishing centers of the world. It does not, however, have the honor of having established the first printing press in the colony. That distinction belongs to Cambridge.

In fact, through some political chicanery, a law was passed forbidding any person to set up a press outside of that town. This was discrimination. The law remained in force until 1674.

The English clergyman Rev. Joseph Glover was a man with a plan. He embarked for Boston in 1639 with the intention of setting up a printing plant. With him he had a printing press, a font of type, four assistants, and a wife. The four helpers were all of one family: Stephen Daye, his sons—Stephen, Jr., and Matthew—and a stepson, William Bordman. Stephen had been a "printer's devil" for a few months. The others knew absolutely nothing of the business.

Had Glover set up his press as he had planned, there is little doubt that he would have been able to train these men in the art and mysteries of the craft; and he would have made them work at it, for the minister was a masterful man. Unfortunately the rigors of the voyage were too severe, and the Rev. Mr. Glover died while the ship was in mid-ocean. Before he left England the parson had already purchased a house in Cambridge, so his widow, when she arrived, moved into it. She had the press set up in her new home and, aided by the Daye family, began the printing business.

Mrs. Glover was an over-kind and inefficient boss; the men were, with one exception, ignorant and lazy. Matthew was the exception. He really tried to do an honest day's work. Stephen, Sr., sat back idly and took what glory there was in the business. He is generally credited with having established printing in the colony.

The results were pitiful. In time they managed to get out a copy of *Freeman's Oath*, an almanac for the year 1639, and the now-famous *Bay Psalm Book*. Their work was unbelievably crude. However, the Dayes had the only press in the colony and what printing there was to be done they did. Ministers and politicians who longed to see their words preserved for posterity patronized the press, poor as it was.

There is a close alliance between education and printing, so President Dunster of Harvard felt it was his duty to welcome the new industry which had opened shop almost in the back yard of his college. Upon his first visit he encountered a pleasant surprise. The widow was much better "set up" than was the type in the press which she controlled. Soon a friendship developed between them which rapidly burgeoned into love. Only two years after her arrival in Cambridge they were married.

Harvard College was now in control of the press of America!

As the bride refused to be separated from her beloved equipment, and since even a college president is easier to move than a printing press, the newlyweds decided to live in her house. All of the Dayes dropped out of the picture except Matthew. He continued to be the colonists' only printer for eleven years, producing smudged pamphlets for Harvard, a few governmental broadsides, and an occasional extra-dry sermon.

When Matthew died at the age of twenty-nine, the job of running the only press in America was given to Samuel Greene. Sam, who had learned the trade from Matthew, was the inept pupil of a none-too-bright teacher. No new type or equipment had been bought in the nineteen years that the press had been in service. The printing was worse than ever. Harvard, which now owned the business, refused to buy new type unless the work improved—and the work could not be improved without new type.

This impasse was solved by an organization with the cumbersome name of "The Society for the Propagation of the Gospel Amongst the Heathen Natives of New England and Parts Adjacent in America." This society, headed by John Eliot, the famous apostle to the Indians, was anxious to have a Bible printed in the Indian language for the use of the natives. The members had money and they were willing to spend it in a good cause. Suddenly Sam Greene found himself supplied with a brand-new press, a generous supply of new type, and an associate printer especially imported from England.

The new printer, Marmaduke Johnson, thoroughly understood the business. In addition he was keen, active, and industrious.

Printing in America was, at last, off to a good start.

Marmaduke was not only a skilled printer but also a shrewd businessman. The terms of his engagement prove him to be that. He insisted upon a written contract. He demanded, and received, "diet, lodging, and washing." He was also to receive forty pounds per year in money—a princely wage for those days. Desirous of fame as well as money, he further stipulated that his name should appear on all of the products of the press.

Marmaduke was well pleased with his contract except for two things—and those he could not change. He was not allowed to work independently. The authorities insisted that he join in partnership with the struggling pressman already on location—Sam Greene. Also, no part of this munificent salary was payable until the Bible was finished—and then he would have to go to England to collect it.

Johnson went into production as soon as his equipment could be set up. He systematized the work on the basis of one page of the Bible each day—set up, printed, and the type cleaned and returned to the case.

This was a solid day's work for two men and gave little time for their outside interests. What leisure they had they devoted to their respective pastimes. Sam was an enthusiastic member of the militia, while Marmaduke, with no less enthusiasm, used his free time in making love to Sam's attractive daughter.

So busy was Mr. Greene with his military duties that it was over a year before he discovered what was going on in his own home. When he did find out, he lost no time in haling Marmaduke into court, charging him with "obtaining the affections of his daughter without his knowledge and concent." In those days that was a felony.

The young printer admitted his guilt and was foolish enough to try to help his case by admitting that he already had a wife in England. The outraged court fined the philanderer five pounds and ordered him to take the next ship back to his wife. Calmly ignoring the court's order, Marmaduke returned to his shop and resumed his work on the Indian Bible.

In spite of the fact that the print shop was almost next door to the court house, it was a year and a half before the court realized that their authority had been flouted. The printer was again ordered to pay his fine and leave at once. However, the politically powerful Rev. John Eliot appeared in his behalf. Eliot pointed out that a good printer was unique in the colony and

The Indian Bible Printed by Samuel Greene for John Eliot

that the Bible was, as yet, unfinished. As a result of this plea, the wayward compositor was granted a year's delay in the execution of the sentence in addition to the year and a half to which he had helped himself.

During the year, the Indian Bible was completed—much to the delight of Eliot; a copy of the psalms was printed; and a book, *Call to the Unconverted*, was published. In the meantime, Marmaduke Johnson's wife in England had died, thereby nullifying the order for his banishment. Also, Greene's daughter had married someone else. All in all it was a good year for Marmaduke.

By this time there was a small fortune in back salary awaiting him in England. He went there, collected what was due him, and spent a considerable part of it in a new press and several fonts of type. With all these improvements he hoped to be allowed to set up his shop in Boston.

The court, however, would not permit any press to be located outside Cambridge, so Johnson established himself there and published, over his imprint, an astonishingly large number of broadsides, pamphlets, and books. He never ceased to importune the court for permission to move to Boston, where he felt his talents would have a wider scope. Finally, in 1674, leave was granted, and the printer joyfully transferred his equipment to the big town. Unfortunately he did not live to see the Boston imprint on any of his work. He died on Christmas Day, 1674.

The business was taken over by John Foster, who is usually noted as the first Boston printer. The Foster Shop was "at the sign of the Dove," which is believed to have been near the corner of Tremont and Boylston Streets.

The first production of this press, and the first book to be published in Boston, was a 63-page copy of a sermon preached at the election of Governor John Leverett.

AN EARLY PLAYBOY

Thomas Morton, who lived out Wollaston way, was a playboy, a sound businessman, and the author of a charming book on early Massachusetts. He knew how to get along with the Indians and was, according to the early settlers, on a much too friendly footing with them.

Morton was one of those strange, little-known characters whom the Puritans found already in residence when they arrived in 1630. He had lived there for years even before the Pilgrims had established their homes in Plymouth.

Gathering a group of boon companions about him, Morton had built a trading post and small settlement on Mount Wollaston which he named Merry Mount. Here he strove with all diligence to make the name a fitting one.

When not engaged in "trafficking with ye Indians" this gay spirit roamed the forest with his dog and gun or embarked in his small sailboat for a day of sport on the bay—fishing and hunting wild fowl. Much of his time was spent in entertaining any wandering hunter, fellow trader, or fisherman who might be passing.

The Indians—particularly the young and frolicsome squaws

—were welcome at all times, and lusty drinking parties often lasted through the night, the next day, and—on particularly festive occasions—into the next week.

When the Puritans arrived in nearby Boston in 1630, it did not take the young men of the town long to discover the delights of Merry Mount. Visits there were surreptitious, of course, but they were, nonetheless, frequent.

Even before the Puritans arrived, the doings at Merry Mount were well known to the Pilgrims, for it was from them that Morton purchased the pitifully small supply of furs obtained by the Plymouth settlers from the animals they managed to trap or shoot.

Governor Bradford of the Pilgrim Colony recounted with considerable horror the festivities in which Morton and his friends indulged.

"In the Spring of 1627," Bradford writes, "they set up a May-pole, drinking and dancing about it many days together, inviting the Indian women for their consorts, dancing and frisking together (like so many faries or furies rather) and worse practices."

The May-pole about which the gaiety centered was described by Morton himself as "A goodly pine tree of 80 foote longe which was reared up, with a pare of buckshorne nayled on somewhat nere unto the top of it: where it stood as a faire sea-marke for directions how to find the way to mine Hoste of Merry Mounte."

A song, composed by "Mine Hoste" himself, was nailed to the May-pole and was sung at intervals—whenever the revelers were in the mood. One of the fifteen verses will indicate the spirit of the song and will probably be all that the reader can endure.

The Songe

Drinke and be merry, merry, merry, boys
Let all your delight be in Hymen's joyes;
Lo! to Hymen now the day is come,
About the merry May-pole take a Roome.

Most historians attribute Morton's downfall at that time to the Pilgrims' hatred of his jolly way of life, but the real reason is that he supplied the Indians with liquor and that he sold firearms, shot, and powder to them. The colonists believed that a drunken Indian was as dangerous as a wild beast—and an intoxicated Indian with a gun was a menace to any man that he might meet. Morton had to be suppressed.

In June 1628 the doughty little Myles Standish, whom Morton called "Captain Shrimpe," was sent with a few soldiers to arrest him. The trader and his friends had armed themselves and prepared to resist. A bloody battle might have ensued but for the fact that the defenders had tried to stimulate their courage with such liberal draughts of liquor that they could not even hold their guns. They were taken without a shot being fired. The only injury suffered by the culprits was that sustained by one man who was "so drunke that he ran his own nose upon the pointe of a sword, but he lost but a little of his hott blood."

The merry rogue was shipped to England but in a short time he was back at his old stand. He was there when the Puritans arrived in Boston. Almost the first official act of Governor Winthrop was to arrest the troublemaker and send him back to England. Some ten years later the offender again returned to Boston, a changed man who was, to the amazement of the Puritans, "sometimes content to drink water."

In spite of his apparent reformation the authorities seized him and, without even the pretense of a trial, threw him into jail, and fined him an amount equal to his entire possessions. Later Morton was released and in some way reached York, Maine, where he died in poverty and disgrace.

A CAPTIVE AUDIENCE

To the Puritans their spiritual leader was a most important personage. The very first question discussed at their earliest meeting in the New World was "How shall the minister be maintained?" They voted that a house should be built for him at public expense and that his salary should be fixed at twenty pounds "until his wife arrived."

The Rev. John Wilson, who was their chosen pastor, was not too happy about the salary. In fact, a few years later when his income had more than doubled, he remarked that nothing in New England was cheap except milk and ministers. Milk was then selling at a penny a quart.

The Rev. John had been educated at King's College in Cambridge, England, and had occupied the pleasant and lucrative position of private chaplain to the Lady Scudamore. This employment terminated somewhat suddenly when Her Ladyship discharged him because he vehemently denounced her and her guests for talking about hawks and hounds on a Sunday.

Mr. Wilson decided to become a Puritan.

The Puritans warmly welcomed their new pastor, and he embarked with them on their great adventure, arriving in Charlestown at about the same time as Governor Winthrop, although on a different ship.

As soon as the little group of pioneers had landed, they gathered together under an oak tree, and in thankfulness for their safe arrival the pastor preached his first hour-long sermon to them. Then they all went to work.

For some time services were held in the open air, but when Mr. Wilson made a hurried trip to London and returned with his wife on May 26, 1632, he found a meeting-house nearly completed on State Street near Washington. Its walls were of mud and it boasted a roof of thatch. Next to it was a dwelling of equal magnificence for the accommodation of his wife and himself. The meetinghouse was of ample size to contain the ninety-four men and fifty-seven women who made up his congregation.

At one side of his lot was a narrow highway known as Crooked Lane. This was soon renamed Wilson Lane in his honor. Many years later this passageway was absorbed as part of Devonshire Street.

During the early part of his pastorate Mr. Wilson enjoyed a rare privilege—a *captive* audience. A law passed May 6,

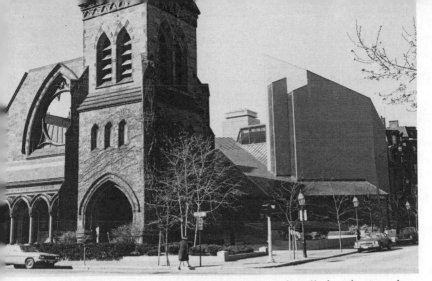

"Sixth in direct line from the first mud-walled gathering place of the Puritans": The First and Second Church

1634, decreed that absence from church should be punished by a fine of ten shillings or by imprisonment for an unspecified time.

During his long life in Boston this first minister was sincerely loved by many and intensely hated by a few. At a meeting of the Puritan soldiers on the Common a gentleman said to him, "Sir, I can tell you a great thing: here is a mighty body of people and there is not seven of them all, but what loves Mr. Wilson."

To this the minister replied, "Sir, there is not so much as one of them all, but Mr. Wilson loves him."

Nevertheless, this great lover was also an accomplished hater. He loathed all those who differed in any way from his own narrow creed and was particularly bitter against Quakers. At the hanging of Mary Dyer on Boston Common he shouted, "I will carry fire in one hand and faggots in the other, to burn all Quakers in the world."

It was his duty and apparently his pleasure to attend all hangings and to vigorously point out to the unfortunate victim the horrible tortures which awaited him in the next world.

Wilson rose to his greatest height of ecclesiastical vituperation in his sentence of excommunication against the unfortunate

Anne Hutchinson, whose only crime was in being a bit too vocal in her religious opinions, which differed from his in several important points.

Pointing a rigid finger at the unrepentant Anne, he thundered, "In the name of the Church I do not only pronounce you worthy to be cast out, but I do cast you out, and in the name of Christ I do deliver you up to Satan, that you may learn no more to blaspheme, to seduce, and to lie; and I do account you from this time forth to be a Heathen and a Publican, and so to be held by all Brethren and Sisters of the congregation and of others; therefore I command you in the name of Christ Jesus and of this church as a Leper to withdraw yourself out of this congregation."

Wilson did not confine his efforts to religion alone; he was also interested in politics. In fact he made what was probably the first stump speech ever given on this side of the Atlantic. During the bitter controversy which resulted in the ousting of Governor Vane in 1637, the vigorous parson climbed up on the limb of a tree on the Common and made a campaign speech which resulted in a victory for Governor Winthrop.

Mr. Wilson was a spiritual leader in the community for thirty-seven years. His pastorate was terminated by his death on August 7, 1677, at the age of seventy-nine. He had seen Boston grow from a primitive settlement into a town of considerable size and dignity.

THE MATHER DYNASTY

Anyone who hopes to understand conditions in early Boston must become acquainted with the ministers of that time.

The pastor was the accepted authority on all matters: religious, political, legal, and medical. It was an age when the minister was more important than the magistrate. The judge could send a miscreant to jail, but the man of the cloth could send him to Hell.

Ministers even dictated how women should dress. Autocracy could go no further.

Almost the only difference between the minister and an absolute monarch was that the office was not hereditary. The Mather family nearly achieved that status.

The "dynasty" of the Mathers in Boston extended through four generations and embraced a period of one hundred and fifty years. There were eleven Mathers trained as ministers in those four generations. Three of them governed churches in England; seven ministered to their flocks in New England; and one, Nathaniel, died a few weeks before he was to deliver his first sermon. Among them they published more than five hundred different works. Most of these were on the subject of religion, but there were also treatises on political problems, legal questions, witchcraft, astronomy, mathematics, the supernatural, science, and medicine.

Verily, the Mathers were versatile.

The first of the clan to come to this country was Richard Mather. He was an English clergyman with Puritanical leanings. He was twice suspended from his church for nonconformity and, foreseeing the trouble which was in store for Puritans under Charles I and Archbishop Laud, he decided to emigrate to America.

The anti-Puritan forces were closing in on him, and it was only by using a disguise and an assumed name that he was able to secure a passage on the *Bristol* for the New World. Still in disguise, Richard landed in Boston August 17, 1635. His fame had preceded him, and he accepted an urgent call to become pastor of the Dorchester Church, where he remained until his death sixteen years later.

The following verses, written in the church register at the time of his death, have been preserved.

> Divine his charms, years seven times seven,
> Wise to win souls from earth to heaven;
> Prophet's reward he gains above
> But great's our loss by his remove.

We may hope that the poet's judgment of character was

better than his mathematics. Mather was seventy-three when he died—which is *not* seven times seven.

Richard was a man of great intellect and vigor. His sons were many. Among them was Samuel, his firstborn, who came from England with his father. Graduating from Harvard in 1643, Samuel was asked to remain with the college as a tutor—the first to be so honored by that institution. His popularity with his students was so great that they wore mourning bands on their sleeves for thirty days after he left the position. He left to become pastor of the New North (The Second Church). He preached there for a few months only and then returned to England where he ultimately became the chaplain to the Lord Mayor of London.

Richard's sixth son, Increase Mather, was born in Dorchester. He was graduated from Harvard in 1656 and took an advanced degree at Trinity College in Dublin two years later.

After preaching in England for three years, he returned to Boston and accepted the position of pastor of The Second Church —where his brother Samuel had preached for a brief time.

He remained as minister to the people of this church for sixty years. Only his death could part him from them. Even when he was offered the high honor of becoming the president of Harvard College, he accepted only with the understanding that he could live in Boston and continue his services to the church. Years later, when Harvard finally issued the ultimatum "Either live in Cambridge or resign from the presidency of the College," he did not hesitate. He chose to resign and continue to devote himself to his parishioners.

Increase lived in a time of great political unrest and unhappiness. The charter which the Puritans had brought with them when they first came, and under which they had lived in contentment for fifty-four years, had been vacated.

In the very year of his ordination Boston ceased to be a chartered colony and became a royal province. Andros was appointed as the first royal governor. He was tactless, arbitrary, and dictatorial. The people hated him. Mather, as the accredited voice of the people, expressed this dislike somewhat pointedly in his sermons. Andros knew of this, and the detestation was returned in full measure.

John Foster, Richard Mather (*1675*)

The colonists at last decided to send a delegate to England who would represent them and their interests—one who could secure for them a charter which would be as nearly like the old one as possible. For this delicate and important mission they chose the most learned and fluent man in the community—Increase Mather. When Andros learned of this plan he issued a writ for the arrest of the minister, but the resourceful divine, disguised as a common sailor, got safely on board his ship, *The President*. He was on his way to England before the writ could be served.

Mather was cordially received in London, was granted several interviews with the King, conducted some adroit negotiations with politicians, and generally made a most favorable impression on all with whom he came in contact.

Having proved himself to be a great statesman as well as an eloquent preacher, he returned to Boston in 1692 bringing with him a new charter which, considering the unfavorable conditions of the times, was remarkably liberal. He could not prevent the change of the colony into a province, but he did secure the incorporation of Maine, Nova Scotia, and the Plymouth Colony into the Province of Massachusetts.

Best of all, perhaps, he was permitted to choose, under certain limitations, the new royal governor. With the approval of the King, Mather selected Sir William Phips, a personal friend, a native of New England, and a man who could be trusted not to forget that he owed his appointment to Increase Mather.

Richard, who as previously noted was the first of the Mathers, had a great love and admiration for his colleague, John Cotton, the pastor of the First Church in Boston. This love must have spread to other members of the Cotton household, for when John died, Richard married his widow, Sarah Cotton. Increase Mather, who was Richard's son by his first wife, carried on the family tradition. In 1662, he married Maria Cotton, the daughter of John Cotton by *his* first wife. Having thus married his stepsister he proceeded to justify his name, Increase, by having seven daughters and three sons.

For his second wife, Increase married Anna Cotton, the

widow of the Rev. John Cotton, III, of Hampton, New Hampshire. She was the grand-daughter-in-law of his first wife's father.

Obviously the Mathers had a Cotton complex. No one expressed the least surprise when Increase named his first son Cotton.

Cotton Mather was an amazingly brilliant and precocious youth. No one appreciated this fact more than the young man himself. In his diary he wrote, "At the age of little more than eleven years I had composed many Latin exercises, both in prose and verse and could speak Latin readily—I had gone through a great part of the New Testament in Greek and I had made some entrance in my Hebrew grammar."

What a Quiz Kid he would have made—and how he would have enjoyed it!

Entering Harvard at twelve, he made a brilliant record in that institution. When he graduated, the president handed him his diploma saying, "The next youth is named Cotton Mather. What a name! Or rather, dear friends, I should have said, 'What names!' I have no slight hope that in this youth these names shall live again, in fact as well as in name—Cotton and Mather."

This high praise was no help to a boy not noted for his modesty to start with.

For a short time Cotton served as a tutor but, in 1675, he became assistant to his father, the pastor of the North Church. Later he became associate, and then pastor himself. Soon he began to consider matrimony, "whereunto," he wrote, "I have had many invitations." The lucky girl was Abigail Phillips of Charlestown.

Cotton Mather was an eloquent preacher, a kindly, albeit stern father to his flock, and an indefatigable worker. He read every book that he could find and his prodigious memory retained it all. Unfortunately, he gave little critical thought to what he read. Anything that was in print he believed without question. Frequently what he read appeared in his own writings as personal observations. "One of my people," he wrote, "killed a rattlesnake with an axe. Before dying, the snake bit the edge of the steele axe which immediately changed color. When next used the discolored part broke off."

Mather sent this story to the Royal Society of London as a bit of his own scientific research. He also reported to the Royal Society that he had discovered, by personal experimentation, that the Devil understood English, Latin, Greek, and Hebrew, but not the Indian language. That was a nice break for the Indians.

Cotton esteemed himself as a physician and wrote a book: *Plain but Potent and Approved Remidies.* One of his prescriptions begins: "Put a half pound of sowbugs alive in a quart or two of wine." For colic he recommended taking the dried dung of a black horse. Hiccoughs could be cured, he claimed, by an infusion of spiders prepared in various nauseous ways. Warts would disappear if the afflicted area was stroked by the dried hand of a man who had been hanged. For baldness, dried and powdered rats were beneficial. Mather did not make up these charming remedies—he read about them somewhere.

Always positive—and sometimes right—Cotton Mather did a prodigious amount of good—and some harm. He visited the sick, comforted the afflicted, and helped the unfortunate. On the other hand, he would relentlessly pursue a poor woman accused of witchcraft; insist that she be hanged; and, before her martyrdom, preach a sermon at her that was worse than the hanging.

Conceit and credulity were his vices; sincerity, piety, charity, and diligence his virtues. The balance is heavily weighted on the better side.

According to his diary, he spent a vast deal of time "bewayling." He "bewayled" his own sins and those of his son, Increase. His own personal sins were chiefly imaginary, but those of his son were really something to wail about. Young Increase was an early, but excellent, example of a juvenile delinquent. After forgiving many of these sins—only to have them repeated—his father finally "cast him forth" and disowned him.

Samuel, the fourth child of the second of Cotton's three wives, also caused considerable "bewayling," but this was only because of his frequent illnesses. Sam was a good boy. Graduating from Harvard in 1723 at the age of seventeen, the lad taught for a few years and then became associate pastor of The Second Church in Boston. This was the same church where three of his illustrious ancestors had served with great distinction.

Tomb of the Mathers: Copp's Hill Burying Ground

Samuel was a man of unusual learning—Harvard granted him the degree of Doctor of Divinity in 1773—but he was not a powerful preacher. Following the family tradition, he published a large number of writings but, unlike his father, he did not venture outside the field of theology.

After nine years as associate pastor, he had difficulties with his colleague, the Rev. Mr. Gee. The claim was made that he was not sound in doctrine nor proper in his conduct. He asked to be dismissed, but the church refused to accept his resignation and ordered an investigation to be made. If there were any spicy details regarding his alleged misconduct they did not want to miss them.

The investigators found that Samuel was not in agreement with some of the religious doctrines of the church but that his personal character and conduct were above reproach. They recommended that he be dismissed and that his salary be continued for one year.

The parishioners were not all against him. Ninety-three of the 353 church members sided with him and left the fold when he did. Encouraged by him, his faithful little flock built a church for themselves at the corner of Hanover and North Bennet Streets. It was called the Tenth Congregational Church in Boston.

The church throve, and he remained its minister until his death in 1785. His last wish was that the church be disbanded and that its members return to The Second Church. Most of them did so.

An inherited taste for book collecting caused Samuel to gather a magnificent library of which he was inordinately proud. In his will he directed that this library be kept intact until one of his sons should be ordained as a minister. Then the entire collection should be given to him. The time never came. None of the sons evinced the slightest interest in theology and none of them became a church leader.

The "dynasty" of the Mathers—as ecclesiastical leaders—was finished.

Copp's Hill Burying Ground overlooks the North End of Boston where the "Church of the Mathers" was located. In the northeast corner of the enclosure is the tomb where lie the mortal remains of the three distinguished Doctors of Divinity who ministered to that church—Increase, Cotton, and Samuel Mather.

xiv. Boston Today

THE RESTLESS CITY

Today's restless cities change constantly. In Boston the changes are now more rapid and more widespread than in many places. This is as it should be. Boston, for all its historic interest, the beauty of its ancient buildings, and the charm and mystery of its narrow and crooked streets was, in some areas, unquestionably drifting into a slum-like decay. When the "New York Streets" area was razed to make room for the Herald-Traveler building in 1954, six dead bodies—obviously of derelicts—were found in abandoned buildings. Another was discovered when, in 1965, the Scollay Square section was demolished. Where such things can happen it is time for change.

Boston's pride in being a unique town was somewhat shaken when a clever etymologist claimed that the word "unique" was derived from the Latin words "unus," one, and "equus," horse. Also some critics said that parts of the city were playing at being primitive for the tourists. There was a growing feeling that something had to be done and done promptly.

During the 1950s Mayor John B. Hynes not only cleaned up the "New York Streets" area of the South End, but also made major changes in the West End including the agonizing uprooting of many families to clear the way for the erection of the dramatic residential towers of Charles River Park.

In 1960 the City Fathers created the Boston Redevelopment Authority and placed at its head Edward J. Logue, who had taken New Haven apart and put it together again in what many felt to be a more interesting and attractive form.

"I think Boston is the most beautiful city that I know," Mr. Logue asserted, and to show that he had given thought to the matter he added, "Hong Kong is my second choice."

Mr. Logue wasted no time. He announced a fifteen-year

"And the Walls Came Tumbling Down!"

plan, organized a corps of 398 full-time and 60 part-time assistants, and began work.

And the walls came tumbling down!

In an incredibly short space of time many areas of Boston began to have the appearance of a city bombed by an especially vicious and implacable enemy. Thousands of buildings were reduced to rubble following the creation of the BRA. In most areas, ancient, unsanitary, and unsafe buildings have been replaced by towering apartment houses and office buildings, and in Scollay Square of unsavory (and sometimes fond) memory a startlingly modernistic Government Center has been built.

Such dramatic and sweeping changes are not made without an accompaniment of grief and repining by the dispossessed, and of bitterness by the lovers of the old order. This bitterness is especially keen in a city where the word *change* might be considered tantamount to the word *sin*. Caustic comments were found scrawled on the walls of many of the condemned houses:

"The rich get richer and the poor get homeless," and "Where now?"

Like some other cities, Boston followed the time-honored method of dealing with its minor historical buildings by letting them fall into picturesque decay. Each passing year has seen the picturesqueness lessen and the decay increase until it at last became evident that their final dissolution could not be far distant. The Redevelopment Authority people have been more direct and forceful. They used bulldozers. They simply cleared away the old substandard buildings in order to replace them with more modern structures.

In recent years, with changing federal priorities limiting the amount of funds available for large-scale urban renewal, the BRA has become more dependent upon private and localized development in the neighborhoods; the obsession with destroying and rebuilding seems to be disappearing in favor of rediscovering Boston's older buildings and rehabilitating what is already at hand for commercial and residential use.

Those buildings of truly great and national historic value have been tenderly cared for by the city government, and many have been designated National Historic Landmarks. The BRA will see to it that they remain and that their surroundings are made more attractive and appropriate. We need have no fear for the future of the Park Street Church, King's Chapel, the Old State House, Faneuil Hall, the Old North Church, and Paul Revere's House. Their historic worth will be respected.

The face of the city is changing with such rapidity that it will not sit still long enough for a portrait, and the only true picture of the Boston of today would have to be a moving picture. A book about it should really be of the loose-leaf type with the possibility of removing and adding pages at least once a week.

In writing of Boston today one must employ some previously unused adjectives: *stimulating, ultramodern, colossal, lofty, stupendous,* and *exciting.* But, thank Heaven, we need not throw into the discard the old stand-bys: *ancient, historic, tranquil, rambling,* and *ivy-grown,* for there will be left much of the delightful old city to continue to charm the antiquarian.

REJUVENATION

Government Center, which covers 60 acres in the old Scollay Square district, attracts a large number of visitors daily. Their comments are varied and often pungent. Some loudly voice criticism, and some who come to scoff remain to praise. Others are stricken dumb with amazement and stand and gaze with wonder and delight. It *is* breathtaking.

The spirit of Boston and its traditional love of good red brick has been featured in the brick-paved plaza which surrounds Boston's impressive City Hall. Perhaps to emphasize the accessibility of our city government, the bricks flow into the building, forming an indoor courtyard. The neighboring John F. Kennedy Federal Building is the business home of more than 4000 federal employees. The 22-story Leverett Saltonstall State Office Building on Cambridge Street houses 39 state agencies, commissions, and divisions with some 3500 employees, and the five-story State Service Center houses both the Division of Employment Security and the Lindemann Mental Health Center; a 33-story office tower designed for the state departments of Health, Education, and Welfare is yet to be built.

Of course, not all of the buildings in Government Center house employees of federal, state, and local government. The 40-story rose-granite headquarters of The New England Merchants Bank is nearby, and is bordered by Washington Mall, which is a major pedestrian link between Government Center and the bustling activity on Washington Street. The curved private Center Plaza Office Building accommodates 4500 office and business workers. Flanked by a ground floor arcade on its outside curve and Pemberton Square inside, this 8-story, 900-foot-long horizontal skyscraper admirably balances the historic Sears Crescent across the way.

While to many, the mention of Government Center brings forth futuristic, spic-and-span, and often sterile visions, its planners have sought to respect the historic character of the area. From many parts of Government Center one is presented with charming views of the Old North, Faneuil Hall, the Old State

Government Center

Keeping an Eye on the City: Samuel Adams

House, Quincy Market, and the Sears Crescent. The Old State House, erected in 1713, held not only the entire state and city governments but the town's private library as well—and even had room for a small market on the ground floor. The contrast between the Government Center of 250 years ago and that of today is, to say the least, noticeable.

Outside of the Government Center area the BRA has viewed much of the Central Business District with a cautious eye, seemingly not in accord with its attitude in other sections of the city. One does not lightly suggest changes in huge department stores, and yet it is obvious that the choking traffic congestion of Washington Street must be relieved to make room for freedom of movement for the vast army of shoppers who swarm in this area. Various solutions have been proposed, and one must have faith to believe that a way will be found. Quite possibly, a section of Washington Street may be closed to vehicular traffic and a pleasant pedestrian mall established where the shoppers may stroll safely and at leisure while investigating the window displays of the shops. This plan is still on the drawing board.

Of course, there has been change in the Central Business District—dramatic change.

The 33-story State Street Bank Building, one of the first skyscrapers in the region, is the business home of 7500 to 8000 persons—more than the population of some towns.

Notwithstanding the high annual rent paid by the tenants of this towering building, its first occupants were two pigeons who built their nest on the lobby floor before it was walled in. The kindly workmen left the space open and even built a convenient perch for the birds. At last the time came when the eviction notice had to be served on the nonpaying tenants. The birds, however, refused to be dispossessed and attempted to peck their way through the solid concrete to their old home.

"Obviously intelligent birds," commented the builders. "They know a good building when they see one." The British Properties, Inc., kept the public informed of the progress of the contest and finally reported that the pair had been caught in a net and "transported to a new home on the Common where bank officials hope they will make all future deposits."

In recent years, other institutions have built mammoth headquarters in the area. The First National Bank Building, the Boston Company Building, One Beacon Street, and the Keystone Building are just a few of the structures which now pierce Boston's skyline, and the Federal Reserve Bank Building, National Shawmut Bank Building, and the Blue Cross – Blue Shield Building are now on their way toward completion.

The reawakened interest in older Boston buildings has brought about some striking changes in the Central Business District. The Old Corner Bookstore at the junction of Washington and School Streets had for years been smothered under huge and defacing advertising signs. An unofficial club for the literary luminaries of Boston in the nineteenth century, this 250-year-old building of much beauty surely deserved a better fate than to be torn down later as an eyesore.

Fortunately, a group of civic-minded Bostonians rallied to

the cause and created "Historic Boston, Incorporated," a nonprofit corporation which raised the necessary money and, on the last day of 1960, took possession of the building. By 1965 they had restored it to its original charm and beauty.

The Boston Globe patriotically established its downtown office on the ground floor and the room was rearranged to resemble as nearly as possible the bookstore of olden days. The desk where Oliver Wendell Holmes frequently worked stands in one corner. A first edition of poems by J. G. Saxe, another of Hawthorne's *The Scarlet Letter,* and many other Old Corner publications by such famous authors as Emerson, Holmes, Whittier, Lowell, and Longfellow adorn the shelves. Altogether there is a collection of several hundred books, all published by Ticknor and Fields from this building. It is interesting to note that the restoration includes lighting fixtures which are exact reproductions of those shown in early pictures of the room.

More recently, rehabilitation by private developers has increasingly caught on as a means of upgrading an area seemingly destined for decay. In the Central Business District, most notably, Old City Hall of French Empire design has been successfully adapted to commercial and office use, the Sears Crescent, once the bookselling center of Boston, has been transformed into an office and restaurant complex, and the Record American Building in Winthrop Square is now being converted to office use.

THE SOUTH COVE

Walking south on Washington Street from the Old Corner Bookstore, the explorer finds himself in a section of the city known to Bostonians as the South Cove, which is roughly bounded by Stuart-Kneeland Street, Hudson Street, the Massachusetts Turnpike Extension, and Clarendon Street. The entire South Cove area was raised from the sea in 1848. Not too long ago, many people who were familiar with the neighborhood felt that it would be a good idea to put it back again.

A Boston newspaper once carried a story about this region which said, "It is the scene of more robberies than probably any other place in Boston. From the first of May to the first of August thirty-six habituees of this district were sent to the Charlestown penitentiary." The article continued, "A thoroughfare that has acquired an obnoxious reputation for houses of ill fame is Indiana Place. Another street of very low moral tone in the vicinity is Compton, formerly Chapman Street." That was in 1895; both streets have since been razed.

The BRA has made extensive changes in the South Cove. Many of the substandard buildings, which comprised nearly half of the total, have been replaced. Two new community housing projects, Tai Tung Village and Mass Pike Towers, have been constructed to relieve some of the congestion produced in Chinatown by the joint encroachment of urban renewal and two traffic arteries that reduced the usable land area considerably. The Tufts–New England Medical Center, a research and teaching hospital offering both health and dental care as well as an outpatient clinic, is another major occupant of the South Cove.

Not all of the efforts to upgrade the South Cove have been so dramatic. There are charming homes in the neighborhood of Fayette, Isabella, Melrose, and Cortes Streets, known as Bay Village. Tradition has it that the artistic brick houses with their arched and recessed doorways and windows were built by the French Huguenots. Many of these buildings have been carefully renovated by their owners, the streets have been improved, and gaslights and brick sidewalks have been installed to accent further the charm of the area. Plants and flowers grow in several of the windows. On Cortes Street, front yards are gay with tiny gardens. It cannot be easy to grow plants in these lots, which are simply sunken areas hardly more than six feet by three with brick floors; but whether grown in boxes, tubs, or pots, they all seem to be thriving.

On Isabella Street is the Catholic Church, Notre Dame des Victoires, which once served only the French immigrants who lived in the neighborhood. Even today the church has many French parishioners.

THE SOUTH END

Gelett Burgess, who lived in Boston's South End in 1900, wrote, "I never saw a purple cow." It is probable though that many who live in this section of the city today have (at certain times) seen such a sight as well as other strange and terrifying monsters, for the police estimate that several thousand "floating" vagrants drift in and out of the region yearly. A very large percentage of these are alcoholics.

Many of the little hidden courtyards of the South End are used as outdoor drinking places and are well paved with "empties," mostly wine bottles. It is an odd fact that the millionaire who wishes to serve his guests the choicest and most expensive liquor will select wine, and the down-and-out whose only desire is to become intoxicated as quickly and as cheaply as possible will also choose wine. It is a truly versatile beverage.

This depressing picture is not, however, the whole story of the South End. A number of streets—Rutland Square, Union Park, and Concord Square among others—contain residential buildings in good preservation and of distinctive architectural quality. Many of them have been renovated in recent years by private developers and families who have reversed the city-to-suburb cycle and want to live in an urban home and enjoy its privileges—including handsome rooms with high ceilings, large windows, and fine old fireplaces.

Sweeping changes have occurred throughout this diverse segment of the city, but the BRA has recognized that some buildings are too useful, too attractive, or too sacred to be uprooted.

More than 250,000 girls from every state in the Union and from fifty-eight foreign countries have called the Franklin Square House their home since it opened its doors to working women and students in 1902. Built shortly after the Civil War, it was for many years Boston's most notable residential hotel. Though its function has changed, this well-loved institution has not been disturbed, nor have its neighbors: the Franklin Square Park, the St. George Cyprian Orthodox Church, the Immaculate

Union Park: The South End

Conception Church, the home of the Jesuit Fathers, and an ancient cemetery where some Bostonians of the early 1800s are at rest. Among others, this graveyard shelters the remains of a considerable number of pirates and other malefactors who were hanged on the gallows, which was conveniently nearby.

Undisturbed, also, have been the many buildings and extensive grounds of the Boston City Hospital and the Boston University Medical Center, both of which are undergoing major expansion, as well as the numerous churches of the area, including the beautiful Cathedral of the Holy Cross at 1400 Washington Street.

While many older buildings have been privately renovated for the use of higher-income residents, the more seasoned inhabitants of the South End who cannot afford high rents have not been ignored. Hundreds of the old and crumbling residences have been replaced by modern, sanitary dwellings which provide clean, low-rental housing; and, in an effort to save the character of the neighborhood, the BRA has sought to rehabilitate a number of the rowhouse blocks for lower-income use as well.

Cathedral of the Holy Cross

Other innovations made recently in the South End include the building of two new schools, several well-located playgrounds, a new library on Tremont and West Newton Streets, and a mammoth wholesale flower market on Harrison Avenue. In addition, the Boston Center for the Arts has taken over the old Cyclorama Building, which now serves as a theater for the performing arts and provides space for art exhibits, classrooms, and studios.

And, though it has not been mentioned as one of the BRA's objectives, these changes have had a tremendous effect upon a large but seldom seen group of old residents. The estimate is that there were about eight rats to every human in the South End before it was revitalized. What happened to them? Where did they go? It is a disturbing thought.

BOSTON'S WINDOW ON THE WORLD

"Boston's Window on the World," as Mayor Collins characterized the Waterfront, has become somewhat dimmed through

Boston's Skyline from Long Wharf

the years. Many of the wharves have been destroyed by fire or decay, and new construction has been sparse. But renewed interest in the Waterfront promises to make this area one of the most exciting in the city.

Private enterprise has developed some interesting and profitable uses for several of the abandoned piers. Harbor Towers, a luxury high-rise apartment complex, has been built on the remains of India Wharf. The massive granite warehouses on Commercial, Long, and Lewis Wharves have been converted into charming apartments, condominiums, and shops. They still smell somewhat of ancient fish, but it makes little difference to those who thrive in this semi-bohemian, semi-nautical type of residence.

The New England Aquarium, which boasts both indoor and outdoor exhibits, an auditorium, the largest glass-enclosed salt-water tank in the world, a mammal pavilion, and even Hoover Harborseal, the duly elected President of the Underwater States of America (New England Region), has been built on Central Wharf. And a harbor-side restaurant and docking facilities for ferry boats are to be built near the present site of Rowe's Wharf.

Under the administration of Mayor Kevin H. White, the BRA has made extensive plans for the rehabilitation of the Waterfront. Still under consideration is the "Walk to the Sea," a proposal that would create an unhampered pedestrian route from Government Center Plaza through Dock Square and the Faneuil Hall Markets and on to the Waterfront.

One major attraction along this proposed route is the six-acre restoration project now under way in the area adjacent to Faneuil Hall, including the 535-foot-long domed Quincy Market building and the North and South Market Street buildings. Erected on the town dock in 1824–26 at a cost of $150,000, the granite Quincy Market was designed by Alexander Parris at the request of Mayor Josiah Quincy to meet the expanding needs of the small marketplace which was then on the ground floor of Faneuil Hall.

Developers are now at work on both the physical and functional restoration of this historic area. Quincy Market is to be revived as a major center for market activity—a huge food bazaar which will flow into North and South Market Streets. Street vendors, flea markets, outdoor entertainment, and open-air cafes will line these highways. The North and South Market Street Buildings will offer shops, offices, restaurants, and night clubs—all of which will bring new life and commerce to the area after years of decline.

RENAISSANCE

About 1900, Boston's North End was an apparently hopeless slum. Buildings were old, dilapidated, and dangerously over-populated. Nowhere else in the city were so many people crowded into so small a space. Indeed, very few places in the United States could show any greater congestion. It seemed to be a bad situation that was bound to grow worse.

What can the impoverished residents of a slum do, except let conditions slide into utter ruin? Not only did banks refuse credit to those who wished to make alterations and improvements in their property, but loans for building in the North End were unattainable from any source. The region lay under a curse— the curse of poverty.

About 1930, however, a strange—almost miraculous— transformation began to take place. Slowly but surely conditions improved. Old buildings were repaired and repainted, and only recently an abandoned macaroni factory, the Prince Building, was converted into a luxury housing unit. The ancient mansions which since the mid-nineteenth century had housed a family in each room were made over into comfortable and sanitary apartments. Attractive substantial houses replaced many of the ruins, and a fierce neighborhood pride replaced the former apathy.

How did this transformation come about? When the Italian immigrant arrived in the North End he had little or no money, but he did have health, stamina, and a powerful desire to succeed. Many of the men living in this section of the city became skilled carpenters, plumbers, decorators, contractors, or masons. If a resident wished to fix up his property and money was scarce, he would trade jobs with a friend. The carpenter would repair a neighbor's house in return for having plumbing installed in his own residence, the only expense for either being the cost of materials. The system worked well, and the Italian community is still in the process of rapidly "unslumming" itself.

Many of the people have prospered to such a degree that they can now well afford to live in any part of Greater Boston that they choose, but they prefer to remain with their old acquaintances. They like it there, and why should they not? The delinquency, disease, and infant mortality rate in the North End are among the lowest in the city, and the death rate, particularly the tuberculosis death rate, compares favorably with that of other sections.

It is true that there are few public parks or playgrounds, except for the new three-acre North End Park below Copp's Hill, but the children play happily on the crowded streets and sidewalks. Under the watchful eyes of friends and neighbors they can come to little harm. Traditionally, the streets are dangerous playgrounds, yet in these active highways, alive with adult observers, the children are really safer than they would be in some of the poorly supervised and little visited public playgrounds.

With the general renewal and modernizing that is going on in the North End it is interesting to find one building where the renewal process was reversed. Here the changes and "improvements" that had been made through the years were stripped away, and the structure restored to its original beauty. St. Stephen's Church at the corner of Hanover and Clark Streets was built in 1805 for a Congregational Society which had previously worshipped in a small wooden church on the same site. It is now the only one remaining of the twelve churches in the city that were designed by the incomparable architect, Bulfinch. It is considered an outstanding example of the Old World grace which marks his work.

Though originally owned and occupied solely by the Congregationalists, and for many years known as "The New North," this church found itself, after the lapse of some sixty years, in the strange position of being a Protestant church in the midst of a community almost solidly Roman Catholic in its faith. The obvious and sensible thing to do was done. About 1863 "The New North" sold the building to the Roman Catholic church, which promptly changed its name to St. Stephen's.

Cardinal Cushing, with a fine feeling for the historic background of the beautiful old structure, and possibly stimulated by the thought that a larger number of tourists than ever would visit the area with the completion of the Government Center, did a marvelous job of restoration.

A few years after it was built, the structure had had to be moved some distance back in order to widen the street, and a number of structural changes were made at that time. The building later was moved forward six feet, nine inches, so that it rested on its original foundations, the ceiling was lowered to its former level, and other alterations brought both the interior and exterior as close to the original design as is possible.

The City of Boston has also done its part in the renaissance

St. Stephen's Church by Bulfinch

of the North End. The little branch library on Parmenter Street which was opened to the public May 5, 1965, is an architectural gem. Brick, glass, ceramics, and Philippine mahogany have been used to produce a novel, but delightful effect. The simple, one-story building is definitely in the Roman tradition. It is perfectly attuned to the spirit of the neighborhood with its deep Italian roots and Latinate feeling. An inner courtyard—lavishly planted, with a pool and plashing fountain in the center—adds charm and color to the main room. Panels of sculptured glass in gay hues are effectively used on the walls.

The Italian atmosphere is continued in the decorations. There is a fourteen-foot diorama of the Ducal Palace in Venice, skillfully and accurately made, with sixteenth-century Venetian figures standing about the courtyard. Brilliant colors in the furniture, the drapes, and the rugs give a vibrant and jewel-like quality to the entire library.

Conditions in the North End are steadily improving. There are still many things "wrong" from the viewpoint of city planners, but the residents are happy, healthy and friendly. Why should they be "relocated" or otherwise disturbed!

THE BACK BAY

Even the beautiful Back Bay section of Boston has been considerably altered in the last few years.

The Prudential Center was built on the site of the Boston and Albany railroad yards. Central to the complex is the 52-story, 750-foot-high Prudential Tower which is the northeastern headquarters of the Prudential Insurance Company of America, and the first of the area's skyscrapers. Included in the center is the huge Sheraton-Boston Hotel and the Hynes Auditorium, which can seat, in its main hall, 5200 persons who, while waiting for the show to begin, may walk about in more than 150,000 square feet of exhibition space. An outdoor skating rink, several apartment buildings, and quality retail shops complete the impressive group.

Trinity Church: Copley Square

Not to be outdone, the John Hancock Insurance Company has built a second skyscraper in Copley Square, the tallest and probably most controversial building in Boston.

Throughout its history, many architects and artists have called Copley Square one of the most attractive in the world, but up until a few years ago its style had become somewhat marred by a multitude of parked cars, by the difficulty of crossing the streets through the busy traffic, and by the city's sometimes unfortunate attempts to beautify the little space in front of the Boston Public Library.

A nationwide contest offering substantial prizes was organized in 1965, and 188 landscape architects and designers vied for the honor of creating a new Copley Square.

The challenge was met and Copley Square has been redesigned, landscaped, and made into an intriguing plaza. Its shape has been changed from a triangle to a rectangle, providing space for a plaza of dark concrete blocks with steps leading down to an open space some five feet below the street level. Here a prom-

Christian Science Center

enade and shallow rectangular pool with illuminated fountain invite visitors to enjoy a few minutes' respite from the traffic of the busy street.

The Boston Public Library has not been ignored. To meet the needs of its ever expanding book collection and increased patronage, a new block-long addition of simple yet monumental style behind the main library opened its doors in 1973.

For years the magnificent and impressive Christian Science Church and its nearby publishing house have been major attractions for both citizens and tourists wishing to see the beauty spots of the city. Now, even this grand religious center has been greatly enlarged. Adjacent to the Prudential Center, a new Christian Science Church Center has been built to serve the growing administrative and publishing needs of the church's worldwide activities. The white-domed Mother Church, still the focal point of the center, is flanked by a 28-story administration building, the Church Colonnade Building which houses some of the publishing activities, and a three-story curved Sunday school which also serves as an auditorium seating over 1000 persons.

An entirely new and spacious public park bordered by linden trees and surrounding a 700-foot by 100-foot reflecting pool completes the picture.

Apart from these more obvious changes, the Back Bay has been less altered than other sections of the city. Here, too, interest has been shown in the revitalization of older buildings by their interior adaptation for contemporary use. The old red-brick fire station on Boylston Street now shares its domain with the Institute of Contemporary Art. The Webster House at the corner of Dartmouth Street and Commonwealth Avenue has been tastefully transformed for office and residential space. The Hotels Vendome and Somerset on Commonwealth Avenue are being converted to condominiums and rental use respectively, and the old Exeter Theater is now undergoing rehabilitation.

The vast and dramatic upheaval of the 1960s has for the most part ended. One hopes that our city planners will continue to look at Boston's buildings with a more cautious and loving eye.

xv. A Last Look

The rehabilitation program for Boston began in 1960 with a modest appropriation of $90,000,000. From that it has grown to a point where few are aware of the immense sums of money committed, or realize the vast areas of Boston that have felt and have yet to feel the impact.

However, with few exceptions, the changes have been made with wisdom and understanding. Very little of historic value, artistic merit, or civic worth has been destroyed. The ancient, dilapidated, and unsanitary buildings of Scollay Square, Skid Row, and the slum sections of South Cove have been razed, and the city has already shown signs of improvement in health, in appearance, and in moral tone by their passing.

Much criticism has been directed at the increasing number of high-rise buildings which are soaring over their neighbors in many parts of the city. Boston is, and always has been, a growing city, constantly in need of more room. For the first two hundred years or so, as more space was needed, the inhabitants solved the problem by leveling hills and filling in coves and bays along the shore line. When all of the shallow bays were filled in and all of the hills lowered to a habitable level, it grew by annexing neighboring towns. Further growth along these lines soon became impossible. The towns on Boston's outer rim are fiercely autonomous and would rather cease to exist than become submerged in another city. The only direction that is left for growth is *up*. High-rise buildings have become a necessity.

From the observation towers of some of the taller buildings, Boston is seen as a pictorial map. It is still a confusing labyrinth of narrow, aimless little streets, unexpected squares, and a wholly irrational intermingling of commercial and residential buildings with an increasing number of lofty residential and commercial skyscrapers scattered throughout the scene. The vivid whiteness of the highly modernistic Government Center presents a contrast with its surrounding buildings which is startling, but not displeasing.

If you would discover the charming, elusive, and unique qualities that combine to form the piquant personality of Boston, study her profile from across the Charles River along that section of Memorial Drive which extends from Harvard University to the Longfellow Bridge. Here is the true revelation of what Boston really is. It is from this vantage point that the departing visitor should take his last look at the city. This is the picture that he should carry away with him to remember and treasure forever.

In the foreground is the placid basin of the Charles, reflecting on its untroubled surface the mood of the day. It is steely gray on cold winter mornings, sapphire blue on languorous summer afternoons, and a riot of kaleidoscopic colors in an autumn sunset. In the spring and summer its surface is dotted with tiny sailboats, racing shells, and little excursion boats making the grand tour from the Embankment to Watertown. Garrulous gulls and ubiquitous ducks are there at all seasons.

Rising in a gentle slope from the opposite shore is the city. To the left are the comfortable homes of Beacon Hill, where the ancient red-brown bricks convey the feeling of peaceful permanence, enduring charm, and old and still sacred traditions. Tier on tier, the houses rise to a summit which is completed by the golden crown of Charles Bulfinch's masterpiece, the inspiring State House, while just beyond, the impressive Government Center marks the beginning of the new and more modern city.

On the right of the picture is the Back Bay. Apartment houses, pleasant parks, and magnificent buildings may be glimpsed in this area.

In the early evening when the lights come on, there is a peculiar poignancy to the scene. There are the soft lights of countless homes, the vertical shafts of radiance which are the skyscrapers, the infrequent splashes of color from advertising signs—fortunately too far off to be clearly read. In the background are festoons of greenish light, the pale aquamarines that adorn the Mystic Bridge—and mystic, indeed, the bridge seems from this vantage point.

The much advertised New York skyline is doubtless the most impressive and stimulating in the world. It shouts at the observer, "Here is the Great City! Come to me! Work! Fight! Taste success! Get rich! Become famous! Have fun! Live it up! But HURRY, HURRY, HURRY!"

In spite of much modernization and its many new and impressive buildings, Boston's skyline conveys no such strident message. The invitation is not raucously shouted but is nonetheless clear and definite: "Here is an old city, a mellowed city. Come to me and enjoy the peace and charm of my ancient streets. Take time to live graciously. Take time to dream."

Yes, the time to dream is still important. The vision itself is of consequence. Boston has ever been sympathetic to the dreamer of dreams and the seer of visions: not the feckless builder of castles in Spain, but the truly great ones of the earth—the dreamers who, through anguish and toil, make those dreams come true. Indeed, the first settlers were those who, in bigoted, intolerant seventeenth-century England, dared to envision a new

Boston's Skyline from Cambridge

land where there would be freedom to worship their God as they saw fit.

It was in Boston that the people first conceived the seemingly fanciful idea of a new republic, free from the tyranny of the mother country. It was here that men first dreamed of the clipper ship with its worldwide trade, of the network of steel that opened the West, of the possibility of transmitting the human voice over wires to the far corners of the earth, of the conquering of pain by the use of drugs, of the abolition of human slavery. These and many other dreams that have had their inception in Boston have, in their unfolding, enriched and expanded the life patterns of the entire world.

It is not by accident that nearly half of those whose names are enshrined in the Hall of Fame for Great Americans were born or lived a part of their lives within sight of the golden dome of the State House in Boston.

Modernizers and city planners will somewhat change the physical appearance of the city. That is inevitable. It has been done in other times and is now unquestionably a desirable thing, but even with its skyline of the future it will still retain its spirit of antiquity, regardless of what changes are made. It will always be the Boston of history and tradition.

Plus ça change, plus c'est la même chose, "The more it changes, the more it remains the same."

Index

Numbers in italics refer to illustrations